ALCIMUS,
ENEMY OF THE MACCABEES

Benjamin Edidin Scolnic

Studies in Judaism

University Press of America,® Inc.
Lanham · Boulder · New York · Toronto · Oxford

Copyright © 2005 by
University Press of America,® Inc.
4501 Forbes Boulevard
Suite 200
Lanham, Maryland 20706
UPA Acquisitions Department (301) 459-3366

PO Box 317
Oxford
OX2 9RU, UK

All rights reserved
Printed in the United States of America
British Library Cataloging in Publication Information Available

Library of Congress Control Number: 2004112310
ISBN 0-7618-3044-8 (paperback : alk. ppr.)

∞™ The paper used in this publication meets the minimum
requirements of American National Standard for Information
Sciences—Permanence of Paper for Printed Library Materials,
ANSI Z39.48—1984

Studies in Judaism

EDITOR

Jacob Neusner
Bard College

EDITORIAL BOARD

Alan J. Avery-Peck
College of the Holy Cross

Herbert Basser
Queens University

Bruce D. Chilton
Bard College

José Faur
Bar Ilan University

William Scott Green
University of Rochester

Mayer Gruber
Ben-Gurion University of the Negev

Günter Stemberger
University of Vienna

James F. Strange
University of South Florida

For Yochanan Muffs, who taught me to think for myself

TABLE OF CONTENTS

Introduction 1
Chapter I
The Historical Background..4
Chapter II The Sources
1Maccabees 12
2Maccabees 25
Josephus 38
Excursus: The Flight of OniasIV to Egypt...50
Are There Rabbinic Traditions That Refer to Alcimus?.............................57
The Importance of Yosi ben Yoʿezer 79
Are There References to Alcimus in the Qumran Scrolls?........................93
Are There Any Ptolemaic and Seleucid Parallels? 108
Chapter III Did Alcimus Write Psalm 79?
The Dating of Psalms...113
When Was the Book of Psalms in Its Final Form?..................................116
The Psalms of *Asaph* 120
Psalm 79 123
Conclusion..136
Chapter IV The Re-evaluation of Alcimus
Who Was Alcimus' Predecessor as High Priest?.....................................138
When Did Alcimus Become High Priest? 143
Who Was Alcimus?..148
Did Alcimus Voluntarily Defile Himself?...150
Was Alcimus a Religious Conservative or a "Hellenizer"?....................156
Did Alcimus Write a Psalm? 159
Alcimus and the *Asidaioi*..161
Was There an Extended *Intersacerdotium* after Alcimus? 165
Re-Evaluating Alcimus 168
Alcimus: Prospects for Future Study 172
Appendix I..173
Bibliography 174
Index 182

ACKNOWLEDGMENTS

I would like to thank:
Dr. Jacob Neusner for his consistent and gratifying support,
Dr. Leslie Wilson for his tireless effort, meticulous care and keen insight,
My friends and students for their questions and feedback.

INTRODUCTION

The Historical Background

The Maccabaean era is a fascinating and significant period of Jewish history. Known mainly because of the holiday of *Hanukkah*, this is the period when the Judeans moved, as Shaye Cohen says, from an ethnos to an ethno-religion, from Judeans to Jews; it was when Jewishness as such began.[1] The beginnings of Pharisaism and Rabbinic Judaism may be traced to this time. The much-discussed sect at Qumran, the writers of the Dead Sea Scrolls, seems to have been born in reaction to events in this era. This period is so interesting and vital to our understanding of the formation of Judaism that it is important to explore every corner and every important personality involved.

Alcimus, as the High Priest after *Hanukkah*, after the restoration of the temple in Jerusalem to proper Jewish worship, should bear some mention in the re-telling of the story. Instead, he has been vilified or ignored. We will show that this is more a result of second-hand prejudice than anything else. Even to those well versed in the history of the Jewish people, the name Alcimus is not at all familiar. While the story revolving around the institution of the holiday of *Hanukkah* is one of the most famous tales transmitted by Jewish tradition and popular culture, the man who was the High Priest of Judaea during the years after that epoch-making event is unknown. Alcimus' enemy Judas Maccabaeus and his descendants the Hasmonaeans considered Alcimus to be an evil man, and since the victors write history, the ancient sources express that prejudice. Most modern scholars, in attempting to reconstruct the history of that period, merely reflect that same attitude.

The modest goal of this study is to examine closely every ancient text that refers or may refer to Alcimus. While we will touch upon many larger issues and themes involved in the reconstruction of this historical period and its literature, we will be forced to wait for other opportunities to discuss matters in the manner they deserve.

---

[1] Shaye J.D. Cohen *The Beginnings of Jewishness: Boundaries, Varieties, Uncertainties* (Berkeley: University of California, 1999).

We shall review many of the important and representative scholarly treatments of this subject. Contrary to most moderns, we will evaluate Alcimus' heritage and loyalty to traditions in a much more positive manner. Most sources and scholars say that Alcimus was a leader of the Hellenizers; we will claim that he was a pious man. Many deny his lineage as a rightful heir to the High Priesthood; we will insist that he was indeed "the seed of Aaron," not just a common priest but also a scion of the Zadokite-Oniad line of High Priests. Many state that he was raised to the High Priesthood because he was acceptable to his pagan sovereigns; we will investigate the possibilities that he was elevated not only because of his heritage but also because of his kinship with a leading sage of the time, his authorship of at least one psalm and his role as a priest who may have already been working within the Temple priestly hierarchy before his initial appointment by Lysias, guardian of Antiochus V.

The most popular model for understanding the events surrounding the rise of the Hasmonaean dynasty, the events commemorated by the Jewish holiday of *Hanukkah*, is that of a revolution.[2] It is a simple fairy-tale with unspeakably evil villains and faithful, heroic heroes. The Seleucid Emperor Antiochus IV *Epiphanes* oppresses the Judaeans, pollutes the Temple with his paganism, and forces the Jews to worship his idols and forsake Judaism. The Judaeans, led by Judas the Maccabee, revolt and, against all odds, defeat the mighty empire. The good guys win and everyone lives happily ever after.

A second model, articulated by the great modern scholar Elias Bickerman,[3] is that of a civil war between Jews who had fully assimilated into the Greek culture ("Hellenizers") and those who refused to forsake their religion, the Maccabees, and their pietist *Asidaioi* supporters. There are villains and heroes in this model, but they are all Jews. The Greek Syrians only become involved at the request of the Jewish Hellenizers.

The problem with the first model is that it does not account for the role of "Hellenized" Jews in these events. The problem with the second model is that it does not account for the many factions among the Judaeans in the 160's BCE and

---

[2] The modern scholar associated with this popular presentation of the *Hanukkah* story is Victor Tcherikover *Hellenistic Civilization and the Jews* (Phil.: JPS, 1961).
[3] Elias Bickerman *The God of the Maccabees. Studies on the Meaning and Origin of the Maccabean Revolt Studies in Judaism and Late Antiquity* 32 (Leiden: Brill, 1979).

Introduction

therefore to the complex meaning of the events of this period. Neither model eschews prejudices enough to emphasize the centrality of a great and impressive tradition, the preservation of the cult through the flexibility of the High Priesthood.

This realization was triggered by two verses in the Book of 1 Maccabees that explain that the High Priest Alcimus was the writer of a psalm. Since this will hardly seem to be a startling or significant fact to most readers, we will need to provide a great deal of background before we explore why Alcimus as a psalm-writer leads us to a different understanding of the Maccabaean struggle.

CHAPTER I

THE HISTORICAL BACKGROUND

In a sense, the entire story of the Maccabaean revolt started and revolved around the actions of the Jewish High Priests.[1] At the beginning of the period, Judaea was ruled by the High Priest Onias III under the oversight of a Seleucid governor. Jason, brother of Onias III and thus a legitimate heir of the Zadokite-Oniad line, bribed Antiochus IV and became the High Priest by promising both additional revenue and the creation of an Antiochene community. Jason, however, only lasted in this position until 172 BCE, when Menelaus stole it from him by offering even greater revenues, then serving as High Priest until 163 BCE. The Hasmonaean revolt, after the rededication of the Temple, nearly folded because of the willingness of the *Asidaioi* to be ruled by the new High Priest, the Syrian-appointed Alcimus, a scion of the Aaronide family. The massacre of sixty *Asidaioi*[2] leaders, meant to frighten and intimidate all opposition, may have also insured the continuation of the revolt, which now became a political one against Seleucid rule. After the death of Alcimus in 159 BCE, there would be no High Priest until 153 BCE when the Maccabaean High Priest Jonathan would rule Judaea.[3] Again, High Priests are central figures in the events of this period.

Let us now give a brief review of these events. Onias III was the recognized authority in Judaea and the heir to the High Priesthood, the powerful institution that exerted religious and sometimes civil authority over the people.

---

[1] I draw on the various histories and other basic works such as Jonathan A. Goldstein, *I Maccabees* The Anchor Bible (Garden City: Doubleday, 1976); E. R. Bevan *The House of Seleucus* 2 vols. (London: 1902); idem *Jerusalem under the High Priests* (London: 1904); G. M. Cohen *The Seleucid Colonies, Studies in Founding, Administration, and Organization* (Wiesbaden: 1978).
[2] I will use this term for the group commonly referred to as the "Hasidim" or "Hasideans." As I will explain below, the latter terms give a characterization to this group that is misleading and unsubstantiated.
[3] Daniel J. Harrington *The Maccabean Revolt: Anatomy of a Biblical Revolution* (Wilmington: Michael Glazier, 1988) 89.

The Historical Background

The chain of events began in 187 BCE when the Syrian emperor Seleucus IV sent his minister Heliodorus to seize money from the treasury of the temple in Jerusalem. Heliodorus' failure to do so was seen as a miracle.[4] This story may revolve around the idea that the temple could not be taken by outsiders because that would be against God's will. Its violation by Jews, as would happen shortly, was even more horrifying in its betrayal of God's will. The Jews themselves would do what outsiders could not do.

Onias III was required to go to the Seleucid capital of Antioch to protect himself against both external and internal pressures.[5] Seleucus IV died in September 175 BCE and his brother Antiochus IV seized power. Antiochus IV, who had been a hostage at Rome[6] was quite enamored with Roman ideals and had created an Antiochene republic on the analogy of the Roman republic.[7]

Onias III's brother Jason ousted him as High Priest in 175-74 BCE by offering Antiochus IV 590 talents[8] and by seeking to become both the High Priest and the founder of an Antiochene community at Jerusalem. Antiochus IV granted Jason these positions and the right to decide who would be the citizens of this community. An Antiochene community meant the establishment of Greek institutions such as the *gymnasium* that were exempt from Jewish law. Meanwhile, Onias III found refuge at the sacred asylum at Daphne.

Antiochus IV, concerned about war with the Ptolemaic empire of Ptolemy VI, strengthened his defenses against this threat. He came to Jerusalem where Jason gave him a magnificent reception.[9] Despite his eagerness to please his emperor,

---

[4] In 2Macc. 3:4-4:1 and Daniel 11:20.

[5] 2Macc.4:1-7.

[6] 1Macc.1:10.

[7] Antiochus IV had served as a hostage in Rome for the Seleucid Empire after it had been defeated by Rome in 190. When he returned to a Seleucid empire that already had many of the necessary features in place, Antiochus IV was very interested in creating his own institutions modeled on those in Rome that he had seen. As Tcherikover points out, there were cities and peoples with substantial autonomy (*Hellenistic Civilization and the Jews* 92-107). These peoples were kept in line by the threat of military colonies of Greeks and Macedonians in their land (cf. Josephus *Ant.* xii 4.1.159). What Antiochus IV brought to this situation was the idea of citizenship in the empire.

[8] 1Macc.1:11-15; 2Macc.4:7-20.

[9] 2Macc.4:21-22.

Jason was himself outbid by Menelaus in 172 BCE and had to flee.[10] Menelaus, however, could not acquire the required money for the emperor and took vessels from the Temple to bribe a royal minister, Andronikos, who was in control while Antiochus IV was away. After Onias III, still in the sanctuary at Daphne, reprimanded Menelaus, Andronikos lured Onias III from the asylum and killed him. Antiochus IV in turn killed Andronikos for this action when he returned to the capital.[11]

Menelaus and his brother Lysimachus, the leaders of the Antiochene community of Jerusalem, continued to infuriate "pious Jews" by taking Temple property and treasures and turning them over to the Greek ruler.[12] These Jews were angry over many trends. They interpreted passages in the *Torah*[13] to mean that Jews should not become citizens of the Antiochene republic. They killed fellow Jews who did become citizens, believing that they were following the laws of the *Torah*.[14] Despite a bloody riot and charges against him, Menelaus survived with the support of the Seleucids. In 170-69 BCE, Antiochus IV was fighting the Ptolemies and invading Egypt.[15] A rumor of the king's death led Jason and his supporters, who thought that Menelaus no longer had his royal patron, to attempt the capture of Jerusalem. Pious Jews did not support Jason and repelled his attack; at the same time, they continued to fight against Menelaus. This would seem to indicate that although Jason was an Oniad, he had ruined his standing with those committed to Judaism as it had been practiced. Menelaus, with the full support of a very alive Antiochus, punished the city and was re-confirmed in his authority.[16] Still, the pious Jews continued to attack and resist Menelaus. Sympathetic to the entreaties of the beleaguered Antiochenes led by Menelaus, Antiochus sent Apollonius the Mysarch on an expedition to punish the pious Jews of Jerusalem, who were massacred in Nisan 167 BCE.[17] New punitive taxes were imposed. Troops manned the *Akra* north of the Temple. Shortly thereafter, Antiochus IV decreed that all Jews in Judaea should stop observing the

---

[10] 2Macc.4:23-26.
[11] 2Macc.4:34-38.
[12] 2Macc.4:39-50.
[13] Ex. 34:15-16 and Deut. 7:2-4.
[14] Exod.22:19 and Deut.13:7-18; cf. Jubilees 23:20.
[15] 1Macc.1:16-20; 2Macc.5:51.
[16] 1Macc.1:20-28; 2Macc.5:1-23.
[17] 1Macc.1:29-40; 2Macc.5:23-27.

The Historical Background

laws of the *Torah*. Instead, they were to follow a new "purified" Judaism with a polytheistic cult.[18] This decree was sporadically and then gradually enforced until on 15 Kislev 167 BCE the "Abomination of Desolation" representing three gods of the imposed cult was placed on the altar for sacrifice in the Temple.[19] The religious persecution was now in full swing throughout Judaea and the Antiochene republic.[20] In late 167 BCE or 166 BCE, Mattathias and his Hasmonaean family began to lead a revolt. The *Asidaioi* were at first reluctant to join this human-led revolt but after more persecution and the massacre of *Asidaioi* on the Sabbath, many did join Mattathias.[21] Mattathias died and his son Judas became the leader, defeating two royal expeditions.

In May/June 165 BCE, Antiochus IV went to fight in the eastern part of the Seleucid empire, leaving the control of the western part of the empire (including Judaea) and half of the army to his young son Antiochus V with Lysias as his guardian and chief minister. They sent Nicanor and Gorgias to crush the rebellion but Judas routed them.[22] This defeat prompted Lysias to fight against Judas himself and the battle of Beth-Zur was fought with heavy losses on both sides. Menelaus and others sought a settlement through negotiations; a letter in the name of the coregent offered the Jews an end to the cult that had been imposed and permission to observe the laws of the *Torah* and amnesty if they would go home by March 27, 164 BCE.[23] The fact that 1Maccabees, which reflects a Hasmonaean viewpoint, does not even mention this offer may indicate that the latter party had already decided to push beyond religious freedom for political independence.

Asidaioi denied Menelaus the right to control the temple and their priests purified the Temple and rid it of the "Abomination of Desolation"[24] building a new altar.[25] Judas chose "blameless priests" to cleanse the Temple and restored

---

[18] 1Macc.1:44-51.
[19] 1Macc.1:54.
[20] 1Macc.1:54-64; 2Macc.6-7; Josephus *Ant.* xii 5.5.257-64.
[21] 1Macc.2:1-48; 2Macc.6:11.
[22] 1Macc.3:38-4:27; 2Macc.8:8-29, 34-36.

[23] 2Macc.11:27-33.
[24] 1Macc.4:42-46; 2Macc.10:3; Daniel 9:27.
[25] 1Macc.4:47-48; 2Macc.10:3.

sacrifice.[26] Judas' men removed the lattice from the Temple Court that had served as apparatus for sacred prostitution (*Megillat Ta'anit*).[27] On the 25th of Kislev in 164 BCE, Judas instituted a holiday of dedication (*Hanukkah*).

Before Antiochus IV died in 164 BCE, he made his young son Antiochus V his co-regent, with Lysias as chief guardian and chief minister. Lysias ended his second expedition to Judaea early in the summer of 162 BCE. He realized that despite his overwhelming military success, internal developments in the empire made it impossible to maintain a large force in Judaea to eradicate the rebels and prevent the resumption of guerilla warfare. Lysias realized that diplomacy would work better than war. He repealed the coercive religious measures that the authorities had been unable to enforce anyway and officially returned the Temple to the Jews. In 163 BCE, Antiochus V deposed Menelaus from the High Priesthood and sent him to Syria for execution.[28] Menelaus served as High Priest from 172 BCE until 163 BCE, an amazing achievement considering the violent and tumultuous nature of these years. Antiochus V appointed Alcimus, a descendant of the Aaronide line and thus a hereditary heir to the High Priesthood,[29] as High Priest and ethnarch.[30] The idea was to place Alcimus in complete charge of Judaea. This was an effort to turn pious Jews away from the rebellion.[31] Antiochus V made full peace with the Jews. Antiochus demolished the wall around the Temple mount.[32] (Antiochus V and Lysias left Jerusalem with their army in order to stop the rebellion of the minister Philip at Antioch.

In early autumn 162 BCE or 161 BCE, Demetrius I *Soter* ("redeemer"), son of Seleucus IV, landed at Tripolis and claimed the kingship after escaping from Rome

---

[26] 1Macc.4:42-53.

[27] *Megillat Ta'anit* is an Aramaic list of thirty-six dates on which Jewish people were not allowed to fast. Some of these dates mark events in the era of the Maccabaean revolt and are thus useful here. *Megillat Ta'anit* seems to have been written between 67-70 CE. See Hans Lichtenstein "Die Fastenrolle" *HUCA* 8-9 (1931-32) 257-351 and Goldstein *I Maccabees* 53.

[28] 2Macc.13:3-8; Josephus *Ant.* xii 9:7.383-85; Daniel 11:24.

[29] The neglected Oniad heir left Judea and eventually established a Jewish temple in Egypt at Leontopolis. I shall discuss this at length below.

[30] Josephus *Ant.* 12.383-5.

[31] *Ant.* xii 9.7.386-88; cf. 2Macc.14:3.

[32] 1Macc.6:55-63; 2Macc.11:22-26; 13:23-26.

The Historical Background

where he had been a hostage.[33] The troops rallied to Demetrius I and killed both Antiochus V and Lysias.[34]

A Jewish delegation led by Alcimus came to Demetrius I and brought charges against Judas the Maccabee and his brothers. Demetrius I accepted the validity of the charges and sent his trusted minister, Bacchides, against Judas, re-confirming Alcimus as High Priest. Bacchides sent a conciliatory message to Judas, who did not accept the gesture as sincere. However, a large delegation of *Asidaioi* did trust Alcimus and said, "A man who is a priest of the stock of Aaron has come with their force; he will not wrong us."[35] Alcimus spoke "soothing words" to them but then arrested and executed sixty of the delegation. The interesting part, for our purposes here, comes in the verse describing Alcimus' action:

> As soon as he had won their trust, however, he arrested sixty of them and had them executed all in a single day, in accordance with the verse which he himself wrote, "The bodies and blood of Your saints they have poured out around Jerusalem, and there is no one to bury them."

These verses are Ps.79:2-3:

> O God, heathens have entered Your domain
> Defiled Your holy temple,
> And turned Jerusalem into ruins.
> They have left Your servants' corpses
> As food for the fowl of heaven,
> And the flesh of Your faithful for the wild beasts.
> Their blood was shed like water around Jerusalem,
> With none to bury them.
> We have become the butt of our neighbors,
> The scorn and derision of those around us.

Since the author of 1Maccabees despises Alcimus, he would not have made up the fact that Alcimus had written this psalm. He is using Alcimus' words against him. At one point, Alcimus had decried the spilling of Jewish blood but now,

---

[33] In place of his uncle Antiochus *Epiphanes*.
[34] 1Macc.7:1-4; 2Macc.14:1-2.
[35] 1Macc.7:12-14.

according to the author of 1 Maccabees, he has been party to the spilling of Jewish blood himself.

That Alcimus is the author of this psalm is the intriguing statement that is at the heart of this study. It will be necessary to examine whether one can accept this fact, to see what commentators throughout the ages have said about the authorship of Psalm 79 and to consider what this might mean for our study of this period.

The role that Alcimus plays in these events is enabled by the acceptance of pious Jews to his appointment as High Priest in the first place. Why did they accept him? The possibilities are that Alcimus a) was of High Priestly stock; b) had other familial credentials; c) had other religious credentials. A combination ofn these three possibilities might also have existed.

It will be our purpose to test all three contentions and to claim that Alcimus was of pedigreed priestly stock, that he was related to a renowned priest and religious leader of the anti-Hellenists and that he was a writer of religious poetry that marked him as a man of piety and spirituality. In the process, we will deal with a number of interconnected issues:

- Who was Alcimus? When did Alcimus become High Priest?
- Why was he chosen by the Seleucids to be High Priest?
- Was he a priest? Was he a Zadokite/Oniad?
- Was he a relative of the sage Yose ben Yoʿezer? Was the brother of Menelaus?
- Who had the authority, from a Jewish perspective, to appoint a High Priest?
- What religious and anti-religious actions did Alcimus take?
- Was he the High Priest of *Hanukkah*, the rededication of the Temple? If not, who was? Was it Judas? Was Judas a High Priest?
- Why did the *Asidaioi* accept him? Did Alcimus kill them?
- Did Alcimus breach the Temple wall? If so, why?
- How did Alcimus die?
- Who succeeded Alcimus? Was there an extended *intersacerdotium*[36] after him?
- Did Alcimus write a psalm? What does Psalm 79 refer to?

---

[36] An *intersacerdotium* is a time interval during which there was no high priest.

The Historical Background

- What is the state of scholarship on the authorship of psalms?
- Is there an irony in the term "Maccabaean psalms"?

There are only a few ancient references to Alcimus. We will carefully cull these sources and examine them in some detail.

CHAPTER II

THE SOURCES

1Maccabees

There is a great deal of scholarly agreement about the nature and purpose of 1Maccabees.[1] Originally written in Hebrew[2] and then translated into Greek, this work is an extremely important source for the events from the Hellenistic reforms in Jerusalem to the death of Simeon, son of Mattathias and the reign of John Hyrcanus.[3] Scholars are generally impressed with its historical accuracy and unity.[4] The author, a native of Judaea, seems to be well informed about the institutions of the Seleucid Empire. The geographical details are almost always precise, with exact names for the sites of important events and battles. The documents that have been interwoven into the narrative may be edited and reworded but scholarship has found them to be basically authentic.[5] The author makes an earnest attempt to provide a chronological framework for his narrative. The nature of 1Maccabees is very much like the books of Ezra and Nehemiah, including documents and letters within the framework, exhibiting a reverence for the glorious past and future of the people. The fight here, as it is in the Book of Daniel, is not only with Antiochus IV but also with all of the empires that have ruled and oppressed the people and the land.

---

[1] Jonathan A. Goldstein, *I Maccabees*; J. C. Danby, *I Maccabees. A Commentary.* Oxford: Blackwell, 1954; J. Efron, *Studies on the Hasmonaean Period* SJLA 39 Leiden: Brill, 1987; Robert Doran "The First Book of Maccabees" in *The New Interpreter's Bible* Vol. IV (Nashville, 1996) 3-178.

[2] An interesting attempt to reconstruct the original Hebrew text has been made by Abraham Kahana *Ha-Sefarim ha-Hitzonim* vol. 2 (Tel Aviv, 1937).

[3] 1Macc.16:23-24 seems to refer to the latter's reign as if it is over.

[4] H. W. Ettelson *The Integrity of I Maccabees* The Transactions of the Connecticut Academy of Arts and Sciences 27 (1925) 249-384; K. D. Schunck *Die quellen des I. Und II. Makkbäerbuches* (Halle: 1954) 7.

[5] Joshua Efron *Studies on the Hasmonean Period* (Leiden, 1987) 14-15 n. 50; M. Stern *Ha Teudot le-Mered ha-Hashmonaim* (Tel Aviv, 1965).

The Sources

In his description of Judas Maccabee's admiration for Roman rule, the author shows his preference for a government of a High Priest and a people's council.[6] The work expresses the attitudes and emphases of the Hasmonaean dynasty.[7] As such, we must read 1Maccabees as an historical work that presents a perspective that, in the case of this study, must be seen as tendentious in its description of Alcimus, his activities, and attitudes.

We will pick up the narrative of 1Maccabees from the point at which Alcimus enters. While Alcimus has already been serving as High Priest for the better part of a year, there is no way to know this from this source. Demetrius I son of Seleucus comes from Rome, has Antiochus V and Lysias killed, and becomes king. It does not take long for the Judaean situation to come to his attention:

> Then all the sinful and wicked men of Israel came before him led by Alcimus, who wanted to be high priest. They brought charges against their people, telling the king, "Judas and his brothers have killed all your friends, and he has driven us from our land."
>
> 1Macc.7:5,6

Alcimus, according to this translation, wants to be High Priest; that is, he is not yet High Priest and has not been High Priest before this. The Greek *hierateuein*, however, is an infinitive and means "to act as priest."[8] Certainly, any diminution of

---

[6] 1Macc.8:14-15.

[7] This has been accepted since the work of Abraham Geiger *Urschrift und Ubersetzungen der Bibel* (2nd ed. Frankfurt/Main, 1928) 206.

[8] See the LXX on the following references where the Greek verb *hierateuein* is used to translate the Hebrew *lekhahen*: Ex. 28: 1, 4; 29:1, 44; 30:30; 31:10; Lev.7:35; 16:32; Num. 3:3; 16:10; 1Sam.2:28; 1Esdras5:39; Sirach 45:15; Hosea 4:6; Ezek.44:13. Goldstein *I Maccabees* 324-25 states that *hierateuein* means either "to be high priest" or "to become high priest." In the former rendering, Alcimus could have come to Demetrius I to be reappointed as high priest by the new Seleucid king. Even though Alcimus has been high priest for some months now (as we shall learn from other sources), this is the first time he is mentioned in 1Maccabees. Since, as we will see from Josephus, Antiochus V already had appointed Alcimus, and since the author of 1Maccabees does mention Alcimus in this chapter and later in Chapter 9, the question is why this earlier appointment was not mentioned. Goldstein suggests that the author may not have recognized Antiochus V's legitimacy or his right to appoint a high priest. See my

Alcimus' legitimacy is consistent with the way he is seen by Judas and his supporters, who are the heroes of this work. They see Alcimus in extremely negative terms. We are not yet told if Alcimus has a priestly or High Priestly pedigree. Alcimus and his allies identify themselves as enemies of the Maccabees and say to Demetrius I:

> "Now, therefore, send a man whom you trust and have him go view all the havoc Judas has wreaked upon us and upon the land of the king's domains, and have him punish Judas and his men and all their abettors."
>
> 1Macc.7:7

To the followers of the Hasmonaeans by whom and for whom this book is written, Alcimus' appeal, which will find a ready response from Demetrius I, would be a terrible betrayal of his people: Alcimus seeks to buttress his own power by bringing in new and more formidable help from the enemies of the Judaeans. Demetrius I chooses Bacchides, one of the king's Friends, governor of the Trans-Euphrates province, to return with Alcimus to Judaea:

> He sent him with the wicked Alcimus, whom he confirmed in the high priesthood, with orders to wreak vengeance on the Israelites.
>
> 1Macc.7:9

Alcimus is "the wicked Alcimus." The translation "confirmed" leaves open the question of whether Alcimus had been High Priest before this point. It is also interesting that while Alcimus and his followers are Israelites as well, the text here makes it seem as if Judas and his followers are the only Israelites.

> They set out on the march with a large force against the land of Judas. Bacchides sent a message to Judas and his brothers, treacherously couched in peaceful terms. However, Judas and his brothers paid the messengers no heed, for they saw how large a Seleucid force had come.
>
> 1Macc.7:10,11

---

discussion below, however, on the ancient Jewish perspective on whether a foreign emperor had the authority to appoint a high priest.

The Sources

Judas has a right to wonder why such a large force would be necessary if peace is the only goal.

This is an important moment because there seems to be a rift between Judas and the *Asidaioi*. The author of 1Maccabees states that while Judas knows that the Seleucids have come to Judaea to wreck and destroy those who are opposed to Alcimus, the *Asidaioi* do not seem to understand what is happening and naively approach those whom they should have known were their enemies.[9] Doran suggests that the disagreement between the *Asidaioi* and Judas was over the acceptance of a foreign army in the land of Judaea. The Judaeans had recently had a terrible experience with the false words spoken by Apollonius the Mysarch:

> ... the king sent a Mysarch against the towns of Judas, and he came against Jerusalem with a strong army. Treacherously he addresses the people in peaceful terms, so that they trusted him, and then he hit the city hard with a surprise attack, killing many Israelites. He plundered the city, set fire to it, and destroyed its buildings and the walls around it. ...
>
> 1Macc.1:29-30

The difference here is that a fellow Judaean and a priest speak the words; the *Asidaioi* believe their countryman. If Alcimus wrote Psalm 79 and if that psalm refers to the event of Apollonius' treachery and ruin of Jerusalem, the *Asidaioi* might not have suspected this betrayal by the man who had condemned those events. Judas, on the other hand, sees the large army and trusts no one.

> Nevertheless, an assembly of men learned in the *Torah* gathered before Alcimus and Bacchides "to seek justice." The *Asidaioi* took the lead among the Israelites in seeking peace at their hands, saying, "A man who is a priest of the stock of Aaron has come with their force; he will not wrong us."
>
> 1Macc.7:12-14

---

[9] Goldstein *I Maccabees* 331 suggests that there is an interesting play here on Zephaniah 1:2-3, that the *Asidaioi* think that the fulfillment of this prophecy is at hand and that therefore Alcimus could be trusted. The idea is that those who knew Scripture were misled by their misunderstanding of it.

It is not clear whether Menelaus was a priest. The *Testament of Moses* (v.4) indicates that he was not; on the other hand, if he were the brother of Simon of the Bilgah clan, mentioned in 2Maccabees[10] as the chief administrator of the Temple, he might indeed have been a priest. If he were not a priest, these texts would have made a great deal of the fact that a non-priest was serving as High Priest. If Menelaus were a priest, what would differentiate Alcimus from his predecessor? And yet the *Asidaioi* clearly see Alcimus' pedigree in a very different light. It would seem that while Menelaus was of priestly stock, Alcimus was of High Priestly stock.

The *Asidaioi* disagreed with Judas in that they were ready to accept Alcimus as High Priest; again, it seems as if Alcimus only becomes the high priest at this point. If he had been High Priest before this point, it would mean that he had already been functioning in this role with at least the tacit cooperation of the people.

> Indeed, Alcimus spoke with them in peaceful terms and swore to them that, "We intend no harm to you or to your friends." As soon as he had won their trust, however, he arrested sixty of them and had them executed all in a single day, in accordance with the verse which he himself wrote, "The bodies and blood of Your saints they have poured out around Jerusalem, and there is no one to bury them."
> 1Macc.7:15-17

As Goldstein states emphatically, "Our verses say, with emphasis, that Alcimus *himself wrote* Ps.79:2-3. Our author loses no love over Alcimus and would not credit him with writing words revered by the pious unless Alcimus was in fact the author of these verses." Goldstein details the various manuscript readings and states that, "modern editors have been correct in taking as most reliable the unidiomatic original text of S, *ton logon hon egrapsen auton*, literally "the verse which he wrote it." As explained above, the heart of this study stems from this fact. Here we see 1Maccabees aiming its harshest possible attack on Alcimus, and yet even at this very point openly speaking of Alcimus as the author of these verses. Actually, v.17 here is a condensation of Ps.79:2-3. If Alcimus wrote the psalm, the reference of what the enemy has done to Jerusalem may be to the sack of Jerusalem by Antiochus IV in 169 BCE or to the expedition of the Mysarch in 167 BCE. The land has been invaded and the Temple defiled, a horror that receives poetic expression:

---

[10] 2Macc.3:4.

The Sources

> It was an ambush against the temple,
> And continually a wicked adversary against Israel.
> They shed innocent blood around the sanctuary
> and defiled the temple.
>
> 1Macc. 1:36-37

We will be treating the subject of Alcimus as psalmist later in this study.

The execution of the *Asidaioi* is a key juncture in the events studied here. The question is: Why did Alcimus arrest and execute the sixty *Asidaioi* representatives? For now, we can only comment on what 1Maccabees says. Alcimus lures the *Asidaioi* into a trap and, apparently with pre-meditation, kills them. Judas, the hero of 1Maccabees, was correct in his suspicions. Alcimus was a traitor to his people. Notice that it is not Bacchides but Alcimus who does the evil and sinister act. While Doran[11] compares this event to the "similar execution" of Judaean leaders by the Babylonians after the fall of Jerusalem in 586 BCE,[12] that action was committed by a foreign conqueror, not a countryman. The crime here would be viewed as much more heinous. Note also that he executes them all in a single day; this is nothing short of mass murder and injustice.

> The fear and dread of them seized the entire people, as they said to one another, "There is no truth or justice among them. They have violated their pledge and their sworn oath." Thereafter, Bacchides left Jerusalem and encamped at Beth-Zaith. Then he sent out orders and had many of the turncoats who had gone over to him arrested, as well as some of our people; he had all these butchered by the great cistern and their bodies cast into it. After putting the country under the control of Alcimus and leaving him troops to assist him, Bacchides returned to the king.
>
> 1Macc.7:18-20

With harsh symbolism, Bacchides prevents the victims from proper burial.[13] Beth-Zaith is south of Jerusalem and on the road to Idumaea. Why does Bacchides need to move in this direction? Had some of the *Asidaioi* fled south? Were other factions rising in revolt? With the religious persecution over, were some of these

---

[11] Doran, *1Maccabees* 95.
[12] 2Kings 25:18-21; Jer.52:24-27.
[13] See Jer.41:7. Archaeologists have found traces of ancient cisterns in the vicinity.

factions resistant to continued foreign rule? One of these factions seems to consist of "turncoats who had gone over to him," a most confusing phrase. Apparently, there were *Asidaioi* who accepted the Seleucid rule but not the legitimacy of Alcimus, especially after the latter's massacre of the *Asidaioi* referred to above. For Bacchides, resistance to either the empire or Alcimus was to be met with death.

For the author of 1Maccabees, on the other hand, anyone who accepted Alcimus and his foreign allies was a "turncoat." To take a step back, however, one must remember that Demetrius I *Soter* is the legitimate king of an empire that has ruled Judaea for some time, an empire that had been accepted by all factions before recent events. Now, any Judaean who continues to accept this empire and its representatives is branded a traitor. The lines are clearly drawn, and those who now do not accept the empire are destroyed.

> Alcimus then faced a struggle for the high priesthood, in which, however, all the troublers of their people rallied to him, overran the land of Judas, and inflicted a great defeat upon Israel. Judas saw all the harm that Alcimus and his supporters had done to Israelites, far worse than anything the gentiles were doing.
> 1Macc.7:21-23

Bacchides left the country under the mistaken impression that the battle had been won and that Alcimus was secure. At first, this seems to be true. But perhaps Alcimus overplays his hand and continues to commit violence against Judas and his supporters and other factions as well.

It is interesting to see how the narrative turns illegitimate political rebellion into legitimate action and the attempt to keep the legitimate political *status quo* as treason. "The troublers of their people" rally to Alcimus; they "overrun" the country and "inflict a great defeat on Israel." "Israel," now, is the citizens of Judaea who support Judas.

Since Bacchides is gone, one has to see the conflict at this point as internally Jewish. This statement brings us into the scholarly controversy about who was more responsible for the damage done to the Judaeans, the Seleucids, or the Jewish Hellenizers.

It is not at all clear what Alcimus and his followers are doing to their countrymen. They may simply be trying to battle the Maccabees and their followers. We are not told what Alcimus "did" to his people. One has to think that if there had

The Sources

been specific and terrible acts, this text would tell us. The dispute seems to be more political than religious.

> Accordingly, he went around the entire territory of Judaea, punishing the turncoats so that they shrank from going out into the countryside. When Alcimus saw the growing strength of Judas and his men, knowing and that he could not cope with them, he went again to the king and accused them of atrocities.
>
> 1Macc.7:24,25

Again, the Seleucids are not directly involved at this moment; this is a civil war. Judas must not be very strong at this point because he cannot engage in pitched battles. Instead, he fights a guerilla war, bottling them up in Jerusalem. Alcimus and the pro-Seleucid Judaeans, who are now losing, go once again to the king. Demetrius sends Nicanor, who proposes peace to Judas.

> Thereupon the king sent Nicanor, one of his high-ranking officers, a hater, and a foe of Israel, with orders to exterminate our people.
>
> 1Macc.7:26

While the author introduces Nicanor as "a hater and a foe of Israel," his own narrative will not support this description.[14] After a peaceful first meeting with Judas, the latter, fearing treachery, refuses subsequent meetings. Nicanor attacks and Judas wins.

> Some time thereafter, Nicanor went up to Mount Zion. Some priests came out of the sanctuary along with some elders of the people to greet him peacefully and show him the burnt offering which was being sacrificed on behalf of the king. He however, mocked them, laughing in their faces and rendering them unclean with his spit. Presumptuously he spoke, angrily swearing that "Unless Judas and his army are delivered into my hands immediately, upon my victorious return I shall burn this temple."
>
> 1Macc.7:33

---

[14] Not to mention the good relationship between Nicanor and Judas that will be described in 2Macc. (see below).

Nicanor goes to Mount Zion but cannot enter the Temple court itself. These restrictions, then, are still in force. The priests in the Temple under Alcimus' tenure offer a burnt offering for the Seleucid king. Nicanor mocks the burnt offering sacrificed on behalf of the king, which one would think he would appreciate. Despite the pro-Seleucid stance of this offering, Nicanor disdains it, probably to show his distrust of those who are adherents of a religion that seems to be provoking such successful revolution against the king. Nicanor goes so far as to threaten to burn the Temple if Judas and his followers are not turned over to him. The priests pray for God to take vengeance on Nicanor. It is striking that if Alcimus and his supporters are in control of Temple worship, the priests are praying for the destruction of Alcimus' benefactor. Nicanor attacks Judas on the 13th of Adar (March 8, 161 BCE); Nicanor is killed and his army is routed.

We shall pass over the alliance made with Rome recorded in Chapter 8[15] and only mention the names of Judas's emissaries to the Romans, "Eupolemus son of John of the clan of Hakkoz and Jason, son of Eleazar."[16] While Jason, son of Eleazar certainly seems to bear a priestly name, we do not know anything about him, except that in the future he may very well be the father of an ambassador who will be sent by the High Priest Jonathan to Rome in the summer of 143 BCE. It is more interesting for our purpose here to note the lineage of the first-named ambassador in 1Macc.8:17, Eupolemus son of John of the Hakkoz clan. The Hakkoz clan has a unique history. In Ezra 2:61-63[17], "the sons of Hakkoz" were one of three priestly clans who were "disqualified for the priesthood" because their genealogical records could not be found. The Persian official at the time, the Tirshatha, ordered them to refrain from eating of the most holy things "until a priest with Urim and Thummim should appear." While it is not clear how the clan of Hakkoz managed to regain full priestly status, 1Chron.24:10 has them fully restored and taking their place in the priestly rotation. Did a priest with Urim and Thummim appear? While this seems far-fetched, something happened and the Hakkoz clan became prominent again. Eupolemus was the son of John who was appointed by

---

[15] Wolf Wirgin "Judas Maccabee's Embassy to Rome and the Jewish-Roman Treaty" *PEQ* 101 (1969) 15-20.
[16] 1Macc.8:17.
[17] See also Neh.7:63-65

The Sources

Antiochus III to be an *ethnos*, a very privileged status.[18] Goldstein suggests that Eupolemus may be the same Eupolemus who wrote an historical work in Greek, *On the Kings in Judaea*, during the reign of Demetrius I.[19] This is a fine example of the waxing and waning of the fortunes of a priestly clan and can serve as useful background for further consideration of the politics in the ancient Israelite priestly world.

We can now continue the narrative of 1Maccabees as it pertains to Alcimus. The embassy to Rome leads Rome to warn Demetrius I that he must not oppress the Judaeans. Demetrius I is apparently unimpressed because he sends an expedition under Bacchides and Alcimus to punish the Jewish rebels under Judas. The punitive expedition is successful and the Jews are massacred at Messaloth-in-Arbela in the Galilee.

> When Demetrius heard that Nicanor and his army had fallen in battle, he sent Bacchides and Alcimus into the land of Judas a second time, and with them the right wing of the army. They went by the road that leads to Gilgal and encamped against Mesaloth in Arbela, and they took it and killed many people. In the first month of the one hundred fifty-second year, they encamped against Jerusalem; then they marched off and went to Berea with twenty thousand foot soldiers and two thousand cavalry.
> 1Macc. 9:1-4

Bacchides and Alcimus reach Jerusalem in the spring of 160 BCE and soon defeat the Maccabee force at Elasa. Judas himself is killed. The survivors are demoralized because of the loss of their leader and go home. Alcimus, with his rival and enemy gone, is in control. As the author of 1Maccabees puts it:

> After the death of Judas, "the wicked sprouted" throughout the territory of Israel, "and the evildoers flourished."
> 1Macc. 9:23

---

[18] As we know from *2Macc*.4:11.

[19] See Goldstein loc. cit. For further study, see B. Z. Wacholder *Eupolemus: A Study of Judaeo-Greek Literature* (New York, 1974) and *Die Fragmente der griechischen Historiker*, ed. by F. Jacoby (Leiden, 1923) 723, F 1-5. Eupolemus may be the Jewish historian the fragments of whose work have been transmitted in Alexander Polyhistor. See Hengel *Judaism and Hellenism* I 92ff.

Goldstein thinks that this is a clear parody of Psalms 92:8:

> A brutish man cannot know,
> a fool cannot understand this:
> though the wicked sprout like grass,
> though all evildoers blossom,
> it is only that they may be destroyed forever.

Goldstein then wonders if Alcimus and "his circle" wrote this psalm, like Ps.79 and perhaps others. We will have more to say about this below.

Alcimus may be a "brutish man" in the eyes of this author, but he has great power and seeks to rid the land of all of Judas' followers. These followers confer the leadership of their struggle on Jonathan, Judas' brother.

It is at this time, between May 2 and May 30, 159 BCE, that Alcimus makes a controversial and confusing move:

> In the year 153[20], in the second month, Alcimus issued an order to tear down the wall of the inner court of the sanctuary, thus tearing down the work of the prophets. Alcimus had already begun the work of having it torn down when he suffered a stroke which put an end to his project. Unable to open his mouth and paralyzed, he could no longer speak or issue a will for his family. So Alcimus died in great agony on that occasion. On finding that Alcimus was dead, Bacchides returned to the king. The land of Judea was undisturbed for two years.
>
> 1Macc. 9:54-57

There is a great deal here that needs explanation. Part of our assessment of Alcimus' character and religious stance depends on our interpretation of v.54. The key phrase is "wall of the Inner Court of the sanctuary." To which court is this a reference? Why did Alcimus do this?

The word "court" is used here either for the area around the innermost building or an area like the "Court of Women." The "Outer Court" would be the "Court of Women"; the "Inner Court" was divided into the "Court of Priests" and the "Court of Israelites." As we will discuss at length in our examination of relevant references

---

[20] The year 153 is according to the Seleucid calendar. For issues of Seleucid chronology and their system of years, see Goldstein *I Maccabees* 544.

The Sources

from *Mishnah Middot* (see below), the barrier that was outside the "Outer Court," the "Court of Women," had already been breached in the time of Antiochus IV.[21] What did Alcimus want to tear down? We will see that Josephus is quite vague in his reference to the barrier that Alcimus wanted to tear down.

Goldstein is certain that even if Alcimus had not been pious[22] he would not have thought about "introducing gentiles or Greek practices to the "Inner Court." Instead, Goldstein thinks that we are reading here about "an internal Jewish controversy, between Jewish sects." Voices as disparate as Ezekiel[23] and the Essenes (as evidenced in the *Temple Scroll*) were intensely concerned with the architecture of the Temple.

It remains to be explained what the author means by "the work of the prophets." It seems difficult to think that the wall is credited to Ezekiel since there are such important differences between the prophet's description of his idealized Second Temple and the Second Temple that was actually built in history. Ezekiel warned against allowing any but Zadokite priests into the "Inner Court"[24] while the author of the book of Nehemiah[25] states that non-priestly male Israelites in a state of ritual purity could enter a part of the "Inner Court." Still, "the work of the prophets" may be a reference to a wall of the "Inner Court" that was supported by the later prophets such as Haggai and Zechariah.

It is interesting to note the text expressly states that Alcimus could not "issue a will for his family." One cannot help but wonder if there is an important implication here that Alcimus does not pass his legacy of the High Priesthood to anyone in his family. His instructions would no doubt have been important because Bacchides and the Seleucids would no doubt have supported them. Indeed, there does not appear to be any reference in any source to Alcimus' progeny. As the High Priest, whether he was considered legitimate by the Hasmonaeans or not, a son of Alcimus might have been someone who would play his part on the political/religious scene.

Now that Alcimus is dead, the Maccabaean revolt seems to be over. "On finding that Alcimus was dead, Bacchides returned to the king. The land of Judas was

---

[21] See 1Macc.1:37..
[22] Goldstein thinks he was, as I shall discuss below.
[23] Ezek.43:8-11.
[24] Ezek.44:10-16; 46:3-9.
[25] Neh.8:16.

undisturbed for two years." The verse is interesting in understanding just how important Alcimus was to all of these events. Does this mean that Alcimus' antagonism to the Hasmonaeans prolonged violent strife between Judaeans? Certainly, that is what the author of 1Maccabees wants us to believe.

We will attempt to answer our list of questions about Alcimus from the perspective of this source:

When did Alcimus become High Priest? Alcimus became High Priest in the autumn of 162 BCE, appointed for the first time by Demetrius I.

Who was Alcimus? Why was he chosen by the Seleucids to be High Priest? Was he a priest? Was he the nephew of Yose ben Yoʻezer? Was he the brother of Menelaus? Alcimus is a priest "of the stock of Aaron." We do not even know his father's name or his priestly clan. We do not know anything else about his lineage except that the *Asidaioi* respected it enough to initially trust him.

What religious and anti-religious actions did Alcimus take? The priests in the Temple under his tenure offered a burnt offering for the Seleucid king. Despite the apparent pro-Seleucid stance of this offering, it is disdained and mocked by the Seleucid general Nicanor. Alcimus wanted to tear down the wall of the "Inner Court" of the Temple, which is seen here as an anti-religious action.

Was he the High Priest of *Hanukkah*, the rededication of the temple? No, the dedication occurred in the winter of 164 BCE and Alcimus, according to this text, only become High Priest in 162 BCE. It is interesting to note that there are many more High Priests mentioned in 2Maccabees than 1Maccabees. The question not only of who was the High Priest for the rededication, but also for the time in between the re-dedication and the appointment of Alcimus, remains open in this text.

Why did the *Asidaioi* accept him? They accepted him because he was of Aaronide descent and they did not believe that anyone of this line could commit evil against then.

Why did he kill them? He killed them in order to weaken the resistance against him. This evil act was a demonstration of Alcimus' falsity and generally abominable character.

Did he write a psalm? According to this text, Alcimus himself wrote Psalm 79. What does Psalm 79 refer to? Since Alcimus wrote it, the reference to what the enemy has done to Jerusalem may be to the sack of Jerusalem by Antiochus IV in 169 BCE or to the Mysarch's expedition in 167 BCE.

The Sources

Can we reconstruct Alcimus' life from psalms? Alcimus wrote a psalm, which means that he was a religious figure with poetic and spiritual feelings and expressions that were well known.

How did Alcimus die? His sudden death was a punishment from God when he attempted to tear down the wall of the "Inner Court" of the Temple.

Who succeeded Alcimus? Was there an extended *intersacerdotium* after him? At his death in 159 BCE, there is no mention of a replacement until the appointment of Jonathan in 152 BCE.

2Maccabees

2Maccabees is an unfortunate name for this totally independent work that is in no way a continuation of 1Maccabees.[26] A native of Judaea wrote 1Maccabees; 2Maccabees is a product of the Hellenistic Jewish diaspora. Where 1Maccabees has a fine sense of geographical details, 2Maccabees has few landscapes and battle scenes. 1Maccabees begins with Antiochus IV's actions against the Judaeans and his profanation of the Jerusalem Temple and ends with the death of Simon in 135/34 BCE. 2Maccabees begins in the reign previous to that of Antiochus IV, that of Seleucus IV and emphasizes the martyrdom of those Judaeans who resisted the oppression by the Seleucids. The work ends after the defeat of the Seleucid general Nicanor and with Judas still alive (161-160 BCE).

While 1Maccabees is clearly written from the viewpoint of the Hasmonaean dynasty, the authorship of 2Maccabees has created a great deal of scholarly discussion. 2Maccabees is an abridgement of a large, five-book work written around 86 BCE by Jason of Cyrene. The abridgement was produced between 78-63 BCE (the epilogue of the abridger indicates that Jerusalem was still in the hands of the Jewish people as of the end of his work, and the Romans under Pompey conquered the city in 63 BCE). 1Maccabees was originally written in Hebrew and then translated into Greek; 2Maccabees was written in the Greek style of its time and abounds in emotion, metaphor, miracles, and graphic descriptions.

The author of 2Maccabees attempts to refute 1Maccabees in certain important ways. 1Maccabees wants to legitimize the Hasmonaean Dynasty, especially in

---

[26] Jonathan A. Goldstein *II Maccabees* The Anchor Bible; Solomon Zeitlin *The Second Book of Maccabees* Dropsie College edition (New York: 1954); Robert Doran "The Second Book of Maccabees" in *The New Interpreter's Bible* (Nashville, 1996) 181-299.

regard to the slight given it by Daniel 7-12. 2Maccabees wants to uphold the view of events and their interpretation in Daniel 7-12. It was not Hasmonaean military might and strategy that brought victory as in 1Maccabees but the martyrdom of the saints that won the day for Israel. While Mattathias and Judas retain the high stature accorded them in 1Maccabees (though we shall try to modify this in reference to Judas), Judas' brothers are tainted by sin.

Recent scholarship has focused on the idea that 2Maccabees may have been written as Temple propaganda.[27] Certainly, there is an emphasis on the cultic, with ritual and holidays such as *Hanukkah* and Nicanor's Day. This is wedded to the focus on Jerusalem and the Temple, perhaps with a negative eye to the Oniad temple in Leontopolis. Momigliano, in a useful essay about 2Maccabees,[28] states that the epitome was written around 124 BCE with the purpose of offering the Jews in Egypt a record of the reconsecration of the Temple in Jerusalem. The epitomist wanted the Egyptian Jews to be loyal to the Temple of Jerusalem and not that of Leontopolis. The latter temple was quite involved in the dynastic struggles raging at that time; the leaders of the party and those who were in control of that temple were one and the same; Onias IV and his sons Chelkias and Ananias supported Cleopatra II and used the temple as a center for the recruitment of Jewish mercenaries. We shall return to the building of the Leontopolis temple below.

That the Jerusalem Temple was ruined but then restored is a centerpiece of the theological message: God was on the side of the faithful Judaeans and against the Hellenizers (such as Alcimus). Thus again, in searching for a more objective perspective on Alcimus, we must separate history from ideology in reading this work. We will pick up the narrative with the first mention of Alcimus. The last two chapters of 2Maccabees[29] cover the same events as 1Maccabees 7, studied above.

> Three years later, Judas and his men received the news that Demetrius son of Seleucus had sailed into the harbor of Tripolis with a strong force and a fleet and

---

[27] Robert Doran *Temple Propaganda: The Purpose and Character of 2 Maccabees* CBQMS 12 (Washington, D.C., 1981).

[28] Arnold Momigliano "The Second Book of Maccabees" in Arnaldo Momigliano *Essays on Ancient and Modern Judaism* ed. by Silvia Berti, trans. by Maura Masella-Gayley. (Chicago, 1994).

[29] 2Macc.14-15.

The Sources

had become master of the country and had done away with Antiochus and his guardian Lysias.

2Macc. 14:1-2.

The phrase "three years later" is important for our purposes because we are interested in Alcimus' role during that period. We need to know as much about the chronology of these years as we can ascertain. 1Maccabees[30] has the accession of Demetrius I Soter in the early autumn of 162 BCE. It is correct, as we know from the fact Demetrius I escaped from Rome after he learned that the Roman ambassador Gnaeus Octavius had been murdered while on an embassy to the Seleucids. The date of this murder has been fixed in 162 BCE.[31] If we go back three years from this date, we are back to the early part of the rebellion under Mattathias (who died 166-65 BCE) and Judas (who defeated different Seleucid expeditions in 165 BCE). The problem is that at the end of the previous chapter of 2Maccabees, we read about the campaign of Antiochus V in 163 BCE. Scholarship has not supplied a satisfactory theory to resolve this discrepancy.[32] It may just be a mistake.

> There was a certain Alcimus, who had previously been appointed high priest but had voluntarily defiled himself during the time of peace.
>
> 2Macc. 14:3

Notice the introduction of this important figure. We do not know what his pedigree is; we do not even know if he is a priest at all. He is "a certain Alcimus." Alcimus seems to reprise the role played by Simon of the clan of Bilgah who, in 2Maccabees[33] is described in a similar way by the author: "There was a certain Simon from the clan of Bilgah." Simon goes to the Seleucid king with self-serving complaints against the true leaders of his people, wreaking havoc with terrible implications.

---

[30] 1Macc.7:1-4.
[31] Elias Bickerman "Makkabäerbucher" in Pauly-Wissowa et al, eds. *Realencylopaedie der klassischen Altertumswiseenschaft* XIV (1930) 783.
[32] Goldstein tries in both *I Maccabees* 91 and *II Maccabees* 478 but fails to solve the riddle.
[33] 2Macc.3:4-6.

To our surprise we learn that Alcimus had been High Priest. If he already had been High Priest, why is he only introduced now? When had he been appointed? We have to assume that Antiochus had appointed him after the demise of Menelaus. Had Alcimus been a part of the temple structure under Menelaus? We also learn that he "had voluntarily defiled himself during the time of peace." If this translation is correct, it seems to indicate that even though it was not under coercion by the Greeks, Alcimus was a willing participant in the "Hellenization" of the Temple. Some seem to think that this defilement is a reference to the murder of the *Asidaioi* that has not yet happened (which does not make any sense) because otherwise, the *Asidaioi* would not have accepted an impure High Priest. If Alcimus had gone through a "voluntary defilement," it could not have been before he first became High Priest. The Seleucids would not have selected a problematic candidate. They wanted a respected and pious priest about whom everyone could agree, one about whom even Judas could not say anything negative.

Some scholars find it totally illogical that the *Asidaioi* accepted Alcimus at a point when, according to their understanding of the text, he was still in a state of defilement. They claim that the writer of 2Maccabees sees defilement as permanent disqualification. If defilement here means what it does in the *Torah*, and Alcimus had served as High Priest or even entered the temple while "unclean," he would have been "cut off."[34] Alcimus could not return to his position if he had been "cut off."[35] Another problem is that, according to both the *Torah* and later rabbinic law, an individual cannot intentionally incur permanent uncleanness.[36]

One theory is that Alcimus never did defile himself in any way and that Jason of Cyrene is creating the defilement in order to pursue his goal of undermining a High Priest that he despised. After all, if Alcimus had truly ritually defiled himself, would 1Maccabees have refrained from saying so? Defilement here means collaboration with the Seleucids, and yet, insofar as such acts are condemned by 1&2Maccabees, they do not constitute ritual defilement. We shall return to this important issue after we have studied other related dimensions of the context of Alcimus' priesthood.

---

[34] Later rabbinic law would condemn Alcimus to "death at the hands of Heaven," which might leave matters, so to speak, up in the air, or lynching, a human and therefore certain punishment (M. *Sanhedrin* 9:6; T. *Keritot* 1:5; BT *Sanhedrin* 82b-83a.)

[35] According to the clear rulings of Lev.22:3 and Num.19: 13, 20.

[36] "Purity and Impurity, Ritual," *Encyclopedia Judaica* XIII (1972) 1405-12.

The Sources

In 1Maccabees, Alcimus approaches Demetrius to gain or regain the High Priesthood. What is different in this text is that there is no massacre of the *Asidaioi* or anything like it.

> Perceiving that there was no way for him to be secure or to have access henceforth to the holy altar, he approached King Demetrius I in about the year 151 and presented him with a gold crown and palm along with some of the customary gifts from the temple.
> 2Macc. 14:3-4

Alcimus has a political problem in that he is not secure in his position. He has also a ritual problem in that he cannot gain access to the holy altar and therefore he cannot act as High Priest. We can readily understand Alcimus' political problem because we know the extent of the power that Judas wielded. However, what has he done to defile himself? Since he is High Priest, who is stopping him if he is defiled? If he is defiled ritually speaking, what can Demetrius do for him?

There are at least two other possibilities. Goldstein voices one explanation: "It would thus appear that Jason's words here are false."[37] The abridger or author of 2Maccabees is artificially creating a defilement that never was. Another theory, given by Doran, is that the text is not speaking of ritual defilement at all but of a disgrace, a disgrace avoided by Judas when he left Jerusalem:

> Judas, also known as Maccabaeus, in a group of about ten, withdrew into the mountains, where he and his men eked out a living like beasts. There they stayed, eating herbs for food, in order to keep clear of defilement.
> 2Macc. 5:27

What they eat or do not eat has nothing to do with the defilement here. They need to stay clear of the uncleanness that is apparently brought by Apollonius the Mysarch. There may be a play on words here since *Mysós* in Greek means "Mysian" and *mysos* means "unclean;" indeed, the Syriac here translates "Mysarch" as "chief of the unclean."

---

[37] Goldstein *II Maccabees* 482.

To return to the problem of Alcimus' defilement, it may be that the author is consciously contrasting the behavior of both Judas and Razis[38] in avoiding defilement and/or disgrace. The problem with this explanation is that it is contrary to the text, which clearly says that Alcimus did not have access to the holy altar because of his defilement. To stay with the meaning of 2Maccabees, then, we have to insist that Alcimus had defiled himself through his actions and that a general state of disgrace is not the sense of the text. We pick up the narrative again; Alcimus is before Demetrius seeking re-appointment. He brings gifts from the temple: a gold crown, a palm, and olive branches.[39] As anxious as he is to regain power, he respectfully bides his time, waiting for the right moment:

> On that day, Alcimus said nothing. However, he found an opportune time for his mad designs when he was summoned by Demetrius to a meeting of the royal council and asked, "What are the present mood and aspirations of the Jews?" He replied, "Among the Jews, those who are called '*Asidaioi*' under the leadership of Judas Maccabaeus, are feeding the flames of war and are in rebellion and refuse to allow your kingdom to become tranquil. As a result, I have been deprived of the distinction of my forefathers (I mean, the High Priesthood).
>
> 2Macc. 14:4-7

A very important question here is: Why does the author omit the massacre of the *Asidaioi*? The event, which is so very crucial in 1Maccabees, is not even mentioned in 2Maccabees. A theory is that the story in 1Maccabees reveals a split between that group and Judas[40] with the *Asidaioi* hoping to find peace with Alcimus and Judas unwilling to negotiate; this split is an embarrassment to the author of 2Maccabees. Instead, the *Asidaioi* are "under the leadership of Judas Maccabaeus." Alcimus makes it seem that it is only Judas and the *Asidaioi* who are causing the problem and that they are distinct from the rest of the nation.[41] The reader of this narrative would think this assessment of the respective popularity of Judas and Alcimus to be untrue, with the nation following Judas and Alcimus as the leader of a troublesome

---

[38] As mentioned above in reference to 2Macc.14:38.
[39] Cf. Simon in 1Macc.13:36-37.
[40] See 7:13; cf. 2:42.
[41] And see below on v.8.

The Sources

minority.[42] Alcimus' speech to Demetrius I is in sharp contrast to that of a hero of this work, Onias III who, when approaching the Seleucid king, acted as a true leader of his people:

> Perceiving how dangerous was Simon's feud and how Apollonius son of Menestheus, the governor of Coele-Syria and Phoenicia, was involved in making Simon's wickedness still worse, Onias journeyed to the king. His purpose was not to bring charges against his fellow Jews but to look to the collective and individual interests of all the people. Indeed, he saw that without provident intervention by the king the commonwealth could never more have peace...
>
> 2Macc.4:4-6

This passage from an earlier chapter in the same work is a model for how a good High Priest should act in approaching the foreign king. Alcimus, when compared to Onias III, is found wanting in every respect. Indeed, Alcimus makes opposition to his High Priesthood to be identical with rebellion against Demetrius. The new king, eager to prove his strength throughout his empire and cognizant that Alcimus was the duly designated appointee of the Seleucid Empire, must take Alcimus' complaint with the utmost seriousness.

A possible explanation of v.7 is that Alcimus has not actually been deprived of the High Priesthood but has been forced to leave his duties in order to come to Demetrius I. This may very well be what actually happened, but it is not the plain meaning of this text, which states that Alcimus had defiled himself and has as a result lost his ability to function in his office.

2Maccabees makes it seem as if Alcimus is by himself in his entreaty to Demetrius; one would never know that he had many supporters and that he was no doubt certainly not alone at the court.

> I have come here now for two reasons: first, because I have the king's interests truly at heart; and second, because I am seeking the welfare of my own countrymen. The folly of the persons I just mentioned has brought upon our entire nation no small misfortune. Please take note of all this, Your Majesty, and take thought for our country, and bring your provident intervention to bear upon the land and upon our sorely beset nation with the ready kindness you show to all, for as long as Judas

---

[42] See 10:14-15 and 12:2.

survives, it is impossible for the commonwealth to have peace." When he had finished speaking, the rest of the Friends, who were ill-disposed toward Judas, were very quick to egg Demetrius on. He immediately appointed Nicanor, who had been commander of the elephant corps, and conferred upon him the title of governor of Judaea and dispatched him with orders to do away with Judas, disperse his men, and restore Alcimus as high priest of the greatest temple.

2Macc. 14:7

The "rest" of the "Friends" would seem to imply that Alcimus was a member of this select group. His Hasmonaean high-priestly successors had this distinction.[43]

Important aspects of the historical events of 162 BCE are missing here, namely the campaign led by Alcimus and Bacchides and anything about Alcimus functioning as the High Priest. As noted above, the execution of the sixty *Asidaioi* leaders is also omitted. The author of 2Maccabees seems to be very careful to paint a picture of Maccabaean control over Judaea. A period in which Alcimus and Bacchides had subdued the country does not fit this picture so it is glossed over. 2Maccabees skips the events covered in 1Macc.7:8-24. Instead, 2Maccabees makes it seem as if Alcimus immediately receives the help of Nicanor.[44] This is how 2Maccabees works: "In the entire narrative of the second book, there is not the slightest trace of internal ranks in the rebel ranks."[45]

Nicanor himself is interesting in that he may be the same Nicanor mentioned in 2Macc.8:9, "Nicanor son of Patroclus, a member of the Order of King's Friends, First Class," and/or in 12:2, "Nicanor the Cypriarch." He is probably the Nicanor of 8:9 on the basis of the references in each passage to the "King's Friends," but not the same as Nicanor the Cypriarch, who was presumably a Cypriot commander of Cypriot mercenaries. 2Macc.8:34-36 speaks of Nicanor's humiliating escape; running from defeat, he sheds his splendid garments and dismisses his attendants, running like a fugitive slave until he reaches Antioch where he professes the might of the Judaean God. Whether he was in fact the same Nicanor is immaterial for our purpose at present, which is to understand the events according to this work. It is clearly the intention here to identify this Nicanor with the one referred to earlier. This is demonstrated by identifying him with the same nasty epithet in 15:3 as had

---

[43] 1Macc.10:20, 11:27, 57, 13:36, 14:38-39.
[44] Covered by 1Macc. in 7:26-32.
[45] Efron *Studies* 26-27.

The Sources

been used in 8:34, *trisalitêrios*, meaning "thrice sinful." There is the possibility of underestimating the artistry of this work that may identify two different Nicanors in creating a powerful literary, and perhaps religiously symbolic, symmetry. As Goldstein states, "Nicanor in his mission, threats and failure has the role played by Heliodorus in 3:7-30, but in his threats, failure and death Nicanor also has the role played by Antiochus IV in 6:1-10:8."[46]

We focus on Nicanor because he becomes an important part of what might constitute a triangle with Alcimus and Judas. He is sent by the king to support Alcimus and destroy Judas.

Yet to the surprise of Judas and the dismay of Alcimus, Nicanor tries the path of peace rather than that of war. One might be inclined to speculate that if Nicanor were the same man who had experienced a terrible defeat just three years earlier, he would be in no rush to engage Judas in battle again. If we leave aside Nicanor's recognition of the Judaean God in 8:36 and transform that religious piety into the kind of respect one warrior might have for another, all of this makes sense. While Judas fears treachery, he comes to a meeting that results in an agreement. Alcimus is clearly not party to the "closed discussions" of v.21. We read about the rather interesting and incongruous friendship between Judas the Maccabee and Nicanor:

> Nicanor spent time at Jerusalem and conducted himself irreproachably. He dismissed the undisciplined mobs that had thronged around him. Continually he kept Judas in his company. He was sincerely fond of the man. He urged him to marry and beget children. He did marry; he experienced tranquility; he partook of life's blessings.
> 2Macc.14:23-25

Judas' willingness to forego his rebellion makes both Nicanor and him appear very reasonable and sophisticated. It as is if to say: "The Maccabees only wanted peace. They did not insist on political independence if the peace would be a true and lasting one. Judas Maccabaeus was like any other normal human being who just wants to have a family and live well."

1Maccabees, we should be reminded, says nothing about this remarkable friendship. We have described the situation as a triangle. If two points of the triangle are too close, where does that leave the other point? As High Priest,

---

[46] Goldstein *II Maccabees* 476.

Alcimus could function in a context of religious freedom and security. Alcimus is not content with this arrangement and feels the need to act. He no doubt feels betrayed by Nicanor and seeks revenge:

> Alcimus, however, on perceiving their mutual goodwill, took a copy of the treaty they had made and came before Demetrius, saying that Nicanor had hostile designs against the state; indeed, he had appointed as his deputy Judas, the plotter against Demetrius' kingdom. The king was infuriated and enraged by the slanders uttered by the arch villain. He wrote to Nicanor, saying that he was annoyed over the treaty and ordering him to make haste to send Maccabaeus in chains to Antioch.
> 2Macc.14:26-27

In an age when every king watched his military leaders very carefully, Alcimus' charges against Nicanor must have been quite disturbing to Demetrius I, who had only been king a short while at this point and who knew all about usurpation. Demetrius I demands that Nicanor send him Judas as a prisoner. Nicanor must do what the king has commanded and must turn on his new friend:

> When this message reached Nicanor, he was perplexed and troubled; should he revoke the terms of the treaty, though the man had done no wrong? Since, however, he could not oppose the king, he sought an opportunity to carry out the order through trickery.
> 2Macc.14:28-29

Judas senses that the friendship has cooled and goes into hiding with his men. The point seems to be that one cannot trust the friendship of foreign leaders; no matter how sincere they may seem, their loyalties will always lie elsewhere. Nicanor goes to the Temple and demands that Judas be turned over to him. He threatens the razing of the Temple and its replacement with a temple to Dionysus. Judas is not there[47] and the priests can do nothing except pray that God will save the Temple from defilement. While it is interesting to note that the Temple does seem to be functioning in proper Jewish fashion under Alcimus' tenure, it is also curious that Alcimus is not mentioned in this story.

---

[47] He is in Samaria, as we learn in 15:1.

The Sources

Nicanor and Judas prepare for battle, Nicanor with blasphemous rantings about attacking on the Sabbath, Judas with prayers to God and quotations from the *Torah* and the Prophets. "He armed each of his men not so much with the security afforded by shields and spears as with the encouragement derived from the good words."[48] This verse is a good example of 2Maccabees' theology; it is God, and not human beings, who makes history.

The text now moves to a very interesting passage about a dream that Judas relates to his men:

> His vision was as follows: he saw Onias, the late high priest, a good man and true, of modest bearing and mild bearing, whose utterances were always fitting, who from childhood had practiced every aspect of virtue. Onias stretched forth his hands to pray for the entire company of the Jews. Thereafter, in the same posture, there appeared a man remarkable for his white hair and his dignity; he had a certain majesty about him, marvelous and magnificent. On being asked, Onias replied, "This lover of his brethren, who offers many prayers for our people and for the holy city, is Jeremiah, the prophet of God." Jeremiah stretched forth his hand to give Judas a golden sword, and as gave it to him, he addressed him as follows: "Take the holy sword as a gift from God, and with it shatter our enemies."
>
> 2Macc.15:12-16

It would seem to be quite ironic for Judas, a rebel against the foreign power, to dream of Jeremiah, who opposed Zedekiah's rebellion against the foreign power of an earlier century.[49] Instead, the point seems to be that the foreign power has forced Judas and his men into their rebellion. In the prelude to Judas' speech to his followers, the narrator tells us that Judas "roused their anger and urged them on, as he held before them at the same time the broken faith of the gentiles and their violation of their oaths."[50] Thus in case anyone would bring Jeremiah to bear against Judas, Judas claims to be the heir of the great prophet and to be worthy of his great legacy. While Jerusalem was conquered and the Temple destroyed in Jeremiah's age, nothing like this will happen again, and Jeremiah himself will sustain Judas with great power.

---

[48] 2Macc. 15:11.
[49] Jer.27:1-18, 28:14, 52:3.
[50] 2Macc.15:10.

While this dream seems to be about Jeremiah, we should emphasize the connection to Onias III. We might suggest the theory that by bringing Onias III into the equation, it is not so much, as Goldstein would have it, to answer the challenge that Onias IV should be the High Priest but to emphasize the idea that the Maccabaean-Hasmonaean line should now be the rightful High Priestly line. The speech links the last legitimate High Priest Onias III with the new legitimate High Priest (in waiting) Judas the Maccabee, all of this as opposed to the High Priest of the moment, Alcimus. Alcimus, who does not seem to be an Oniad in this work, is but an interruption in the orderly succession from the Oniads, represented by Onias III in the dream, to the Hasmonaeans, represented by Judas, the recipient of the dream. They are both in a succession from Jeremiah who, not coincidentally, was a priest but not of the High Priestly line.

The dream is not only a rally cry for the troops who are about to go to battle. It is about the legitimacy of the High Priesthood of Judas the Maccabee who, we will assert, was the *de facto* High Priest during the restoration of the Temple in Jerusalem and the institution of *Hanukkah*. He may also have expected to be the High Priest of the next era. He may have been as angry about the appointment of Alcimus by Demetrius I (and before him, by Antiochus V) as Alcimus was about his continuing challenge. We also suggest that the "voluntary defilement" of Alcimus was the result of a challenge to his authority by the supporters of Judas in his campaign to gain or re-gain the High Priesthood.

It is instructive to note that this abridgement, at least, ends with the death of Nicanor.

> Such was the outcome of the affair of Nicanor. From that time on, the city has been held by the Hebrews.
>
> 2Macc.15:37

Since Judas would die in the spring of 160 BCE and Alcimus would live until May 159 BCE, the writer/abridger sees Alcimus as a Hebrew who rules in proper fashion over the city and state of the Jewish people. The work ends with Alcimus functioning as High Priest over a fully functioning temple in Jerusalem.

We return to the questions that we ask of every source.

When did Alcimus become High Priest? He had been High Priest under Antiochus V after the removal of Menelaus (163-62 BCE), had voluntarily defiled himself and lost the High Priesthood, and is re-appointed by Demetrius I (162 BCE). Alcimus here is High Priest for four straight years under the reigns and approval of both Antiochus V and Demetrius.

Who was Alcimus? Why was he chosen by the Seleucids to be High Priest? Was he a priest? Was he an Oniad? Was he the nephew of Yose ben Yoʿezer? Was he the brother of Menelaus? He is only "a certain Alcimus."

What religious and/or anti-religious actions did Alcimus take? His voluntary defilement seems to involve some kind of action that leads to ritual impurity, rendering him unfit for the duties of the High Priest.

Was he the High Priest of *Hanukkah*, the rededication of the Temple? No; *Hanukkah* is instituted in 2Macc.10:3-7 and Menelaus is removed in 2Macc.13:3-8. Alcimus becomes High Priest after the latter date.

Neither source has anything to say about the period between the departure of Antiochus V and Lysias from Jerusalem early in 162 BCE and the seizure of the Seleucid kingship by Demetrius I about a year later. This may be an indication that both 1 and 2Maccabees drew from a common source that also had nothing to contribute about this time. Another possibility is that it does not suit the purposes of these sources to discuss a time when Alcimus was High Priest and when there was peace and security. Instead, these sources want to demonstrate the need for the Hasmonaeans and the terrors brought on by "Hellenizing" Judaeans.

In comparing the two sources on Alcimus that we have treated so far, it is important to distinguish between a High Priest *de jure* and a High Priest *de facto*. We are interested in the period between the death of Menelaus and the death of Alcimus. Menelaus was High Priest from 172 BCE to 163-162 BCE. In 164 BCE, after the victories of Judas against Nicanor, Gorgias, and then Lysias, pious Jews stopped Menelaus from retaining control over the Temple. Menelaus was still High Priest according to the Seleucids, but after Lysias left the country assuming that Menelaus would be in control both politically and religiously, Judas and his pro-Jewish followers were in control as either predicted or explained in Daniel 11:24.[51] The restoration of the Temple to proper Jewish worship and the events of *Hanukkah* occurred in late 164 BCE. Menelaus was deposed during the expedition of Antiochus V and Lysias which lasted from around June 163 BCE to January-March 162 BCE. At some point during this campaign, Antiochus V selected Alcimus, a

---

[51] See Goldstein *II Maccabees* 376.

religious priest, as the new High Priest, hoping to have someone in the office that had not rebelled against him. Alcimus was a fascinating choice. Antiochus V could have selected Onias IV, who went to Egypt. Antiochus V and Lysias left Jerusalem to crush the rebel Philip at Antioch. Antiochus V made full peace with the Jews, but before he went, knocked down the wall around the Temple mount.[52] At this point, with Judas having acted as *de facto* High Priest, he had to deal with a *de jure* and *de facto* High Priest in Alcimus.

Quite instructive is the example of Simon the Hasmonaean who, according to 1Maccabees became High Priest when he was proclaimed leader and High Priest first by "the people."[53] Josephus also indicates that Simon was appointed High Priest by the multitude.[54] It is only later that he is recognized by Demetrius II[55] and only in his third year that he gained approval from the priests and the other leaders of the nation.[56]

The point is that a High Priest had several constituencies in the sense that he needed the approval of the foreign power, the priestly aristocracy and the people. Simon could function to at least a certain extent with the approval of the people and without the appointment of the foreign ruler and the Temple aristocracy. Alcimus had the appointment of one foreign power, Antiochus V, but seems to have lost control over the Temple indicated by his "voluntary defilement," and the acceptance of the people. Judas, on the other hand, had control over the temple, at least for a while, and the acceptance of many of the people, but never had the appointment of the foreign power.

Josephus

Josephus, claiming to be a proud descendant of Jonathan the Hasmonaean, is clearly pro-Hasmonaean in his works.[57] That Josephus is extremely proud of his

---

[52] 2Macc.11:22-26; 13:23-26.
[53] 1Macc.14:35; 13:2.7-8.
[54] *Ant.* 13.213.
[55] 1Macc.14:38.
[56] 1Macc.14:29-45.
[57] J. A. Montgomery "The Religion of Flavius Josephus" *JQR* 11 (1921) 277-305; H. Rasp "Flavius Josephus und die Religionsparteien" *ZNW* 23 (1924) 27-47; F.J. Foakes Jackson *Josephus and the Jews* (London, 1930) Steve Mason "Was Josephus a Pharisee? A Re-Examination of *Life* 10-12" *Journal of Jewish Studies* 40 (1989) 31-45; idem

priestly heritage[58] is also very important for our considerations here. Josephus looks on the priestly theocracy as the ideal form of government, a superior constitution that is divinely sanctioned and unique in the Greek-speaking East.[59] In fact, Josephus seems to have coined the word *theocracy*.[60] In his interpretation of Deut.17:14f., a key passage concerning the institution of the kingship, Josephus insists that Moses intends any monarchy to share power with the High Priest and the people's council. If the people want a king, he insists, "Let him do nothing without the high priest and the senators."[61] He thinks of the priests as the rightful aristocrats of Judaea. As opposed to the usual concept of Jewish history that sees the ideal political situation as that with an Israelite ruler as king governing an independent state, Josephus reads the same history with different eyes. Moses received the laws from God and transmitted them to the High Priest to keep them safe.[62] The High Priest and the priests formed a senatorial aristocracy in the period of Joshua and the Judges.[63] Samuel does not so much object to the idea of a king as he does have a strong commitment to aristocracy.[64] After a long and eventually disastrous period of monarchy that culminates in the Babylonian Exile, the Judaeans return to the proper priestly aristocracy.[65] Josephus is careful to tell his reader the identity of the High

---

"Josephus, Daniel, and the Flavian House" in F. Parente and J. Sievers, eds. *Josephus and the History of the Greco-Roman Period* (Leiden, 1994) 161-191; idem "The Contra Apionem in Social and Literary Context" in L. Feldman and J. R. Levison eds., *Josephus' Contra Apionem: Studies in its Character and Context with a Latin Concordance* ... (Leiden, 1996) 188-95; T. Rajak *Josephus: The Historian and His Society* (London, 1983); Shaye J. D. Cohen "History and Historiography in the *Contra Apionem* of Josephus" in *History and Theory 27: Essays in Jewish Historiography* (1988) 1-11; idem *Josephus in Galilee and Rome: His Vita and His Development as a Historian* (Leiden, 1979); Seth Schwartz *Josephus and Judaean Politics* (Leiden, 1990).
[58] *The Jewish War* 1:3. I use the translation by H. St. J. Thackeray *The Jewish War Books III –IV* (Cambridge: Harvard, 1997).
[59] Steve Mason "Josephus and Judaism" *The Encyclopedia of Judaism* Vol. II (Jacob Neusner, Alan J. Avery-Peck and William Scott Green, eds.) (New York, 1999) 554-55.
[60] *Contra Apion* 2.17:21-23.
[61] *Ant.*4.8.17.
[62] *Ant.*4.304.
[63] *Ant.*4.223; 5:15, 43, 55, 135.
[64] *Ant.*6:36.
[65] *Ant.*11.111.

Priest throughout *Antiquities* and even provides a partial summary at the halfway mark.[66] It was a family of priests that fought Antiochus[67] and created the Hasmonaean dynasty.[68] If Aristobulus had not changed the nation into a monarchy, the priestly theocracy would have continued to rule well.[69] In case anyone has missed the point, Josephus provides a full list of High Priests at the end of the work.[70]

Antiquities, the first edition of which was completed by 94 CE,[71] is a very important source for our considerations in more specific ways as well. Books 12-14 narrate the events from the time of Alexander's death (c.323 BCE) to the passing of Antigonus, the last Hasmonaean king (c.38 BCE). Josephus seems to have had access to 1Maccabees.[72] There has been a long-standing debate on whether Josephus had access to the Hebrew original, which still existed in Origen's era (c.184-254 CE).[73] Some say that he paraphrased from that original on many occasions, while others say that he only had the Greek translation. Whatever the case, Josephus needed to modify the text in certain respects when it came into conflict with his beliefs; it was still his most important source for the period that we are examining here.

2Maccabees, on the other hand, was more problematic for him and scholars from Geiger[74] on have shown that he found it to be unreliable. For instance, the positive evaluation of Onias III in 2Maccabees presented Josephus with a problem, for he wanted to show that all of the later Oniads were unworthy of the High Priesthood, thus clearing the way for the rise of the Hasmonaean High Priests. This

---

[66] *Ant.*10.149-153.
[67] *Ant.*1.36.
[68] *Ant.*1.53, 68.
[69] *Ant.*1.70.
[70] *Ant.*20.224-51.
[71] *Ant.*20.267.
[72] Cohen *Josephus* 46; Isacc Gafni "On the Use of 1 Maccabees by Josephus Flavius," (Hebrew) *Zion* 45 (1980) 81-95; Sievers *The Hasmoneans and Their Supporters* 12 n.51.
[73] Compare Goldstein *I Maccabees* 14-15 with Heinrich Bloch *Die Quellen des Flavius Josephus in seiner Archäologie* (Leipzig, 1879) 80-90, H. J. Cadbury *The Making of Luke-Acts* (N.Y., 1927) 169-79 and the bibliography and warnings of Shaye J. D. Cohen *Josephus in Galilee* 44-45, esp. n. 77.
[74] Geiger *Urschrift und Ubersetzungen der Bibel* 2nd ed. Frankfurt am Main, 1928) 229.

The Sources

also would have been a response to those who would have preferred Onias IV to those who actually ascended to the position. In the beginning of 2Maccabees, Jason of Cyrene glorifies Onias III for piety that brought Jerusalem the blessings of peace.[75]

2Macc.15, as we have seen in the last section, glorifies Onias III and makes Judas his legitimate successor. For Josephus, however, this was unacceptable. If 2Maccabees says that Onias III was pious and successful in negotiating peace and religious freedom for his people, Josephus is careful to tell us that Onias II caused the people to suffer at the hands of the Samaritans[76] and that he failed to pay Ptolemy the appropriate tax money.[77] His method was often subtle. We turn now to the relevant passages from Josephus about Alcimus while clarifying this point about his attitude towards the Oniads. We pick up the narrative in 163 BCE when Antiochus V removes Menelaus from office:

> After doing this, he returned to Antioch, taking with him the high priest Onias, who was also called Menelaus. For Lysias had advised the king to slay Menelaus, if he wished the Jews to remain quiet and not give him any trouble; it was this man, he said, who had been the cause of all of the mischief by persuading the king's father to compel the Jews to abandon their fathers' religion. Accordingly, the king sent Menelaus to Beroea in Syria, and there had him put to death; he had served as high priest for ten years and had been a wicked and impious man, who in order to have sole authority for himself had compelled his nation to violate their own laws.
>
> *Ant.*12.9.7.383-385[78]

It is striking that Josephus says that Menelaus was called Onias and even more strange that he makes Menelaus Onias III's brother. Is it possible that Menelaus did take this famous name of his High Priestly predecessors? Is it also possible that Menelaus was the brother of Onias III? Earlier, Josephus explains the succession of the High Priesthood among three brothers:

---

[75] 2Macc.3:1-2.

[76] *Ant.*12.4.1.156.

[77] *Ant.*12.158. For these and other examples, see Goldstein *II Maccabees* 549.

[78] Josephus *Jewish Antiquities Books XII-XIII* Loeb Classical Library trans. by Ralph Marcus (Cambridge: Harvard, 1998) 199. All translations of Josephus are from this series.

> About this same time the high priest Onias also died, and Antiochus gave the high priesthood to his brother; for the son whom Onias had left was still an infant ... Jesus, however, —this was the brother of Onias — was deprived of the high priesthood when the king became angry with him and gave it to his younger brother, named Onias; for Simon had three sons, to each of whom the priesthood came, as we have shown. Now Jesus changed his name to Jason, while Onias was called Menelaus.
>
> *Ant.* 12.5.1.237-239[79]

Josephus is consistent on these two points, as he is in *Ant.* 20:10:1:

> ...and then the forementioned Antiochus and Lysias the general of his army, deprived Onias, who was called Menelaus, of the high priesthood, and slew him at Berea and driving away the son [of Onias the third,] put Jacimus into the high priest's place, one that was indeed of the stock of Aaron, but not of the family of Onias. On which account Onias, who was the nephew of Onias that was dead and bore the same name with his father, came into Egypt ...[80]

Considering the conventions of the day, it would seem to be plausible that Menelaus could have taken the name Onias upon his accession, as kings such as the Ptolemies would do (Ptolemy VI and Ptolemy VIII were brothers who were co-kings). Antiochus IV had an older brother named Antiochus. A list of the High Priests of the period beginning with Onias I, however, would seem to contradict this possibility:

Onias I
Simon I
Eleazar
Manasses
Onias II
Simon II
Onias III

---

[79] *Jewish Antiquities Books XII-XIII* 121.
[80] *Jewish Antiquities Book XX* 45.

The Sources

Jason (Joshua)
Menelaus
Alcimus (Joiakim)
Jonathan

Note that, with the exception of Onias III and IV, there do not seem to be a father and son who bear the same name. With the possible exception of Onias III and Menelaus (whom Josephus calls Onias as well), there do not seem to be two brothers with the same name. It is possible that Onias IV only took the name after death of his father. In a study of the names of the High Priests of the Persian period,[81] we showed that these priests were only given names of grandfathers who had passed away. It would be safer to support Josephus on these matters if we had Judaean parallels; still, the Seleucid and Ptolemaic models are interesting. It is not impossible that Menelaus took the name Onias upon becoming High Priest (and see the next section). If so, why was he not called Onias by 1 and 2Maccabees? Certainly, in the case of 2Maccabees, the answer is clear: its association with Menelaus would tarnish the name of Onias. This would also explain why, if Menelaus were the brother of Onias, 2Maccabees would gloss over this fact. Josephus, on the other hand, would be only too happy to tarnish the Onias name in order to pursue his pro-Hasmonaean goals.

The High Priest chosen after the death of Menelaus was Alcimus, also called Jakeimos. While it seems to be a small detail here, it is significant for our purposes that Josephus mentions that Alcimus "also called Jakeimos." Alcimus would seem to be Greek for the Hebrew name Eliakim and Jakeimos for the Hebrew name Yakim. The names are obviously similar; what is interesting is that Josephus would mention the variations. Menelaus and Onias are completely different names and if Josephus is correct that Menelaus had or took the name Onias, it is important for purposes of clarification. Such small variations as Alcimus/Jakeimos would not seem to be worthy of mention. He does not tell us, for instance, that Onias was also Yoḥanan. One wonders if there is not more to this; that, for instance, Alcimus was known as Jakeimos in certain circles. Indeed, we will examine rabbinic references to Yaqim below.

---

[81] *Chronology and Papponymy: A List of High Priests of the Persian Period* (Atlanta, 1999).

Then Onias, the son of the high priest, who, as we said before, had been left a mere child when his father died, seeing that the king had slain his uncle Menelaus and had given the high priesthood to Alcimus, although he was not of the family of high priests, because he had been persuaded by Lysias to transfer the office from this house to another, fled to Ptolemy, the king of Egypt. And being treated with honour by him and his wife Cleopatra, he received a place in the nome of Heliopolis, where he built a temple similar to that in Jerusalem. Of this, however, we shall give an account on a more fitting occasion.[82]

Josephus states that Alcimus did not come from the Oniad family. It as if to say: "Menelaus was bad but at least he came from the right stock." While this is an issue for Josephus and, of course, for the would-be Onias IV, it does not seem to bother the religious factions, who, one might think, would be quite willing to be finished with the Oniads considering the actions of Jason and, if Josephus is right, Menelaus. This feeling no doubt influenced the Seleucids who could have chosen Onias IV over the outsider Alcimus. While Onias IV had not reached physical maturity in 170 BCE when his father Onias III was killed, he was not so young at this later point (163-62 BCE) that he could not have become High Priest.[83] So why did Antiochus V not select the natural heir Onias IV? It is possible that they knew or suspected that he had pro-Ptolemaic tendencies. This theory seems to be based on the fact that he eventually settled in Egypt under Ptolemy VI *Philometer* where he founded a Jewish temple at Leontopolis. On a more human level, it would have been completely understandable if Onias IV blamed the Seleucids for his father's death, even though he must have known that Antiochus IV had killed his father's murderer, Andronikos. He might still have been angry that his father had lost the High Priesthood to his uncle Jason in the first place.

Another possibility is that a prominent family such as the Oniads had a power base of their own, their outstanding heritage; Alcimus would be a singleton, without the same kind of internal standing and power base. Josephus relates that after two years of Antiochus V's reign, the king was overthrown and killed by Demetrius I. The narrative continues with Alcimus' entreaties to the new emperor and closely resembles 1Maccabees but is very different from 2Maccabees in that it relates the mission of Bacchides and the massacre that ensued:

---

[82] *Jewish Antiquities Book XII* 201.
[83] *Ant.* 15:3.51-56; BT *Hullin* 24a-b; *Sifra Emor* 3:1 to Lev.21:17.

The Sources

> About the same time Demetrius, the son of Seleucus, escaped from Rome, and occupying Tripolis in Syria, placed the diadem on his own head ...Then there came to him in a body many of the wicked and renegade Jews, among whom was the high priest Alcimus, and they accused their whole nation, especially Judas and his brothers, saying that they had killed all the king's friends, and had destroyed all those in the kingdom who were of his party and awaited his coming, and had driven the present speakers out of their country and made them aliens in a strange land; and now they requested him to send one of his own friends and learn from him what bold crimes had been committed by Judas and his men.
>
> 12.10.1.391-92[84]

Josephus seems to know and borrow from Alcimus' speech in 2Macc.14:6-10:

> And so Demetrius, being roused to anger, sent out Bacchides, a friend of King Antiochus Epiphanes, and a worthy man, who had been entrusted with the government of all Mesopotamia, and giving him a force of soldiers, and putting Alcimus under his protection, instructed him to kill Judas and the men with him. Thereupon Bacchides set out with his force from Antioch, and when he came to Judaea, sent to Judas and his brothers to discuss friendship and peace, for he planned to take him by deceit. But Judas did not trust him, for he saw that he had come with such an army as one has when going to war, but not when making peace. Some of the citizens, however, giving ear to the peace proposals made by Bacchides, and believing that they would suffer no harm at the hand of Alcimus, who was their countryman, went over to them; and after receiving oaths from both men that neither they themselves nor those who were of their mind should suffer in any way, put themselves in their hands. But Bacchides made light of his oaths, and killed sixty of them; and so, by not keeping faith with the first, deterred the others who were thinking of going over to him from doing so. And when, after marching out of Jerusalem, he came to a village called Berzetho, he sent his men to seize many of the deserters, and some of the people, and after killing all these, commanded all who lived in the country to obey Alcimus; and leaving him with enough of an army to enable him to keep the country under his control, he returned to Antioch to King Demetrius.

It is very important to notice that it is not Alcimus who commits the heinous execution of those who had come to him in peace, but Bacchides; also notice that

---

[84] *Jewish Antiquities Books XII-XIII* 204.

there is nothing specific about the *Asidaioi* as those who were massacred (it is "some of the people"). So while Josephus has clearly derived his material from 1Maccabees here, why does he deliberately make these changes? Both the Hasmonaeans and the *Asidaioi* are Josephus' heroes and he, like Jason of Cyrene, the author of 2Maccabees, does not want to describe a split between the two groups. He therefore omits any reference to the trust that the *Asidaioi* put in "a priest of the stock of Aaron" in 1Maccabees 7. Alcimus, to this point, has misrepresented the actions of Judas to Demetrius I but he has not yet done anything violent. Once Bacchides has left and he is in charge, however, this will change:

> But Alcimus, wishing to strengthen his authority, and perceiving that by making the people feel friendly toward him he would govern with greater security, led them on with kind words, and speaking to everyone in a pleasant and gracious manner, very soon indeed acquired a large body of men and a force behind him, who were for the most part from the irreligious and renegades....[85]

Josephus, like our other sources, is hardly presenting objective history. Alcimus' supporters cannot be peace-loving Judaeans who simply want to live their lives, especially now that they have their religious autonomy again. Alcimus slays "many of the good and holy men of the country," who are the supporters of Judas:

> ...and these he used as his attendants and soldiers in going through the country; and all those whom he found in it siding with Judas he slew. When Judas, therefore, saw that Alcimus had now become powerful and had put to death many of the good and pious men of the nation, he also went through the country, and put to death those who sided with the enemy. And when Alcimus saw that he was not able to withstand Judas, but was inferior to him in strength, he decided to turn for help to his ally King Demetrius. Accordingly, he went to Antioch and roused the king's anger against Judas, at whose hands he said in his accusation, he had suffered many injuries, which would become still greater unless Judas were first caught and brought to punishment by having a strong force sent against him.[86]

Demetrius responds to Alcimus' new appeal by sending him Nicanor, whom engages Judas in battle, only to lose at Capharsalama. There is nothing here about

---

[85] *Jewish Antiquities Books XII-XIII* 207.
[86] *Jewish Antiquities Books XII-XIII* 208-09.

The Sources

the peace treaty or about the friendship that grew between Nicanor and Judas nor the peaceful interval before Alcimus induced Demetrius to force Nicanor to move against Judas. It is not at the end of the friendship but after a losing battle that Nicanor threatens the Temple:

> And again, as Nicanor was coming down from the *Akra* to the temple, he was met by some of the priests and elders, who greeted him and showed him the sacrifices which they said they were offering to God on behalf of the king. Thereupon he fell to cursing them, and threatened that, if the people did not give up Judas to him, he would pull down the temple when he returned. After making these threats, he left Jerusalem, while the priests burst into tears in their distress over his words, and supplicated God to deliver them from their enemies.[87]

Judas defeats Nicanor and there is peace again; however, Alcimus cannot leave well enough alone:

> As the high priest Alcimus was planning to pull down the wall of the Holy Place, which was very old and had been erected by the ancient prophets, a sudden stroke from God seized him, by which he was brought speechless to the ground, and after suffering torment for many days, he died, having been high priest for four years. And when he died, the people gave the high priesthood to Judas.... [88]

Alcimus here dies before Judas; this is very different from 1Maccabees[89] in which Alcimus dies after the death of Judas.[90] It seems as if Josephus may have reversed the order of their deaths so that Judas could become the High Priest. As Shaye Cohen puts it, "Alcimus has to be removed from this world before his time."[91]

Josephus' version of Alcimus' death seems to be deliberately vague when he induces a controversy concerning the "Inner Court": "the walls of the sanctuary" in the translation here is an interpretation; the Greek original says "walls of the holy

---

[87] *Jewish Antiquities Books XII-XIII* 211-12.
[88] *Jewish Antiquities Books XII-XIII* 215-16.
[89] 1Macc.9:54-57.
[90] Mentioned in 1Macc.9:18.
[91] Cohen *Josephus in Galilee* 46.

place." We discussed this problem in our discussion of the 1Maccabees parallel above. Josephus mentions the barrier separating the area of the "Inner Court" of the Temple that is restricted to priests in two other places in the *Antiquities*. In 8:3.9.95, he speaks of a wall "called *geision* in our native language and *thrigchos* ['cornice' or 'barrier'] in Greek" that existed in Solomon's temple to bar non-priests from the sacred area. In 8.13.5.373 he speaks of "a wooden lattice around the altar and the sanctuary extending up to the *thrigchos*" that was built by Alexander Jannaeus to bar non-priests. Goldstein is correct in his admission that we simply do not know whether this *geision* was early or late or whether it was a rectangle (around the altar and the sanctuary) or a linear shape. He is weaker in guessing that the reference to the wall as built by the prophets is a way of saying that the prophets did not argue against the wall. We are left with the impression that such barriers were the very stuff of sectarian controversy, and that there were different attitudes toward what barriers were necessary in order to bar non-priests.

All of this begs the question that we need to answer here. What was Alcimus doing and why was he doing it? Clearly, both 1Maccabees and Josephus think that God struck him down for his action. And yet it is God who strikes him down; there is nothing here about a popular clamor against him for what he is doing. We shall return to this issue below.

- When did Alcimus become High Priest? After the disposal and exile of Menelaus.
- Who was Alcimus? Why was he chosen by the Seleucids to be High Priest? Was he a priest? Was he an Oniad? The nephew of Yose ben Yoʿezer? The brother of Menelaus? He was a priest, of the stock of Aaron but he was not an Oniad. He was not a brother of Menelaus. We do not know of any connection to Yose ben Yoʿezer. He seems to have been chosen as a pious man of the right stock who was neither a Hasmonaean nor a "Hellenizer."
- What religious and anti-religious actions did Alcimus take? We see proper sacrifices being conducted at the Temple during his term and we do not see any improper worship during this time. His doomed effort to break down the wall around the altar seems to be against a religious stance of barring non-priests from the most sacred area. The next section about *Middot* 2:3 will deal with this problem at length.

The Sources

- Was he the High Priest of *Hanukkah*, the rededication of the Temple? No, he was selected after that event.
- Why did the *Asidaioi* accept him? The *Asidaioi* are not mentioned in this context. Instead, Bacchides leads a mission in whom "some of the people" put their trust.
- Why did he kill them? Bacchides killed those who trusted in that mission.
- Did he write a psalm? There is nothing either to support or reject this possibility.
- How did Alcimus die? He is struck down by God for his act of breaking down the wall around the sanctuary. Josephus makes Alcimus die earlier in order to create a time for the High Priesthood of Judas.
- Who succeeded Alcimus? Was there an extended *intersacerdotium* after him? Josephus states that Judas became High Priest after Alcimus' death. The *intersacerdotium* happened after the death of Judas. This makes very little sense, since there would have been many eligible Hasmonaean candidates, beginning with Jonathan and Simon, Judas' brothers.

EXCURSUS: **The Flight Of Onias IV To Egypt: Does It Imply That Alcimus Was A Zadokite Or A Non-Zadokite?**

When did Onias IV leave for Egypt? If, as Josephus says, it was upon the appointment of Alcimus, we may ask what this may imply about Alcimus' lineage. One position is that as long as Menelaus, a non-Zadokite, was the high priest, Onias IV (or, if he was still alive, Onias III) might have stayed in Syria as a kind of legitimate High Priest in Waiting. On the accession of a different Zadokite, Alcimus, Onias IV would give up his hopes of becoming high priest in Jerusalem under the Seleucids and go to Egypt to build a temple under the Ptolemies. The other position would take the opposite view, that with the accession of still another non-Zadokite after Menelaus, Onias IV left for Egypt for the same reason.

Onias IV's founding of a Jewish temple at Heliopolis in Egypt is a fascinating aspect of this period.[1] While archaeological evidence is uncertain,[2] there are references from Josephus and the Talmud to consider.

Scholars have noted the somewhat curious fact that Josephus begins and ends his story of the Jewish war against Rome with references to the temple at Leontopolis.[3] Hayward suggests that the persistence of the Jews in *philoneikia* or "party strife" is what leads to the "ultimate undoing of the whole Jewish nation in its war against Rome in 66-70 CE."[4] In *War*, based on Josephus' references, there is

---

[1] Robert Hayward "The Jewish Temple at Leontopolis: A Reconsideration" *JJS* 33 (1982) 429-43; Joan E. Taylor "A Second Temple in Egypt: The Evidence for the Zadokite Temple of Onias " *JSJ* XXIX 3 (1998) 298-322.

[2] W.H. Flinders Petrie *Egypt and Israel* (London: S.P.C.K., 1923) 108-09 may have discovered the foundations of this temple at Tell el-Yehudiyyeh, but see Andre Barucq "Leontopolis" in *Supplement au Dictionnaire de la Bible V* (1957) 359-72; Mathias Delcor "Le Temple d'Onias en Egypte" *RB* 75 (1968) 188-203 and Roland de Vaux in an afterword to this article, 205.

[3] *BJ* I.31-33; VII. 420-436; *AJ* XII. 387-88; XIII 62-73, 285; XIV.131-32; XX. 235-37; *Contra Apionem* II. 49-56.

[4] Hayward "The Jewish Temple at Leontopolis" 431.

The Flight Of Onias IV To Egypt

war against Rome in 66-70 CE."[4] In *War*, based on Josephus' references, there is uncertainty about the identity of the founding high priest. Josephus states that Onias III, son of Simon II, escaped to Egypt to the protection of Ptolemy VI and was given authorization and support by that king to build a temple in Egypt:

> The high priest Onias made his escape to Ptolemy and, obtaining from him a site in the nome of Heliopolis, built a small town on the model of Jerusalem and a temple resembling ours.
>
> *BJl* 33[5]

> Onias, son of Simeon, and one of the chief priests at Jerusalem, fleeing from Antiochus, king of Syria, then at war with the Jews, came to Alexandria, and being graciously received by Ptolemy, owing to that monarch's hatred of Antiochus, told him that he would make the Jewish nation his ally if he would accede to his proposal. The king having promised to do what was in his power, he asked permission to build a temple somewhere in Egypt and to worship God after the manner of his fathers; for, he added, the Jews would thus be still more embittered against Antiochus, who had sacked their temple at Jerusalem, and more amicably disposed towards himself, and many would flock to him for the sake of religious toleration.
> Induced by this statement, Ptolemy gave him a tract, 180 furlongs distant from Memphis, in the so-called nome of Heliopolis. Here Onias erected a fortress and built his temple (which was not like that in Jerusalem, but resembled a tower) of huge stones and sixty cubits in altitude. The altar, however, he designed on the model of that in the home country, and adorned the building with similar offerings, the fashion of that the lamp stand excepted; for instead of making a stand, he had a lamp wrought of gold which shed a brilliant light and was suspended by a golden chain. The sacred precincts were wholly surrounded by a wall of baked brick, the doorways being of stone. The king, moreover, assigned to him an extensive territory as a source of revenue, to yield both abundance for the priests and large provision for the service of God. In all this, however, Onias was not actuated by honest motives; his aim was rather to rival the Jews at Jerusalem, against whom he harboured resentment for his exile, and he hoped by erecting this temple to attract the multitude away from them to it. There had, moreover, been an ancient prediction

---

[4] Hayward "The Jewish Temple at Leontopolis" 431.
[5] See Schurer *The History of the Jewish People in the Age of Jesus Christ* revised and edited by G. Vermes and F. Millar Vol. I (Edinburgh, 1973) 46-48.

made some 600 years before by one named Esaias, who had foretold the erection of this temple in Egypt by a man of Jewish birth.... The duration of the temple from its erection to its closure was three hundred and forty three years.

BJ VII 423-432, 436[6]

In the second citation, Josephus presents remarkable detail concerning the structure and appurtenances of this temple. He may have gathered these details from a description of the temple as it is given in documents sent by the Roman officers Lupus and Paulinus to Vespasian; these officers closed the temple down.[7]

Despite all of these details, however, there is an important contradiction within the writings of Josephus. In *War*, it is clear that it is Onias III, son of Simon II, who is the founding high priest of the temple in Egypt. In *Antiquities*, however, it is Onias IV, Onias III's son, who founds this temple:

> Then Onias, the son of the high priest, who, as we said before, had been left a mere child when his father died, seeing that the king had slain his uncle Menelaus and had given the high priesthood to Alcimus, although he was not of the family of high priests, because he had been persuaded by Lysias to transfer the office from this house to another, fled to Ptolemy, the king of Egypt. And being treated with honour by him and his wife Cleopatra, he received a place in the nome of Heliopolis, where he built a temple similar to that in Jerusalem.
>
> AJ XII:9:7

> Now the son of the high priest Onias, who had the same name as his father, having fled to King Ptolemy surnamed Philometer, was living in Alexandria, as we have said before; and seeing that Judaea was being ravaged by the Macedonians and their kings, and desiring to acquire for himself eternal fame and glory, he determined to send to King Ptolemy and Queen Cleopatra, and request of them authority to build a temple in Egypt similar to that at Jerusalem, and to appoint Levites and priests of his own race. In this desire he was encouraged chiefly by the words of the prophet Isaiah, who had lived more than six hundred years before and had foretold that a

---

[6] The long period is obviously incorrect because it would mean that since the temple was destroyed in 74 CE, it was built in 269 BCE. Instead, the figure seems to be reckoned as a fulfillment of Isa.30:26. See the interesting discussion in Hayward "The Jewish Temple at Leontopolis" 436-37.

[7] Thackeray *Josephus War* Vol. 3 625; S. A. Hirsch "The Temple of Onias " 53-54.

temple to the Most High God was surely to be built in Egypt by a Jew. Being, therefore, excited by these words,

AJ XIII:3.1

Josephus cites a letter written by Onias to Ptolemy and Cleopatra in which he asks permission to build a temple:

...in the likeness of that at Jerusalem, and with the same dimensions...that the Jewish inhabitants of Egypt may be able to come together there in mutual harmony and serve your interests.

AJ XIII:3.2

The king and queen give him permission and he builds the temple. Josephus refers the reader to his *War*. The fact that Josephus connects the two passages in his works makes it all the more strange that he should contradict himself about the identity of the high priest involved. His confusion may be due to the circumstances of what happened, or did not happen, to Onias III in Syria. 2Maccabees[8] tells the story that Onias III, the son of Simon II and high priest in the time of Seleucus IV (c.180 BCE), abandoned his father and grandfather's loyalty to the Seleucids and became a follower of the Ptolemies. His relatives, the Tobiads, sided with the Seleucids. One of the Tobiads, Simon, the captain of the Temple, told King Seleucus of money in the Temple that belonged to Hyrcanus, his half brother and an agent of the Ptolemies. Onias III did not allow Seleucus' agent Heliodorus to take the money. Simon accused Onias III who had to go plead his case in Antioch. Heliodorus assassinated Seleucus whose brother Antiochus IV *Epiphanes* became king.

The question is what happened to Onias III at this point. 2Maccabees[9] says that he was assassinated in Antioch after leaving the asylum of Daphne. A case could be made, however, that he fled to Egypt and eventually built the temple at Leontopolis.[10] In this theory, the former story was made up in order to discredit the

---

[8] 2Macc.3:10 ff.

[9] 2Macc.4:33 ff.

[10] *BJ* VII:10:2; M. *Menahot* 13:10. This possibility has been supported by F. Parente "Onias III's Death and the Founding of the Temple of Leontopolis" in F. Parente and J. Sievers (eds.) *Josephus and the History of the Greco-Roman Period: Essays in Memory*

temple in Leontopolis. If it were Onias III, a *bona fide* High Priest of Judaea, who founded the temple in Egypt, it would be a legitimate sanctuary. It would be more palatable to say that Onias III was killed and that Onias IV founded the temple.[11] If Onias III was not killed in Syria at all but fled to the safety of Egypt, this does not mean that there was no Onias IV. One can accept a historical Onias IV without assuming that he was the founder of the temple in Heliopolis.[12] The murder of Onias III would be easier to accept than the renegade building of a rival temple to the one in Jerusalem. The building took place in a period when there was great enmity between the Ptolemies and the Seleucids. It is important to remember that Onias III was a loyalist to the Ptolemies and that he had found himself in difficulties with the Seleucids because of that loyalty. It would have been only a just reward for Onias III to be given a temple to replace the one he had lost because of his alliance with the Ptolemies.

An interesting piece of evidence occurs in Theodorus of Mopsuestia's commentary on Psalms (late 4th century CE). There, a re-telling of this period that follows the account of 2Maccabees omits the assassination of Onias III in Daphne and instead includes the building of the temple in Egypt by Onias III.[13] Taylor wonders whether Theodorus had a different version of Jason of Cyrene's complete work or of 2Maccabees.[14]

---

of Morton Smith [Studia Post-Biblica, 41] Leiden: Brill, 1994 and V. Keil "Onias III – Märtyrer oder Tempelgründer" *ZAW* 97 (1985) 221-33 but rejected by M. Stern "The Death of Onias III" *Zion* 25 (1960) 1-16 (in Heb.).

[11] S. B. Hoenig ("Onias " *IDB* vol. 3 603) suggests that there may have been a rumor that Onias III had been assassinated. The rumor may have started because of the death of a delegation favoring Jason over Menelaus.

[12] It is true that Goldstein (*I Maccabees* 58 ff.) assumes an Onias IV to the extent that he even creates a chronicle by this high priest as a primary source for I (or II) Maccabees. Goldstein's reconstruction of the chronicle of Onias IV is ingenious but quite idiosyncratic and has not won scholarly acceptance.

[13] Friedrich Baethgen "Siebenzehn makkabäische Psalmen nache Theodor von Mopsuestia" *ZAW* 1886 193-288, esp. 267-83; Fausto Parente "Le témoignage de Théodore de Mopsueste sur le sort d'Onias III et la fondation du temple de Léontopolis" *REJ* 154, 3-4 (1995) 429-36.

[14] Taylor "A Second Temple in Egypt" 298-303.

The Flight Of Onias IV To Egypt

I turn now to the Talmudic passage BT*Menahot* 109b in which it is clearly Onias III who builds the temple in Leontopolis.[15] It is the succession from Simon II to Onias III that is the basis for this Talmudic story:

> In the hour of his departure [from this life], he said to them, "My son Onias shall assume the office [of high priest] after me." His brother Shime'i, who was two years and a half older than he, was jealous of him and said to him, "Come and I will teach you the order of the Temple service." He thereupon put upon him a gown, girded him with a girdle, placed him near the altar, and said to his brethren the priests, "See what this man promised his beloved [his wife] and has now fulfilled: 'On the day in which I will assume the office of High Priest I will put on your gown and gird myself with your girdle.'" At this his brethren the priests sought to kill him. He fled from them but they pursued him. He then went to Alexandria in Egypt, built an altar there, and offered thereon sacrifices in honour of idols.

In the Talmudic discussion, Rabbi Judah b.Ila'i argues with R.Me'ir and states that the roles of the two characters should be reversed. Shime'i, not Onias, was the victim of the subterfuge. According to R.Judah, when the priests were about to kill Shime'i, he explained what had happened and how Onias had tricked him. The priests then went after Onias, who fled to Egypt and built an altar to God in Alexandria.[16] R.Judah's version makes more sense. In this account, Simon the Just, who would be Simon II, not Simon I, was not going to make his eldest son Onias III the high priest. There is, to be thorough, evidence that this is a story about Simon I and that it was Onias II who built this temple.[17] To return to R.Judah's version, Onias, feeling wronged, felt the justification to attempt to discredit his rival.

Notice again that it is Onias III, not Onias IV, who builds the temple in Egypt. If there is an Onias IV, as Josephus says, he has the same name as his father. It is possible that Onias IV was given this name only after his father died and that Onias was a kind of throne-name.

---

[15] M.*Menahot* 13:10; BT*Menahot* 109ab; cf. alsp M. Yoma 6:3; Meg.10a; Avod. Zar. 52b.
[16] See also *PT Yoma* 33b.
[17] See Delcor "Le Temple d'Onias " 189 for further discussion and bibliography.

Scholars are quick to criticize Josephus for his confusion in saying that Menelaus was also named Onias.[18] Perhaps, however, Josephus thinks that when Menelaus seized the high priesthood, he took the name Onias as his own.[19] Or perhaps Josephus wants to tarnish the Onias name with the brush of Menelaus.

I now return to the question of this section: Does any of this imply anything about the lineage of Alcimus? Goldstein thinks that Onias IV left Judaea for Egypt because Alcimus was not a member of the Zadokite-Oniad line. But it is just as possible that Onias IV (or III) realized that he could not counter the claims of a fellow Oniad as he had hoped to with another non-Zadokite candidate. If it were Onias III, he would be reaching a certain age (he had been deposed in 174 BCE; it was now 163-62 BCE) and knew it was now or never. Assuming a term for Alcimus like that of Menelaus, he could not afford to wait a decade to determine if he would become the high priest after the new appointee.[20] The probability is that, despite the confusion of the sources, it was Onias IV who left for Egypt to find his destiny, implying that Alcimus was a Zadokite and a legitimate and formidable heir to the high priesthood.

---

[18] Lester L. Grabbe *Judaism from Cyrus to Hadrian: Volume One: The Persian and Greek Periods* (Minneapolis, 1992) 281.
[19] He may have taken the name after the death (or assumed death) of Onias III.
[20] Emile Puech "Le grand prêtre Simon (III) fils d'Onias III, le Maître de Justice?" *Antikes Judentum und frühes Christentum* (1999) 137-158,

ARE THERE RABBINIC TRADITIONS THAT REFER TO ALCIMUS?

There are only two passages in rabbinic literature that may refer to Alcimus. It is striking to begin with that there are only two possibilities; however, we will test the validity of these two connections. For the rabbis, Alcimus' impact on important events in recent history should have been clear. We will begin with a suggestion and return to its validity below: If the rabbis were so angry with the Hasmonaean kings that they had little to say about them, how much the less would they emphasize historical figures who make the Hasmonaeans look good?

Middot 2:3

Middot 2:3 is a reference that is often cited as referring to Alcimus. The historical interpretation given to this *mishnah* is that Alcimus broke into the *soreg*, one of the approaches to the Temple, in order to remove the wall which non-Judaeans were forbidden to pass. The *soreg* was breached in thirteen places, infuriating the *Asidaioi*. When Alcimus died suddenly, it was interpreted as an act of retribution. This interpretation is based on two passages, one from 1 Maccabees and the other from Josephus, which we will cite again for convenience and for the merit of juxtaposition:

> In the year 153, in the second month, Alcimus issued an order to tear down the wall of the inner court of the sanctuary, thus tearing down the work of the prophets. Alcimus had already begun the work of having it torn down when he suffered a stroke which put an end to his project. Unable to open his mouth and paralyzed, he could no longer speak or issue a will for his family. So Alcimus died in great agony on that occasion.
>
> 1Macc.9:54-56

> As the high priest Alcimus was planning to pull down the wall of the Holy Place, which was very old and had been erected by the ancient prophets, a sudden stroke from God seized him, by which he was brought speechless to the ground, and after suffering torment for many days, he died, having been high priest for four years. And when he died, the people gave the high priesthood to Judas....
>
> *Ant.*12:10:6

These passages agree that Alcimus was going to tear down the wall of the sanctuary but was miraculously stricken by God for his sinful action. Both passages refer to this wall as being ancient.

The *mishnah* from Tractate *Middot* does not contain *Gemara* (later rabbinic explanations); therefore, we are completely dependent on the *mishnah* itself (and later commentaries) for our understanding. The tractate presents the measurements of the principal parts of the Temple in Jerusalem. It assumes the existence of the Temple. *Middot* may have been included in the *Mishnah*, which was compiled after the destruction of the Temple, as a plan for the rebuilding of the Temple at a future date.[1] The first chapter describes the places where the priests and Levites kept watch in the Temple and the various gates. The second chapter, from which our *mishnah* comes, gives the measurements of the Temple Mount and its divisions, the *ḥel* and the *ʿazarah*, the "Women's Court," and so on. The third chapter describes the sacrificial altar and what surrounded it. The fifth and last chapter furnishes more information about the *ʿazarah* and its chambers.[2]

Here are two translations of the *mishnah*, the first leaving a couple of terms in the original, the second by Jacob Neusner with more explanation in brackets:

> Within it was the *soreg* ten handbreadths high. There were thirteen breaches in it; these had originally been made by the kings of Greece; and when they repaired them they enacted that thirteen prostrations should be made facing them. Within this was the Hel, which was ten cubits [broad]. There were twelve steps there. The height of each step was half a cubit and its tread was half a cubit. All the steps in the Temple were half a cubit high with a tread of half a cubit, except those of the porch. All the doorways in the Temple were twenty cubits high and ten cubits broad except those of the porch. All the doorways there had doors in them except those of the porch. All the gates there had lintels except that of Taddi which had two stones inclined to one another. All the original gates were changed for gates of gold except the Gates of

---

[1] Jacob Neusner *Judaism: The Evidence of the Mishnah* 372.

[2] The flat temple mount area, about 4 times the area within the *soreg*, was surrounded by a wall, with a covered porch on the interior. The south (main entry) porch, the Royal Portico, was the most elaborate. Towers at each southern corner were the temple pinnacles, the easternmost having a commanding view of the world outside the walls of Jerusalem, overlooking the Kidron Valley.

References to Alcimus in the Qumran Scrolls

Nicanor, because a miracle was wrought to them. Some say, however, it was because the copper of them gleamed [like gold].[3]

2:3 A. Inside it [the Temple mount, surrounding the inner area which contained the women's court and the Temple court] is a latticed railing, ten handbreadths high.

B. There were thirteen breaches in it which the kings of Greece opened up. They went and closed them up again and decreed on their account thirteen prostrations. Inside it is the rampart, ten cubits [wide]. And there were twelve steps there [leading up from the rampart to the women's courtyard]. The height of each step is a half-cubit, and its tread, a half-cubit. All the steps which were there [within the Temple mount] were a half a cubit in height and a half-cubit in tread, except for those of the porch [which had a tread of a cubit]. All of the entrances and gates which were there were twenty cubits high and ten cubits wide, except for that of the porch. All the entrances which were there had doors, except for that of the porch [M. 3:7]. All the gates which were there had lintels, except for the Taddi gate, which had two stones leaning against one another [as a pointed arch]. All the gates which were there were changed [and covered] with gold, except for Niqanor's gate, because a miracle was done with them [M. *Yoma*.3:10]. And there are those who say, "Because their bronze shone like gold."[4]

The *mishnah* requires a great deal of explanation. The entire enclosure of the "Court of Women" and the "Inner Courts" was shielded by a huge retaining wall. The wall created what was in effect a fort during some of the wars that directly affected the Temple Mount. According to Josephus, it was forty cubits (66 feet) high. Around the wall ran the *ḥel*, a level promenade that ran around the *ʿazarah*, the "Women's Court." The purpose of this wall is not known since there was no higher degree of holiness involved until one reached the *ḥel*. The *ḥel* was a rampart or bulwark that was 14 cubits (23 feet) wide. Steps led down to the "Courts of the Gentiles," the "Outer Courts." The wide platform was used for gatherings and crowds. It also had many storerooms and chambers for stocks of grain, wine, and oil.

Beyond these steps that led down to the "Courts of the Gentiles" and within the wall of the Temple Mount was the *soreg*. The *soreg* was 10 *ṭepaḥim*, which has

---

[3] *The Babylonian Talmud Seder Kodashim: Middoth* III trans. and ed. by I Epstein (London: Soncino, 1948) 7.

[4] Jacob Neusner *The Mishnah: A New Translation*: Middot *loc. cit.*

been estimated to be about five feet high.[5] The *soreg* may have been a kind of latticework; this notion is based on the fact that the root *sarag* means, "to entwine." Josephus, however, states that the *soreg* was made out of stone. Placed at regular intervals were elegant *stelae*, carved stone slabs that bore Greek and Latin inscriptions that prohibited Gentiles from entrance to the internal sacred courts (Greek *hieron*). Josephus mentions the *soreg* several times,[6] emphasizing the point that it bore warnings against trespass on holy ground on pain of death. Two relevant Greek inscriptions with the same content have been unearthed:[7]

> No foreigner is allowed within the balustrade surrounding the sanctuary and the court encompassed. Whoever is caught will be personally responsible for his ensuing death.

The *mishnah* mentions that there were "thirteen prostrations" in the Temple. Whenever the priests would pass by one of thirteen specific places in the Temple, they would bow down. According to Jewish traditional commentary based on different references in the *Gemara*, the thirteen prostrations were performed at the thirteen places in the *soreg* where the Greeks made breaches, which the Maccabees repaired. The prostrations at those places were instituted as a sign of gratitude to God for the victory over the Greeks.

Numbers Rabba 7:8 is quite clear and helpful in this regard. In discussing gradations of holiness, Israel is holier than all other countries, Jerusalem more holy than the rest of Israel, and the Temple Mount holier than the rest of Jerusalem. The latter statement is proved by the fact that while people afflicted with venereal disease can enter Jerusalem, they cannot enter the Temple Mount. The *midrash* then goes further and explains that the *ḥel* is holier than the rest of the Temple Mount, which is proved by the fact that non-Jews and unclean people may enter the Temple Mount but may not enter the *ḥel*. Further gradations of holiness are found as one gets closer to the Holy of Holies through the *ʿazarah*, the "Men's Court," the "Court of the Priests," and so on. When the breaches were later repaired,

---

[5] *Ant.* 8.3.9. See also Benjamin Mazar *The Mountain of the Lord: Excavating in Jerusalem* (Garden City, 1975) 113.

[6] *Ant.* 15: 417 etc.; *The Jewish War* 5: 193-200.

[7] Charles Clermont-Ganneau found one in 1870; the other was discovered near the Lion's Gate in 1935 in fragmentary form. See Mazar *The Mountain of the Lord* 114.

References to Alcimus in the Qumran Scrolls

worshippers in the ʿ*azarah* were instructed to make thirteen prostrations facing the breaches. Within this area was the *ḥel* (the rampart or level promenade in front of the "Inner Temple Court") that was ten cubits wide. What follows are details about the steps and doors and their measurements. Of further interest here is the statement that "all the original gates were changed for gates of gold except the Gates of Nicanor, because a miracle was wrought to them. Some say, however, it was because the copper of them gleamed like gold."

The Gate of Nicanor is an important and well-known point in the structure of Temple holiness. We learn this from *Numbers Rabba* 9:13,16, 24 and 33 where we learn that the rituals of the suspected adulteress (Numbers 5:15) are performed at the Nicanor Gate. It is also called the "eastern gate," or "the great gate." It was made of Corinthian brass and was regarded as the principal gate on account of its greater height (50 cubits) and width (40 cubits) and from its being more richly decorated with precious metals.[8] The reference to the Gates of Nicanor leads us to BT*Yoma* 38a, where we find a commentary on a *mishnaic* statement (*Yoma* 3:10): "As to Nicanor, miracles were done at his doors. And they remembered him with honor." The *Gemara* recounts that when Nicanor went to Alexandria to get doors for the great eastern gate of the Temple court, a great storm rose up in the sea to drown him (a legend that sounds quite similar to the Biblical story of the prophet Jonah). The sailors threw one of the doors into the sea but it did not stop the sea from raging. When they were about to throw in another door, Nicanor clung to the door and told them to throw him in with it, which they did. The sea immediately calmed down. Even though he was still alive (and very much like Jonah in his consternation over the gourd; Jonah 4), Nicanor was despondent over the first door that had been lost (apparently he got back aboard the ship with the second door intact). As the ship arrived at the Acre harbor, the first door reappeared and came up from under the sides of the boat. The *Gemara* tells us that others (even more clearly working with the Jonah tale) say that a monster swallowed the door and spat it onto the dry land. The story is referred to here because all the Sanctuary doors were changed to golden ones except those of Nicanor because of the miracles that had been wrought to bring them to Jerusalem. Others insist that they did not need to

---

[8] It may be the gate referred to in Christian Scriptures as the "gate of the temple which is called Beautiful" (Acts 3:2).

be replaced with golden ones because the bronze that they were made of already possessed a golden hue.[9]

"Methinks the lady doth protest too much": The tradition that Nicanor brought his miraculous doors from Egypt does not have an iota of historicity. It is so completely artificial, so obviously a secondary development of the Jonah story that one is forced to wonder what it is attempting to obscure. The tradition that there was a wealthy Alexandrian Jew named Nicanor who funded this gate sounds like an invention born from necessity because the truth, that a Greek general funded the gate, was too difficult to bear. It is at least plausible to suggest therefore that the reference in the *Mishnah* is to the Nicanor whom we have studied above. It is certainly striking, and to some, disconcerting, that a gate would be named for a Seleucid general who would become such an enemy of the people, an evil oppressor of the Judaeans. Actually, as we have seen, the picture of Nicanor in 2Maccabees is quite complex. We see his friendship with Judas and his temporary benevolence. We even have an earlier passage concerning his repentance and apparent conversion to the faith in the "One God." As we mentioned above in discussing 2Maccabees,[10] Nicanor, after being defeated by Judas,[11] runs from defeat until he reaches Antioch where he professes the might of the Judaean God.

It would be interesting if *Mishnah Middot* contains references to two historical personages involved in the Maccabaean period, Nicanor and Alcimus.[12] In fact, we have by no means proved that the "Gate of Nicanor" is connected to the Seleucid general.

More important here is the question: Does *Middot* 2:3 refer to Alcimus? "The thirteen breaches in it had been made by the kings of Greece." This is taken as a

---

[9] The same passage in *Numbers Rabba* 7:8 provides another interesting breakdown of holiness, with an explanation of three camps: The Israelite camp is from the gates of Jerusalem to the Temple Mount; from the gate of the Temple mount to the Gate of Nicanor is the Levitical camp; and from the Gate of Nicanor inwards is the camp of the Divine Presence.

[10] 2Macc.8:34-36.

[11] See also 1Macc.3:38-4:25.

[12] For the reasons why the Rabbinic sages did not transmit much about the period of the Hasmonaeans, see A. L. Hilbis "The Hasmoneans According to the Talmudic and Midrashic Sources" *Sinai* 8 6-22.

reference to the passage about Alcimus' death in 1Maccabees[13] cited above. If it is about Alcimus, the question becomes: Why does the *mishnah* say "the kings of Greece" and not Alcimus? A rather weak answer is that perhaps it was simply too difficult for the Rabbinic writer of this *mishnah* to admit that a High Priest of the Jews could have done this thing.

It appears unlikely that the *mishnah* is about Alcimus at all. After all, the passages in 1Maccabees and Josephus tell us that Alcimus did not succeed in his attempt to destroy the wall. It is entirely possible that it was indeed "the kings of the Greeks," or their representatives, and not Alcimus who created the breaches. Indeed, the chronology of the period seems to refute the Alcimus alternative. What is at stake is the evaluation of Alcimus and his role in preserving the sanctity of the Temple.

First, we will make the usual case that does connect Alcimus to *Middot* 2:3 as a part of a bigger historical theory about this period. The theory begins with background about the Seleucid attitude toward the exclusionary policies of the Jerusalem Temple, an attitude that changed in Maccabaean times, thus creating a crisis. Previous Seleucid emperors had taken a posture of great sensitivity to the question of Gentile access to the Sanctuary. In a royal edict, Antiochus III displayed his concern to preserve the ritual purity of the Jerusalem Temple. Such edicts were not demonstrations of royal magnanimity; a foreign king would not have addressed himself to the concerns of a subject people unless he knew exactly the issues that were close to the heart of that people. Ritual purity in the Temple was a prime concern of the priesthood, and in this case the edict was the result of negotiations with a delegation of which the priest Yoḥanan was the chief. Interestingly, we know from 2Maccabees that Yoḥanan was the father of Eupolemus, who has been mentioned above as a member of Judas' embassy to the Romans.[14] Here is Antiochus III:

He also published a decree, throughout his kingdom, in honour of the temple, as follows:

> It shall be lawful for no foreigner to come within the limits of the temple round about; which thing is forbidden also to the Jews, unless to those who, according to

---

[13] 1Macc.9:54-5.

[14] On Eupolemus, see above in my discussion of the embassy to Rome in 1Maccabees.

their own custom, have purified themselves. Nor let any flesh of horses, or of mules, or of asses, be brought into the city, whether they be wild or tame; nor that of leopards, or foxes, or hares; and, in general, that of any animal which is forbidden for the Jews to eat. Nor let their skins be brought into it; nor let any such animal be bred up in the city. Let them only be permitted to use the sacrifices derived from their forefathers, with which they have been obliged to make acceptable atonements to God. And he that transgresseth any of these orders, let him pay to the priests three thousand drachmae of silver.[15]

Ant. 12:145f.

This edict prohibits all foreigners from access to the sanctuary and also prohibits them from bringing meat and skins and breeding unclean animals in Jerusalem. In other words, only animals that could be sacrificed could be brought and kept in the city. At a later date, the Romans would also recognize this privilege.[16] Violation of these prohibitions would be punished with serious fines. The priest Yoḥanan represented the High Priest Simon, who thus set a kind of model for how a High Priest should protect the Temple and its city from contamination. To use a Talmudic expression, the prohibition of unclean animals in the city was "a fence around a fence"; if the animals could not be brought into the city at all, they certainly could not be brought near the Temple.[17] Contacts with the Gentile world may have been seen by some religiously problematic in that they could lead to assimilation and Hellenization.[18]

Economically speaking, however, this policy could not have been good news. Trading caravans would need to avoid the city. If one were more "progressive" and less influenced by these religious considerations, the sanctification of the entire city

---

[15] E. Bickerman "Une proclamation séleucide relative au temple de Jérusalem" *Syria* 25 (1946/48) 67-85; Marcus in *Josephus* VII, Loeb Classical Library (London, 1961) 701ff.

[16] Hengel *Zeloten* 219f.

[17] The fact that all of this had been worked out made the acts of the High Priest Jason even worse: "He cast away the humane royal concessions gained for the Jews by John, the father of the ambassador Eupolemus, who negotiated the treaty of friendship and alliance with the Romans. Overthrowing the civic institutions of the *Torah*, Jason brought in new usages which were contrary to the law" (2Macc.4:11).

[18] For instance, the traditional Jewish hymn *Ma'oz Tzur* contains these words: "Greeks gathered against Me then in the days of the Hasmonaeans, they breached the walls of My towers and defiled all the oils." This seems to be a reference to *Middot* 2:3.

References to Alcimus in the Qumran Scrolls

was economically destructive and problematic to one who wanted to be part of the world. There were clearly two sides to this argument. In the reign of Antiochus IV, the pro-Hellenization side asserted itself in new ways.

The *mishnah* states that the kings of the Greece opened the breaches which were then closed by the Maccabees in their repair and rededication of the Temple. If so, to whom would "the kings of the Greeks" specifically refer? We would suggest the Mysarch Apollonius who, in 168-167 BCE, came to Jerusalem with an army. He apparently came on a peaceful mission.[19] There does not seem to have been a rebellion that brought him to the city. The Judaeans actually went to watch his troops parade;[20] this would indicate that there were no precipitating problems. Still, Apollonius commits great and dramatic offenses to the sensibilities and control over the Judaeans. He burns parts of Jerusalem, tears down walls and builds a new fortified quarter called the *Akra*.[21] Most important here, control of the Temple is given to Jewish and non-Jewish "Hellenizers" who stop the traditional sacrifices:

> Forces will be levied by him; they will desecrate the temple, the fortress; they will abolish the regular offering and set up the appalling abomination.
>
> Daniel 11:31

> Her temple was deserted like a desert;
> Her festivals were turned into mourning,
> Her Sabbaths into cause for mockery,
> Her glory into cause for contempt.
>
> 1Macc.1: 39

In this context, the theory is that some would want to make breaches in the *soreg* as part of a political and religious program of "Hellenization." The exclusion of Gentiles from the Temple proper illustrates the concept of the Jews as a chosen, separated people. The gradation of the courts and their restricted access emphasized group distinction within Judaism. The inaccessibility of the "Holy of Holies" to all except the High Priest on one day of the year, and the various barriers which prevented common people from approaching the place of the Divine Presence, was

---

[19] According to both 1Macc.1:30 and 2Macc.5:25.
[20] 2Macc.5:26-26.
[21] 1Macc.1:33.

a continual object lesson on the holiness of God and His separation from sinners. The function of the *soreg* that made it a specific target of the Greeks and supporters of "Hellenization" was that it delineated the area into which non-Jews were permitted entry into the Temple. Non-Jews were allowed to come to the Temple to pray to God and to bring sacrifices but they could not continue past the *soreg*. Only those of the Jewish nation were permitted further. The Greeks were not against the existence of the Temple but were against any distinction made between them or any other nation and the Jewish people. They therefore breached the barrier placed in the Temple specifically for that purpose. Tearing down the *soreg* was very symbolic of the whole effort to force Jews to assimilate, to blur the line between Jew and non-Jew—the very separation indicated by the *soreg*.

Why thirteen breaches? Why not just tear down the whole thing? Was a king of Greece or Alcimus doing something ceremonial, breaching it in different places in order to make a symbolic show or point? The thirteen breaches the Greeks made in the *soreg*, and the thirteen repairs that the Maccabees later made, in a sense reflect the essence of the real battle between the Greeks and the Jews at that time. The holiday of *Hanukkah*, according to this theory, should be seen not only as the rededication of the Temple to the worship of God but also to restrict it again to Jews. If we follow this theory, we must also see the other side and view the *soreg* and the graded distinctions of the Temple from the perspective of those who would disagree with all such distinctions. In this regard, a glance at Christian texts will be instructive. When Jesus died, "the curtain of the temple was torn in two from top to bottom,"[22] signifying that the way was now open for immediate access to God.[23] Paul was accused of violating the sanctity of the holiest of places by bringing a Greek into the Temple.[24] Christianity made the statement that all class distinctions are obliterated—those that existed between Jews and Gentiles:

> For there is no distinction between Jew and Greek; the same Lord is the Lord of all and bestows his riches upon all who call upon him. For every one who calls upon the name of the Lord will be saved.
>
> *Romans* 10:12

---

[22] *Matthew* 27:51.
[23] According to *Hebrews* 10:19-20.
[24] Acts 21:17-29.

References to Alcimus in the Qumran Scrolls

—those between men and women:

> There is neither Jew nor Greek, there is neither slave nor free, there is neither male nor female; for you are all one in Christ.
>
> *Galatians* 3:28

—those between priests and laymen:

> To him who loves us and has freed us from our sins by his blood and made us a kingdom, priests to his God and Father ...[25]
>
> *Revelations* 1:6

One might reason that this is another viewpoint that would cast Alcimus' actions in a very different light. Indeed, from this alternate perspective, Alcimus was doing something heroic.

This is the prevalent theory, one that makes sense in terms of what seemed to be the Antiochene program and the Maccabaean reaction to it. And yet even if we accept this theory, *Middot* 2:3 does not seem to have a reference to Alcimus. In evaluating his actions as High Priest, we may state that he may have unsuccessfully attempted to break down a wall but he was not responsible for the breaches in the *soreg*, breaches that were made and then repaired *before* he became High Priest. In the prevalent theory, the ongoing controversy between those who would guard the specifically Jewish character of the innermost parts of the temple and those who would allow all people to enter those parts, the breaches were made, repaired, and then a new attempt was made by Alcimus to symbolically tear down the separation. At least according to our sources, he died in the attempt.

As we have indicated, it is unlikely that Alcimus' action in attempting to break down the wall has anything to do with the above. Following Goldstein, we will suggest the theory that Alcimus was a priest who believed in the exclusively Jewish nature of the holiest places in the Temple. His issue had nothing to do with Jews and Gentiles but about priests and non-priests, about whether non-priests were allowed to be anywhere in the "Inner Court." The word "court" is used here either for the area around the innermost building or an area like the "Court of Women."

---

[25] The separation between the Jews and Gentiles accomplished by the *soreg* may also referred to in *Ephesians* 2:13-14.

Benjamin E. Scolnic

The outer court would be the "Court of Women;" the "Inner Court" was divided into the "Court of Priests" and the "Court of Israelites." The *soreg*, the barrier that was outside the "outer court," the "Court of Women," had already been breached in the time of Antiochus IV. This is what *Middot* 2:3 and 1Macc.1:37 refer to. What did Alcimus want to tear down? Goldstein is correct in stating that even if Alcimus were "not pious he still would not have thought about "introducing gentiles or Greek practices to the "Inner Court." Instead, Goldstein thinks that we are reading here about "an internal Jewish controversy, between Jewish sects."

Voices as disparate as Ezekiel[26] and the Essenes (as evidenced in the *Temple Scroll*) were intensely concerned with the architecture of the Temple. 1Maccabees 9's reference to "the work of the prophets" may or may not be a reference to the passage in Ezekiel where he warns against allowing any but Zadokite priests into the "Inner Court."[27] Ezekiel certainly makes a powerful statement about this issue:

> Thus said the Lord GOD: Let no alien, uncircumcised in spirit and flesh, enter My Sanctuary—no alien whatsoever among the people of Israel. But the Levites who forsook Me when Israel went astray...shall suffer their punishment. They shall be servitors in My Sanctuary, appointed over the temple gates...But the levitical priests descended from Zadok, who maintained the service of My Sanctuary when the people of Israel went astray from me—they shall approach Me to minister to Me; they shall stand before Me to offer Me fat and blood—declares the Lord GOD. They alone may enter My Sanctuary and they alone shall approach My table to minister to Me; and they shall keep My charge.
>
> Ezek.44:10-16

> The gate of the inner court which faces east shall be closed on the six working days; it shall be opened on the Sabbath day and it shall be opened on the day of the new moon. The prince shall enter by way of the vestibule outside the gate, and shall attend at the gatepost while the priests sacrifice his burnt offering and his offering of

---

[26] Ezek.43:8-11.

[27] It is hard to dismiss the fact that there are such important differences between the prophet's description of his idealized Second Temple and the Second Temple that was actually built in history. "The work of the prophets" may have nothing to do with Ezekiel at all and may be a reference to a wall of the "Inner Court" that was supported by the later prophets such as Haggai and Zechariah. But see the evidence of the *Damascus Document* below.

References to Alcimus in the Qumran Scrolls

well-being; he shall then bow low at the threshold of the gate and depart....The common people shall worship before the LORD on Sabbaths and new moons at the entrance of the same gate....And as for the prince, he shall enter with them when they enter and leave when they leave.

Ezek.46:1-10

The Zadokite priests have a special state of holiness; they, and only they, shall enter the "Inner Court." As clear as these instructions are, however, this does not mean that Ezekiel was followed on this matter. Indeed, in post-exilic times, non-priestly male Israelites in a state of ritual purity could enter a part of the "Inner Court:"

So the people went out and brought them, and made themselves booths on their roofs, in their courtyards, in the courtyards of the House of God, in the square of the Water Gate and in the square of the Ephraim Gate.

Neh.8:16

Could it be that in a later time of crisis, this matter of architecture and sanctity became a raging issue? Alcimus, far from being a "Hellenizer," might have acted to say that there is no need for a wall at all because, following Ezekiel, non-Zadokite priests were not to be allowed anywhere in the "Inner Court." One begins to wonder if the reference to the wall as "the work of the prophets" in 1Maccabees and Josephus is not a refutation of the idea that the wall is against the work of the prophet Ezekiel.

Alcimus' action had nothing to do with the *soreg* mentioned in *Middot* 2:3, which barred Gentiles from the structures which surrounded the "Court of Women." That was a very different issue, the one that in the prevalent theory enveloped Alcimus' action. Instead, Alcimus' action was not about allowing non-Israelites in at all but about removing the barrier separating the area of the "Inner Court" restricted to priests to that open to all Israelites. Without that wall, non-priests could not have even come that close to the Holy of Holies. This was not about being exclusively Jewish; of that, contrary to the usual theory, there was no question. This was about the rights of access of non-Zadokite priests. As long as there was a wall, these non-priests could get close; without the wall, they could not go into the "Inner

Court" at all.[28] Thus, Alcimus' action has been misinterpreted by mistakenly connecting it to *Middot* 2:3. Actually it was a move that was pro-Zadokite priest, and perhaps, anti-Hasmonaean.

We present the possibilities again:

1. The usual theory—Alcimus as *soreg* breaker
2. An intermediate theory—Alcimus did not breach the *soreg*, but his attempt to break down a wall was an anti-exclusionary Jewish move.
3. The proposed theory—that Alcimus' action was a pro-priestly move.

Whatever the case, the issue of Temple architecture was of great symbolic import. It is possible that there is a connection to the evidence from the Dead Sea Scrolls, where there are negative references to a group called "the Builders of the Wall." The phrase seems to come, again, from Ezekiel[29] but there it is a metaphorical passage about the flimsy wall the people built out of false prophecies. In the "Document of the Damascus Covenanters," there are a number of references to this group.[30] Goldstein suggests that there may be a connection between the criticism of "The Builders of the Wall" and the story about Alcimus: "Did the hated sect get that name because of its theory that Israelites should be admitted to an area of the "Inner Court" marked off by a barrier?"[31] This would put Alcimus in the middle of a (perhaps) long-standing sectarian controversy.[32] The evidence from the *Damascus Document*[33] is suggestive:

> 'The builders of the wall'.... who have followed after 'Precept'—'Precept' was a spouter of whom it is written, *They shall surely spout (*Mi.2:6).
>
> CD 4:19

---

[28] See *The Jewish War* 5.5.6.226; *Ant.* 8.3.9.95.
[29] Ezek. 13:10.
[30] *CD* 4:19, 8:12, 18, 19:25, 31. See Chaim Rabin *The Zadokite Documents* 2nd ed. (Oxford, 1958).
[31] Goldstein *I Maccabees* 393.
[32] Chaim Rabin *Qumran Studies* (New York, 1957) 54.
[33] Citations are from Geza Vermes *The Complete Dead Sea Scrolls in English* (New York, 1997). Words are italicized by Vermes and are scriptural references.

References to Alcimus in the Qumran Scrolls

They have not kept apart from the people ... and have willfully rebelled by walking in the ways of the wicked of whom God said, *Their wine is the venom of serpents, the cruel poison (or head) of asps* (Deut.32:33). The *serpents* are the kings of the peoples and their *wine* is their ways. And the *head of asps* is the chief of the kings of Greece who came to wreak vengeance upon them. But all these things the *builders of the wall and those who daub it with plaster* (Ezek.13:10) have not understood because a follower of the wind, one who raised storms and rained down lies, had preached to them (Mic.2:11), against all of whose assembly the anger of God was kindled.... Because God loved the first (men) who testified in His favour, so will He love those who come after them, for the Covenant of the fathers is theirs. But he hated the *builders of the wall* and His anger was kindled (MS. B: against them and against all those who followed them); and so shall it be for all who reject the commandments of God ...

CD 8.18ff.

The builders of the wall have not understood the meaning of history because of the false teacher who preached to them. There is no definitive connection to Alcimus, but again, this material is suggestive. An alternate theory would have to explain the meaning of "Builder of the Wall"; at least, in this theory, we know what wall is referred to and we know who the builders are, namely, those who would allow non-priests to enter the "Inner Court" of the Temple.

We will return to the Dead Sea material below in our discussion of the "Teacher of Righteousness."

In the sources studied thus far, Alcimus is portrayed as a traitor and collaborator. His so-called voluntary defilement was his political collaboration made into a religious evil. And yet we think of Judas' friendship with Nicanor as described in 2Maccabees during the very time that Alcimus was High Priest; Judas was not "defiled" by this contact. Political controversy is turned into religious controversy. A tentative position on the basis of 1Maccabees, 2Maccabees and Josephus is that Alcimus never did anything against Judaism, but that he was anti-Maccabee. These sources show him appealing for help from the Seleucids against the Maccabees. Alcimus did see Judas as both a personal threat and as bad news for the Judaeans. We certainly have sources that place Alcimus in bitter rivalry with Judas. We now turn to a source that places Alcimus in opposition to an early sage, Yosi ben Yoʿezer.

Benjamin E. Scolnic

Genesis Rabba

Another interpretation of AND HE SMELLED THE SMELL OF HIS RAIMENT is that it refers to such as Joseph Meshitha and Jakum of Zeroroth. Joseph Meshitha: When the enemies desired to enter the Temple mount, they said: Let one of them [the Jews] enter first.' Said they to him [Joseph]: 'Enter, and whatever you bring out is yours.' So he went in and brought out a golden lamp. Said they to him: "It is not fitting for a common person to use this, but go in again and what you bring out will be yours'; he, however, refused. R.Phinehas said: They offered him three years' taxes, yet he still refused. 'Is it enough that I have angered my God once,' he exclaimed, 'that I should anger Him again!' What did they do to him? They put him in a carpenter's vice and sawed him in sunder, while he cried out, 'Woe, woe that I angered my Creator!' Jakum of Zeroroth was the nephew of R.Jose b.Jo'ezer of Zeredah.[34] Riding on a horse he went before the beam on which he [R.Jose] was to be hanged,[35] and taunted him: 'See the horse on which my master has let me ride, and the horse upon which your Master has made you ride.' 'If it is so with those who anger Him, how much more with those who do His will,' he replied. 'Has then any man done His will more than thou?' he jeered. 'If it is so with those who do His will, how much more with those who anger Him,' he retorted. This pierced him like the poison of a snake, and he went and subjected himself to the four modes of execution inflicted by the Beth din: stoning, burning, decapitation, and strangulation. What did he do? He took a post and planted it in the earth, raised a wall of stones around it and tied a cord to it. He made a fire in front of it and fixed a cord in the middle [of the post]. He hanged himself on the post, the cord was burnt through and he was strangled. The sword caught him, while the wall [of stones] fell upon him and he was burnt. Jose b.Jo'ezer of Zeredah[36] fell into a doze and saw his [Jakum's] bier flying in the air. 'By a little while he has preceded me into the Garden of Eden,' said he.

Genesis Rabba LXV:22

In both of the stories here, the traitorous Jews, Joseph of Meshitha[37] and Jakum of Zeroroth, do something evil and then decide that they cannot do any more. It is

---

[34] A town in Peraea.
[35] According to 1Macc.7:16, he was executed with a number of others, by Bacchides the Seleucid general.
[36] Note that the version of *Midrash Rabba* says that he was dying.
[37] We do not seem to know anything else about this figure.

References to Alcimus in the Qumran Scrolls

important to note that Joseph of Meshitha's action here is defilement of the Temple, a central charge against Alcimus in some of our other sources. How is this passage a commentary on "smelling the smell of his raiment?" It would seem that God, like Isaac, smells the raiment of Esau on the body of Jacob, Jewish figures represented by Joseph of Meshitha and Alcimus. This passage is connected to others about repentance: Joseph of Meshitha and Alcimus metaphorically wear the clothes of the heathen but then repent of their ways.

Jacob Neusner discusses this passage[38] and gives a critical evaluation of the tradition. He points out that it has no connections to other traditions about Yosi b. Yoʻezer and appears to echo some of the late legends of R. ʻAqiba's martyrdom. He discounts the identification of Yakim of Ṣerurot with Alcimus or any historical conclusions made thereby. Here is Neusner's translation as it appears in that book:

> VI.i.1.A. Yaqim of Ṣerurot was the nephew of R. Yosi b. Yoʻezer of Ṣeredah. He was riding on his horse.[39] He went before the beam on which [Yosi] was to be hanged.

---

[38] Jacob Neusner *The Rabbinic Traditions About the Pharisees Before 70* (E J Brill, 1971) 176-77.

[39] Goldstein (*I Maccabees* 335) mentions that one commentator, Theodorus (on *Bereshit Rabbah* p. 742, line 6) states that the sin was that he was riding on his horse on the Sabbath. This is another example of how Jewish tradition expands on the evil of the figures it sees as villains. Indeed, this is how the story has been passed down in Jewish traditional circles. In a lesson on transforming others, Rav Chaim Shmuelovitz offers some advice: "These ideas were demonstrated brilliantly by Rabi Yosi ben Yoʻezer as he was being led out on a horse to be executed. His irreverent nephew approached him, riding a horse on the Sabbath, and taunted him saying, "Look at the horse that my master gives to me and look at the horse that your Master gives to you!" Rabi Yosi overlooked the incredible audacity of this nephew taunting him at such a time and focused all of his compassionate thoughts on utilizing this opportunity to influence him. He turned to his nephew and said, "If Hashem does that for those who anger Him, imagine what will be done for those who fulfill His will." His stunned nephew responded, "Is there anyone who fulfilled Hashem's will more than you?" Rabi Yosi then moved in for the kill. "If Hashem punishes the wrongs of those who fulfill His will, imagine what will be done to those who anger Him." The words found their mark, entering this nephew like the venom of a snake. He repented completely and entered the "World to Come" even before his uncle, Rabi Yosi."

He said to him, "See the horse on which my master has set me, and see your horse on which your master has set you."

He said to him, "If he does thus to those that anger him, how much the more [good will he do to] those that do his will."

He said to him, "Has any man done his will more than you?"

He said to him. "If [he does] so to those that do his will, how much the [worse will he do to] those that anger him."

The matter pierced him like the poison of a snake, and he went and brought on himself the four modes of death inflicted by the court: stoning, burning, decapitation, and strangulation.

B. What did he do? He brought a post and planted it in the earth, raised around it a wall, and tied on it a cord. He made a fire in front of it and set a sword in the middle [of the post]. He hanged himself on the post, and the cord was burned through, and he was strangled. The sword caught him, while the wall [of stones also] fell on him, and he was burned.

Yosi b.Yo'ezer of Ṣeredah dozed and saw his bier flying through the air.

He said, "By a brief hour has he preceded me to the Garden of Eden."[40]

Notice that Alcimus refers to Yosi as "my master." The story would make sense in the context of the events of 162 BCE. Alcimus is saying, "My earthly master, that is the Seleucid king Demetrius, has given me authority and glory, while your pious service to your Master, God, has brought you to this terrible fate."

Alcimus taunts Yosi that no one has done more for his God than him. If Yosi b.Yo'ezer were the most pious man of his generation, this would fit with the rabbinic references about the grape-clusters and Yosi's extraordinary piety (see below). Alcimus still goes to the Garden of Eden because of his repentance.

This question before us is whether this text is significant for the study of Alcimus' life. Neusner denies this in the most emphatic terms:

> This is a singleton, appearing in a late compilation, with no connections in theme or in detail to any antecedent traditions on Yosi b.Yo''ezer. We do not know how the story was shaped and have no idea whatever as to the sources of Yosef b.Yo'ezer's

---

[40] *Gen. Rabba.*65:27, ed. Theodor-Albeck, II, pp.742 1.5 through 744, 1.1 = Midrash on Psalms 11:7, Braude, I, pp. 166-7. Neusner cites the part of the passage at issue but does not start at the beginning of the text. The second story is the parallel to the first and therefore is instructive.

References to Alcimus in the Qumran Scrolls

supposed martyrdom. As it stands, the story stands quite apart from, and outside of, the other traditions on Yosef b.Yoʻezer. Had Yaqim been associated with any ancient worthy, it would not have made any difference for the substance of the story, which apparently is an echo of one of the several ʻAqiba martyrdom legends. Part B is interpolated, a gloss explaining the foregoing.
The identification of Yaqim of Serurot with Alcimus of 1Macc.7:16 and the further allegation that Alcimus was Yosi's nephew (!) are groundless; the various historical opinions based on that identification are absurd.[41]

And yet, would rabbinic tradition make up a connection between one of its first heroes, Yosi b.Yoʻezer, and a traitorous High Priest? As we shall see, Yosi b.Yoʻezer was a very significant figure in rabbinic history and it is fair to suggest that we would have some tradition about his death, especially if he was a martyr. The "grape clusters" tradition (see below) speaks of his death and does mourn his passing, testifying to his greatness and erudition.

It may be unfair to say that because the story is a singleton, it is not true. One does understand, again, why Neusner says this. While other traditions have their parallels, versions and cross-references, the fact that the story only exists in this later compilation does make it seem less authentic than the others. Yet following Neusner's own chart of the references about the Yosi's, we see that there are other singletons as well. Also, we cite Neusner's references because he shows that a version of the story is presented in *Midrash Tehillim*. While the latter work is probably an even later compilation than *Genesis Rabba*, it is, nevertheless, another witness of our text. It may also be unfair to assume that because the story is found in a late compilation, the story itself is necessarily late. It may be that the text is used here because of its ending about the Garden of Eden, as the section in *Midrash Tehillim* is concerned with matters of death and the afterlife. we cite it here because of its interesting variations, especially at the beginning and end of the passage:

> The upright shall behold his face (Ps.11:7). The Sages say that during a time of religious persecution a decree was issued for the hanging of Jose ben Joʻezer. Jakum of Serorot, the nephew[42] of Jose ben Joʻezer of Seredah, rode by on a horse, as Jose ben Joʻezer, bearing the beam for the gallows, was going forth to be hanged. Jakum

---
[41] Neusner *Rabbinic Traditions* I 77.
[42] Some versions say "stepson"; see Goldstein *I Maccabees* 334.

said: "Look at the horse that my master gives me to ride, and look at the horse that thy Master gives thee to ride." Jose ben Joʿezer replied, "If so much is given to such as thee who provoke Him, how much more shall be given to those who obey His will!" Jakum asked: "Has any man been more obedient to the will of God than thou?" Jose ben Joʿezer replied: "If so much is done to those who are obedient to His will, how much more shall be done to those who provoke Him!" This answer went into Jakum like the venom of a snake: He went away and imposed upon himself the four death penalties of stoning, burning, beheading, and strangulation. How did he do it? He got a beam and drove it into the ground. To the beam, he firmly tied a rope. He placed sticks of wood in a row and built a wall of stones over them. Then he piled up fuel in front of the beam and put a sword, pointing upward, in the midst of the fuel. After lighting a fire under the sticks of wood beneath the stones, he hanged himself from the beam and thus strangled himself. The rope broke, and he fell into the fire, the sword met him, and the wall of stones tumbled upon him. The soul of Jakum departed, and because of his repentance he was received. Jose ben Joʿezer, in the drowse of death, spied Jakum's bier flying through space and said: "See ye, this man by a brief hour precedes me into the Garden of Eden."

Braude's note states that, "The Syrian general Bacchides crucified Jose ben Joʿezer. Jakum may be the notorious High Priest so named, or the governor Alcimus."[43] It is another example of scholarly prejudice that Alcimus is referred to as "the notorious High Priest." We do not know why Braude would call Alcimus a "governor" nor do we know how Braude knows that Bacchides crucified Yosi. Still, the idea that Bacchides crucified Yosi would be a fascinating connection to the killing of the *Asidaioi*. One might have thought of the massacre as being one dramatic event. Alternatively, what if, after the shocking event, Yosi, as the leader, was hanged in public?

This new beginning may be considered a gloss, but compare the two initial sentences:

Yaqim of Ṣerurot was the nephew of R. Yosi b. Yoʿezer of Ṣeredah. He was riding on his horse. He went before the beam on which [Yosi] was to be hanged.
Genesis Rabba

---

[43] William G. Braude *The Midrash on Psalms* (New Haven, 1959) 431.

The Sages say that during a time of religious persecution a decree was issued for the hanging of Jose ben Joʿezer. Jakum of Ṣerorot, the nephew of Jose ben Joʿezer of Ṣeredah, rode by on a horse, as Jose ben Joʿezer, bearing the beam for the gallows, was going forth to be hanged.

Midrash Tehillim

Obviously, the superior text is the second one. It is no doubt later; glosses have become part of the text. The earlier text, then, seems to assume more recognition of the subject and the events to which the text refers. The ends of the two versions are also instructive:

Yosi b.Yoʿezer of Ṣeredah dozed and saw his bier flying through the air. He said, "By a brief hour has he preceded me to the Garden of Eden."

Genesis Rabba

The soul of Jakum departed, and because of his repentance he was received. Jose ben Joʿezer, in the drowse of death, spied Jakum's bier flying through space and said: "See ye, this man by a brief hour precedes me into the Garden of Eden."

Midrash Tehillim

Neusner is working within rabbinic traditions and as such can make such claims about the historicity of this passage. Once we broaden the context to the other extent literature, however, it is not implausible to consider certain connections between the various materials.

While Neusner is adamantly dismissive, Goldstein, on the other hand, has a great deal to say about this passage. First, he agrees with the scholarly identification[44] of Alcimus with the Yaqim in this story. He also accepts the familial connection between Alcimus and Yosi b.Yoʿezer, stating that whether Alcimus were a nephew, as both of the versions of the story say, or a stepson, as some manuscripts of *Midrash Tehillim* have it, Alcimus "could well have been strongly influenced by the sage." On weaker ground, Goldstein also feels that the wall that falls on Yaqim in the story ("He placed sticks of wood in a row and built a wall of stones over them") may be an echo of the death of Alcimus when he tried to knock

---

[44] Geiger *Urschrift* 64.

down the wall in the Temple.[45] This point is tenuous, at best: The passage seems to be working to show that Alcimus killed himself by all four modes of execution, including stoning. Since it is hard to stone oneself, the falling wall seems to be the method that the story conjures up to fulfill this mode. This story does not seem to have anything to do with the wall of the Temple; in fact, it seems as if this story does not know about the stroke that Alcimus suffered because of his action there.

An intermediate position is that of Hoenig[46] who does not think that Yaqim was the nephew of Yosi b.Yo‛ezer but who does accept the historical usefulness of the story in *Genesis Rabba*.

Looking at the story as a possible witness to the life of Alcimus, it is clear that it describes Alcimus as very evil. The taunting by a total stranger would be bad enough; by a nephew and fellow-priest it is horrible. On the other hand, a ruptured relationship between famous uncle and famous nephew would be just the motivation for this kind of taunting.

There is something eerily familiar about the story. Alcimus sounds uncomfortably like the infamous Jew in the anti-Semitic legends of "the Wandering Jew" who mocks Jesus on his way to the Cross. Alcimus' suicide reminds one of Judas' suicide as reported in Christian Scriptures. One wonders if this tradition was not an inspiration for the obviously artificial story of Judas in the Christian Scriptures, an infamous and destructive tale that is based on the story of David and Aḥitophel in 2Samuel.

Returning to the matter at hand we also have to deal with Alcimus' repentance and his frantic attempt to achieve atonement (in the Psalms version, this repentance seems to be accepted). Why allow repentance? Part of it may just be the premium placed by the rabbis on repentance, as if to say: "If Alcimus could repent and go to Heaven, how much the more so all of us who are not sinners in his category?" Perhaps, however, there is another possibility, that Alcimus is given the opportunity to repent because of his original piety. Yosi talks to Alcimus, using his former loyalty to God to try to show him the error of his ways. Yosi's incredible heroism and faith at the hour of his martyrdom win Alcimus back to God. If there is the

---

[45] Goldstein *I Maccabees* 393.
[46] Sidney B. Hoenig *The Great Sanhedrin. A study of the origin, development, composition, and function of the Bet Din Ha-Gadol during the Second Jewish Commonwealth* (Philadelphia, 1953) 29ff.

References to Alcimus in the Qumran Scrolls

family relationship, if Yosi is the uncle or stepfather of Alcimus, this repentance would be especially gratifying to Yosi. Or if Yosi's support were one of the bases for Alcimus' rise to prominence, the repentance would be all the more gratifying.

Yosi b.Yoʿezer is a priest.[47] It is likely that Yosi's brother was Alcimus' father, as the priesthood was passed down in a patrilineal line. Indeed, it may be that Alcimus' emergence was partly due to his connection to his famous and trusted uncle. This makes Alcimus' betrayal of the *Asidaioi* all the worse.

In order to understand this passage fully, we will briefly survey what we know about Yosi b.Yoʿezer from rabbinic sources.

The Importance of Yosi Ben Yoʿezer

Jacob Neusner[48] has studied three chains of Pharisaic tradition: the authorities who decreed concerning the laying on of hands, those who issued decrees, and those who gave moral apophthegms. Let us begin with the most famous of the relevant passages, that which lists the authorities that pronounced moral apophthegms.

> A. Yosi b.Yoʿezer of Ṣeredah and Yosi b.Yoḥanan of Jerusalem received [it] from them. Yosi b.Yoʿezer says, "Let your house be a gathering place for sages. And wallow in the dust of the feet. And drink in their words with gusto."
>
> ʾAvot 1:4

This citation must be read in its context. Neusner's form-critical reading of the first chapter of *ʾAvot* must be summarized here in order to appreciate the importance of Yosi b.Yoʿezer[49] in the justly famous chain of tradition. One cannot appreciate Neusner's reading without at least listing the necessary parts of the entire passage according to his breakdown:

---

[47] See below on *Mishnah Hagigah* 2:7: "Yosef b.Yoʿezer was the [most] pious man in the priesthood."

[48] Jacob Neusner *The Pharisees: Rabbinic Perspectives* (Hoboken, N.J., 1973) 10-22.

[49] S. Safrai "The Teaching of the Asidaioi in Mishnaic Literature" *JJS* 16 (1965) 15-33; Jacob Neusner *Rabbinic Traditions about the Pharisees before 70*. 3 volumes (Leiden, 1971); idem *The Idea of Purity in Ancient Judaism* (Leiden 1973).

Benjamin E. Scolnic

A. Moses received the *Torah* from Sinai and handed it on to Joshua, Joshua to the Elders, the Elders to the Prophets, and the Prophets handed it on to the men of the Great Assembly.
B. They said three things, "Be deliberate in judgment, raise up many disciples, and make a fence around the *Torah*."
2. Simeon the Just was of the remnants of the Great Assembly. He used to say, "On three things the world stands: on the *Torah*, on the [Temple-] service, and on deeds of loving kindness."
3. Antigonus of Sokho received from Simeon the Just. He used to say ...
4. A. Yosi b.Yoʿezer of Ṣeredah and Yosi b.Yoḥanan of Jerusalem received [it] *from them* (my italics). Yosi b.Yoʿezer says, "Let your house be a gathering place for sages. And wallow in the dust of the feet. And drink in their words with gusto.
5. Yosi b.Yoḥanan of Jerusalem says ...
6. Joshua b.Peraḥiah and Nittai the Arbelite received from them. Joshua b.Peraḥiah says ...
7. Nittai the Arbelite says ...
8. Judah b.Ṭabbai and Simeon b.Shetaḥ received from them. Judas b.Ṭabbai says...
9. Simeon b.Shetaḥ says ...
10. Shemaʿiah and Abṭalion received from them. Shemaʿiah says ...
11. Abṭalion says
12. Hillel and Shammai received from them. Hillel says ...
13. He used to say ...
14. He used to say ...
15. Shammai says ...
16. Rabban Gamliel says ...
17. Simeon his son says ...
18. Rabban Simeon b.Gamliel says, On three things the world stands: on truth, on judgment, and on peace, as it is written, *Execute the judgment of truth and peace* (Zech.8:16)."

Neusner shows that the basic form of the original passage is found in #4-12 and is quite fixed. The names of the two sages receive the *Torah* from their predecessors, and three of each sage's famous sayings are recorded. The pairs end with Hillel and Shammai. Rabban Gamliel is not said to have received from Hillel and Shammai and "Simeon his son" is not said to have received from his father. Since Simeon in #17 is the same person as "Rabban Simeon b.Gamliel" in #18, one is struck with the new form of his name. Also, the saying in #18 is a direct counterpart to #2; both speak of the three things on which the world stands. Simeon

References to Alcimus in the Qumran Scrolls

the Just says that the world stands on the *Torah*, Temple service, and deeds of loving kindness. Rabban Simeon b.Gamliel says that the world stands on truth, judgment, and peace. Following Morton Smith, Neusner explains that the latter is a post-135 CE version of the former, with *pax Romana* replacing "the brotherhood of Israel." When #18 was written to balance and change #2, #2 must have been the first saying in the list. At this point in the analysis, it seems that what is now #1 must have been added and placed at the beginning of the list. Still, #2 does not fit with what Neusner has established is the form of the list, represented by #4-12. #2, concerning Simeon the Just, and #3, Antigonus of Sokho, were added to the list. Since rabbinic tradition ignores Antigonus and basically just has legends about Simeon, Neusner comes to a clear conclusion:

The original list began just as the rabbinic legal traditions began: with the two Yosi's. The appeal to Simeon the Just, perhaps known from Ben Sira, was motivated by the desire to attach this legal tradition to the last great member of the legitimate Jerusalem priesthood before its fall.

A chronological problem is that the basically unknown Antigonus is supposed to cover the century between Simeon the Just and the Yosi.[50] The larger problem is that the two Yosi's receive the *Torah from them*. Clearly, they did not inherit from Antigonus (an individual). Also, #4 cannot be the beginning of the list. They must have received the *Torah* from the men of the Great Assembly. In this reconstruction, the original reading would have been:

A. Moses received the *Torah* from Sinai and handed it on to Joshua, Joshua to the Elders, the Elders to the Prophets, and the Prophets handed it on to the men of the Great Assembly.
4. A. Yosi b.Yoʻezer of Ṣeredah and Yosi b.Yoḥanan of Jerusalem received [it] from them. Yosi b.Yoʻezer says ...

This simple structure was broken to insert Simeon the Just, who, though a righteous High Priest, places *Torah* above Temple service. The point is made that

---

[50] Antigonos of Sokho seems to be the first noteworthy Jew who bears a Greek name. There is an interesting tradition in *ʾAvot of Rabbi Nathan* 5 that Antigonos had two disciples, Zadok and Boethus, who rejected their master's teaching and lapsed into heresy. From these arose the Sadduceeans and the Boethusians; both denied the doctrines of the immortality of the soul and of the resurrection of the dead.

even while the Temple was in its heyday, *Torah* was already attaining precedence. It is as if Simeon the Just looks ahead to the corruption of the High Priesthood by his successors. Those successors are not the heirs of Simeon the Just; as the list makes clear; his heirs are the early sages and the rabbis.[51]

One of the two other chains of Pharisaic tradition lists the authorities that made statements about the laying on of hands.[52] Perhaps the first *halakhic* dispute was between Yosi ben Yoʿezer and Yosi ben Yoḥanan. The dispute went on for many generations concerning *sᵉmikhah*, the laying of hands on sacrifices during festivals:

---

[51] I do wonder why Onias III does not have a place in all this. Perhaps it was a resistance to anything connected to Onias IV and his temple. Still, as I discussed above, 2Maccabees does try to connect the legitimacy of Onias III to the legitimacy of Judas the Maccabee and his Hasmonaean successors as high priests.

[52] For a historical interpretation, see Louis Ginzberg "The Significance of the Halachah for Jewish History," *On Jewish Law and Lore* (Philadelphia, repr. 1962) 77-126. The laying on of hands was a way to increase the return of the Jews to Judaea. Ginzberg does not support this statement with historical information or corroboration. Neusner (*Rabbinic Traditions about the Pharisees* 341) refutes Ginzberg's assumption that the Hasmonaeans were subservient to the Pharisaic sages. Though Ginzberg claims to be speaking in historical terms, he does not substantiate how all of this worked in real terms or what the relationship between the kings and the sages was.
Another interpretation is that of Solomon Zeitlin "The Semikah Controversy between the Zugoth" *JQR* 7 (1916-1917) 499-517. Zeitlin does not think that "the laying on of hands" concerns the laying on of hands on sacrifices in the Temple on the holidays. Instead, he concludes that "the laying on of hands" concerns the acceptance of the authority of the "sages in their innovations in the *Torah*." I do not think that this mistaken notion even makes sense; all of the mentioned sages acted on their authority to make innovations. In a later work, *The Rise and Fall of the Judaean State. A Political, Social and Religious History of the Second Commonwealth* (Phil., I, 1962; II, 1967), Zeitlin states that the controversy about the laying of hands concerned whether people were allowed to lay their own hands on the sacrificial animals; if they could not do so, they could not bring the animals and would not make pilgrimages. So the House of Hillel would allow the people to lay on hands. According to Zeitlin, the Shamma'ite view that the people could not lay hands on the sacrificial animals prevailed and as a result the Temple was deserted on the holidays.

References to Alcimus in the Qumran Scrolls

Yosi b.Yoʻezer says (*'mr*) [on a Festival-day] not to lay (*lsmk*) [hands on the offering before it is slaughtered]. Yosi b.Yoḥanan says to lay on [hands]. Joshua b.Peraḥiah says not to lay [hands]. Nittai the Arbelite says to lay [hands]. Judas b.Ṭabbai says not to lay [hands]. Simeon b.Shetaḥ says to lay [hands]. Shemaʻiah says to lay [hands]. Abṭalion says not to lay [hands]. Hillel and Menaḥem did not differ, but Menaḥem went forth, and Shammai entered. Shammai says not to lay [hands]. Hillel says to lay [hands]. The former were $n^e si\ 'im$, and the latter fathers of the court (*'bwt byt dyn*).

Mishnah Hagigah 2:2

R.Meʾir's list in *Tosefta Hagigah* 2:8[53] is different in certain respects but our point, that Yosi b.Yoʻezer is the first link on the chain, is unchanged.

Similarly, the other chain of Pharisaic tradition, lists Yosi b.Yoʻezer as the first in the chain of authorities making decrees:

Mishnah: And these are the laws stated in the upper chamber of Hananiah b.Hezekiah b.Garon, when they went up to visit him. They took a count, and the House of Shammai outnumbered the House of Hillel. And on that day they enacted eighteen measures. **Gemara:** And what are the eighteen measures? We learned ...one's hands.] And the hands. Did the students of Shammai and Hillel [so] decreed [it], as it is taught (*dtny'*) Yosi b.Yoʻezer of Ṣeredah and Yosi b.Yoḥanan of Jerusalem decreed (*gzr*) [the capacity to receive] uncleanness (*twm'h*) upon the land of the peoples and on glassware.[54] Simeon b.Shetaḥ ordained (*tqn*) a marriage-contract for the wife and decreed (*gzr*) [the capacity to receive] uncleanness upon metal utensils. Shammai and Hillel decreed uncleanness on hands.

BT*Shabbat* 14b

---

[53] *Tosefta Hagigah* ed. Saul Lieberman 382-83, lines 40-44.
[54] Again, for a historical interpretation, see Ginzberg *The Significance of the Halachah for Jewish History* 77-126. Ginzberg thinks that the Yosi's declare uncleanness on both foreign countries and glassware in order to attempt to stem the tide of emigration from Judaea at the time of the persecutions of Antiochus IV. By saying that would-be emigrants would be going to an impure place, Ginzberg theorizes, the Yosi's were trying to keep them in their homeland. Ginzberg also thinks that glassware was expensive but might be preferred to locally made earthenware and metal dishes because the former could not become impure but the latter could. Neusner retorts that glassware was cheap and that the masses did not keep the purity laws (Neusner *Rabbinic Traditions about the Pharisees* Vol. III 338-339).

> Did not R.Zeʿira b.Abuna in the name of R.Jeremiah say, "Yosef b.Yoʿezer of Ṣeredah and Yosi ben Yoḥanan of Jerusalem decreed uncleanness upon the land of the peoples and upon glass utensils." R.Yonah said, Rabbi Judah b.Ṭabbai . R.Yosi said, "Rabbi Judah b.Ṭabbai and Simeon b.Shetaḥ decreed uncleanness on metal utensils. "Hillel and Shammai decreed concerning the cleanness of the hands."
>
> PT *Shabbat* 11a

Let me explain why all of this is so important for our purpose here. All three chains of Pharisaic tradition begin with Yosi b.Yoʿezer. Yosi b.Yoʿezer was a priest and sage. He was the true heir of the chain of tradition. And his decrees are important, cherished, and transmitted faithfully:

> Testified R.Yosi b.Yoʿezer of Ṣeredah about (1) a *qamsa* locust, that it is clean [for eating]; and about (2) liquid in the slaughterhouse, that it is insusceptible to uncleanness; and (3) that one who touches a corpse [alone, and not what that person in turn will touch] is unclean. And they called him Yosi the Easy-going.
>
> M. *Eduyyot* 8:4

The liquids in the slaughterhouse of the temple are not subject to defilement. He testified on all three *halakhic* issues regarding purity and impurity, ruling all of them as permissible, so he was called by his generation *Yosi Sh^{e}raya*, "Yosi the Permitter."

Neusner's analysis of this tradition is striking:

> Yosi b.Yoʿezer's uncleanness decrees represent another tradition attested at early Yavneh. Eliezer and ʿAqiba refer to it. The little list has not been revised to conform to mishnaic conventions; it is kept in Aramaic, for one thing, and does not use the terms nearly everywhere predominant: *ṭmʾ/ṭhr*. I think we have here something more than a merely generalized tradition that Yosi issued uncleanness rulings with respect to the Temple cult. It may be a tradition formulated with some precision and deriving from the earliest, pre-Hillelite stratum of Pharisaic materials. It stands apart in form and language from everything else; and since it has an early attribution, we may take for granted that the form and language are not only different from, but earlier than, the Yavnean revision of the antecedent traditions. On that

References to Alcimus in the Qumran Scrolls

basis, of course, we cannot claim we have Yosi's *ipsissima verba*. But we may well have a remnant of a very old tradition indeed.[55]

Neusner 's method takes him to this positive conclusion about Yosi b.Yo'ezer. Yet he is unwilling to move from this conclusion to a historical connection.

Yosi b.Yo'ezer's greatness is established by many other rabbinic texts. Later generations said that the two Yosi's taught *Torah* like the greatest rabbi of them all, Moses:

> When Yosef ben Yo'ezer of Seredah and Yosef b.Yohanan died, the grape clusters came to an end. What are the grape clusters? A man in whom are all things. And Rav Judah said in the name of Samuel, "All the grape clusters who arose for Israel from the days of Moses until Yosef b.Yo'ezer died *learned Torah like Moses our rabbi.* Henceforward they did not learn *Torah* like Moses our rabbi." In a *mishnah* we learned: There was no reproach in all the grape clusters that arose for Israel from the days of Moses until Yosef b.Yo'ezer of Seredah. Henceforward there was reproach in them…[Here a story is told of a certain *hasid* in whom was found only a single matter of reproach, that he reared a small goat in Palestine, which is forbidden.][56] And it is an established fact with us that wherever we deal with *a certain hasid*, it refers to either R.Judah b.Baba or R.Judah b.Ila'i.[57] Now [these] rabbis lived many generations after Yosef b.Yo'ezer. R.Joseph said, "[It is the] reproach of the laying on of hands [controversy]." But does not Yosef b.Yo'ezer himself differ with reference to the law of laying on of hands? When he differed it was in his later years, when his heart had weakened.[58]
>
> BT *Temurah* 15b-16a

The death of Yosi b.Yo'ezer is nothing short of a turning point in history. These are not mere compliments. He is part of the first pair. Learning would never be the

---

[55] Neusner *The Rabbinic Traditions about the Pharisees* 251.
[56] One wonders whether the small goat that the *hasid* reared does not symbolize Alcimus.
[57] The question is why the story of this *hasid* appears here. It is possible that Yosi as *hasid* and these other stories of *hasidim* are brought in connection with each other.
[58] What if the apparently weak harmonization of "his heart had weakened" is not just the usual reconciliation of contradiction but also a reflection of his weakened state when he was older?

same after him. He is also the last grape cluster. Yosi ben Yoʿezer and Yosi ben Yoḥanan were called "grape clusters" because of their profound erudition and piety:

> When Yose b.Yoʿezer of Ṣeredah and Yose b.Yoḥanan of Jerusalem died, the grape clusters ceased, as it is written, There is not a cluster to eat, my soul desireth the first-ripe fig (Micah 7:1).
> *Mishnah Soṭah 9:9*

In discussing the work of the Ushan school,[59] Neusner reviews Gary G. Porton's work on the "grape clusters." Porton has shown that Bar Kokhba was the first to use the grape cluster on his coins. Using the same symbol to make an important point, the rabbis characterized the Pharisaic masters as the "grape clusters," in order to say, "Blessing will be found through sages, not messiahs." The idea is that there have been disputes and controversies since the days of the end of the "grape clusters." Everyone between the time of the last "grape clusters" and the time of Usha, even the great sages such as Hillel, has been unworthy of the holy spirit.

This periodization of history leads one to the understanding that from the time of Moses to the time of Yosi b.Yoʿezer, "grape clusters," men who bore the special grace of God, brought blessing to Israel. The Yosi's were the last of these special men; when they died, the blessing was lost to Israel. Now, however, Judah b.Baba, who ordained the remaining students of ʿAqiba, has restored the blessing of the grape cluster. Usha can bring blessing into the future; in a sense, the blessings of the past have been restored, and one can now feel the continuum once again from Moses to the Yosi's to Usha.

We now return to the attempt to understand Yosi b.Yoʿezer. Yosi was, first of all, not only a priest, but because of his carefulness in the laws of purity and impurity, he was called "the pious one in the priesthood."

> Yosef b.Yoʿezer was the [most] pious man in the priesthood, yet for them that ate of hallowed things, his apron counted as suffering madras-uncleanness.
> *M. Hagigah 2:7*

When did Yosi b.Yoʿezer live? While the lists of Pharisaic tradition would certainly put him early, that is, in the first part of the 2nd century BCE, there are

---

[59] Neusner *The Rabbinic Traditions about the Pharisees before 70* 282-86.

rabbinic traditions that would seem to put him much later in time. We need to place Yosi b.Yo'ezer in a historical period in order to test the possible historical validity of an Alcimus - Yosi b.Yo'ezer connection/confrontation.

Yosi b.Yo'ezer of Ṣeredah and Yosi b.Yoḥanan of Jerusalem decreed uncleanness on the land of the people and glassware.

> But the rabbis of the "eighty years" [before the destruction of the Temple] did so, for R.Kahana said, "When R.Ishmael son of R.Yosi fell ill, they sent to him, 'Rabbi, tell us two or three things you stated in your father's name." "He replied, "Thus did my father say, One hundred and eighty years before the destruction of the Temple the wicked kingdom spread over Israel. " Eighty years before the destruction of the Temple uncleanness was imposed on the land of the peoples and the glassware. "Forty years before the destruction of the Temple the Sanhedrin went into exile and took its seat in the trade halls..." And should you say, They [Yosi b.Yo'ezer and Yosi b.Yoḥanan] flourished during these eighty years also, it was taught: Hillel and Simeon Gamliel and Simeon ruled as patriarchs during the [last] century of the Temple's existence. Thus Yosi b.Yo'ezer of Ṣeredah and Yosi b.Yoḥanan were much earlier.
>
> BT*Shabbat* 15a

At first, it seems as if we must place Yosi b.Yo'ezer in a later period; this passage, however, takes care of its own difficulty and restores Yosi to an earlier chronological period.

Another problematic text is found in BT*Bava Bathra* 133b, where Yosi ben Yo'ezer seems to give all of his property to the sanctuary and leaves nothing for his son because of his unworthy behavior:

> The question was raised: Do rabbis [behind the Mishnah-ruling] actually disagree with Rabbi Simeon b.Gamliel or do they not?[60] Come and take note: Joseph b.Yo'ezer had a son who did not behave properly[61]. He had an attic full of *denarii*,

---

[60] Do the rabbis agree that it is right to disinherit one's wicked children or not? The Mishnah (8:5) states:
   He who writes over his property to others and left out his sons, What he has done is done. But sages are not pleased with him. Rabban Simeon b.Gamliel says, "If his sons were not behaving properly, his memory is for a blessing."

[61] Neusner's translation here has a typographical error; his text says "property."

which he consecrated to the Temple. [The son] left home and married the daughter of the wreath-maker of King Yannai. His wife gave birth to a son. He bought a fish for her. When he opened it up, he found a pearl in it. She said to him, "Don't show it to the king, they'll take it from you in exchange for a trifling sum. Rather, take it to the Temple treasurers, but don't suggest a price, since if you make an offer of a price to the Most High, it is as binding as actually delivering the goods in a secular transaction. So let them set the price." They valued it at thirteen lofts[62] of *denarii*. They said to them, "Seven of them are in hand, and the remaining six are not in hand." He said to them, "The seven hand over to me, and as to the six, lo, they are sanctified for Heaven." They went and wrote, "Joseph b.Yoʿezer brought in one, but his son brought in six." There are those who say, "Joseph b.Yoʿezer brought in one, but his son took away seven." Now, since the story says, "he brought in," it is to be inferred that [the father] had acted properly. To the contrary, since the story says, "he took out." it is to be inferred that the son did not act rightly! Thus, on the basis of the facts that are in hand, it is not possible to draw a reliable conclusion. So what is the upshot of the matter? Come and take note of what Samuel said to R.Judah, "Sharp-wit! Don't get involved in transfers of inheritances, even from a bad son to a good son, all the more so from a son to a daughter."[63]

The *Mishnah* contains a statement by R.Simeon ben Gamliel that if children do not conduct themselves in a proper manner, they do not deserve to inherit the estate from their righteous parents. To defend this controversial position, the story is told of Yoseph ben Yoʿezer who had a son who did not conduct himself righteously. First, he married the daughter of the wreath-maker of a wicked king. The wickedness of the king is further demonstrated by the son's wife's statement that the king will cheat her husband on the price of the pearl. The wife herself is clever to a fault; she insists that her husband not offer a price lest he not get all that he might out of the deal. The Temple, however, will be fair in its pricing. The very fair price that is set is thirteen lofts of *denarii*; the immediate problem is that this is such a huge amount of money that even the Temple treasury cannot pay Yoseph's son the set amount. Yoseph's son very piously and generously decides that he will take the seven lofts available and consecrate the other six lofts to the Temple. The officials

---

[62] A preferable translation would be "lifts", as in the amount a man can lift.
[63] Translation is by Jacob Neusner *The Talmud of Babylonia: An Academic Commentary XXII Bavli Tractate Baba Batra B. Chapters VII through XI* (University of South Florida, 1996) 392.

of the Temple are obviously approving of this great and charitable act. They say that Yosef b.Yoʿezer brought in one loft of *denarii* and his son brought in six lofts. This apparently means that while Yoseph was a charitable man, his son is even more charitable. In an effort to criticize the son, others say that while his father gave all that he had to the Temple, his son was quite willing to take a fortune away with him. As it stands now, it is not clear what this story means, and the *Gemara* quite explicitly struggles with it. If the point is that one does not have to give money to a wayward son, why does the son wind up with such a fortune? And why does such a terrible son accept a little more than half of the value of the pearl, giving the rest to the Temple?

Neusner says that the tradition about Yosi disinheriting his son is represented by sentences found at the beginning and the end of the passage: 1. *Yosef b. Yo ʿezer had a son who did not behave properly*; 2. "Yosef b.Yoʿezer brought in one, and his son took out seven." The story in between these sentences should illustrate how the son behaved badly by taking in contrast to his father who gave. Instead, the story illustrates how well the son behaved; he gave more than his father did. Neusner concludes that later rabbis did not understand which sentences (B and F) encapsulated his story.

Our understanding of the story is very different from Neusner's. In our view, the rabbis did indeed disagree with Rabbi Simeon b.Gamliel. They thought that one should not disinherit one's wicked children. Yosi's son behaved badly by marrying the wreath-maker of an evil king. God puts a pearl in the fish so that the son could be tested. He not only passes the test; he surpasses his father in charity and devotion to the Temple. Do not disinherit your son, even if he behaves badly; he may change his ways. This is a story of repentance, like the story of Jakum in the *Genesis Rabba* tradition. In fact, it may be a parallel story to the one about Alcimus' repentance. Interestingly, and perhaps not coincidentally, Neusner states that these two stories are the only two examples of biography in the Yosi traditions.[64]

There is another issue involved in this story. Is Yosef ben Yoʿezer here the same as the Yosi ben Yoʿezer about whom we are studying? The problem is the reference to King Yannai, Alexander Jannaeus, which would put him in a later period. It is

---

[64] Is any way to connect this story of Yosi b.Yoʿezer to his nephew, or perhaps his stepson, Alcimus. What did the son do wrong? Was he a Hellenist? Was he a "collaborator" like his cousin Alcimus?

possible that we should not take the end of the *Genesis Rabba* story seriously at all and that Yosi should be dated later. Alexander Jannaeus (103-76 BCE) was the son of John Hyrcanus I, husband of Alexandra Salome;[65] and father of Hyrcanus II and Aristobulus II during whose struggles the Romans under Pompey would gain entry and conquest. Yannai was declared king of Judaea by the widow of Aristobulus but against the wishes of the Jewish religious community. In spite of his success in ruling and defending the country,[66] the Pharisees did not accept him. The reason may have been that Alexander Jannaeus could be called a progressive, embracing the Hellenization moving through the Near East. Toward the end of his career, Yannai became cruel, executing many Jews in retribution for offenses, real and imaginary. Josephus writes about Alexander Jannaeus and states that he turned against the Pharisees and had hundreds crucified. One wonders whether the report that Yosi b. Yoʿezer was crucified somehow became intertwined with the reports of these crucifixions by Alexander Jannaeus, and that Yosi b. Yoʿezer was thus placed in this, the incorrect time period:

> Now as Alexander fled to the mountains, six thousand of the Jews hereupon came together [from Demetrius] to him out of pity at the change of his fortune; upon which Demetrius was afraid, and retired out of the country; after which the Jews fought against Alexander, and being beaten, were slain in great numbers in the several battles which they had; and when he had shut up the most powerful of them in the city Bethome, he besieged them therein; and when he had taken the city, and gotten the men into his power, he brought them to Jerusalem, and did one of the most barbarous actions in the world to them; for as he was feasting with his concubines, in the sight of all the city, he ordered about eight hundred of them to be crucified; and while they were living, he ordered the throats of their children and wives to be cut before their eyes. This was indeed by way of revenge for the injuries they had done him; which punishment yet was of an inhuman nature, though we suppose that he had been never so much distressed, as indeed he had been, by his wars with them, for he had by their means come to the last degree of hazard, both of his life and of his kingdom, while they were not satisfied by themselves only to fight against him, but introduced foreigners also for the same purpose; nay, at length they reduced him

---

[65] It is possible that Yannai married the widow of Aristobulus, Alexandra.
[66] He spent his career defending his nation against invaders and expanding the nation of Judaea. The Nabatean king, Obedas I, stopped Alexander Jannaeus' move to the east.

to that degree of necessity, that he was forced to deliver back to the king of Arabia the land of Moab and Gilead, which he had subdued, and the places that were in them, that they might not join with them in the war against him, as they had done ten thousand other things that tended to affront and reproach him. However, this barbarity seems to have been without any necessity, on which account he bare the name of a Thracian among the Jews whereupon the soldiers that had fought against him, being about eight thousand in number, ran away by night, and continued fugitives all the time that Alexander lived; who being now freed from any further disturbance from them, reigned the rest of his time in the utmost tranquility.

(*Ant.*13:14)

A better response is that the rabbis simply have their chronology wrong, as they do in connecting Joshua b.Peraḥiah with Jesus.[67] Goldstein suggests that it is also possible that we need to read the *Genesis Rabba* story differently and say that Yose ben Yoʿezer was not killed at that point, and that part of the point of the Jakum story is that the mocker died and not the hero. The text, however, states:

Yosi b.Yoʿezer of Ṣeredah dozed and saw his bier flying through the air. He said, "By a brief hour has he preceded me to the Garden of Eden."

That is, Yosi knew that he was about to die and said so as he was about to expire. The *Midrash Tehillim* version is even clearer in this respect, saying that Yosi was in "the drowse of death." Indeed, the reason that Yosi could see Jakum's bier flying through the air is because he was in a twilight zone of death. We have to understand what it was about Yosi b.Yoʿezer that made the event of his death such a turning point. History would never be the same after his death. Perhaps the manner of his death contributed to this. The trauma of his brutal death may have led to the kind of additional fame that is accorded a martyr. The story transmitted in *Genesis Rabba/Midrash Tehillim* may be a reflection of the process by which Yosi b.Yoʿezer's fame grew. Could it be, as *Genesis Rabba/Midrash Tehillim* have it,

---

[67] Neusner *The Rabbinic Traditions about the Pharisees* 310. For a peculiar interpretation, see H. J. Zimmels "Jesus and 'Putting up a Brick,'" *JQR* 43 (1952-53) 225-28. Zimmels thinks Jesus worships not a brick but a fish.

that he was crucified by his nephew, the man in whom he and his colleagues and supporters had placed so much hope?

Alcimus, Yosi b.Yoʿezer's nephew, should have been the righteous High Priest, another Simeon the Just. Instead, at least according to his detractors such as the Hasmonaeans, he took a different path. So the rabbis, rather than the high priestly line, became the most important chain of tradition in a Judaism that became Rabbinic.

ARE THERE REFERENCES TO ALCIMUS IN THE QUMRAN SCROLLS?

Of all the issues that have swirled around the publication and interpretation of the Dead Sea Scrolls,[1] perhaps no topic has proved as interesting and controversial

---

[1] Michael Avi-Yonah, and Zvi Baras, eds. *Society and Religion in the Second Temple Period, World History of the Jewish People*: First Series: Ancient Time (Jerusalem: Massada Publishing, 1977); George J. Brooke, "The Pesharim and the Origins of the Dead Sea Scrolls," in *Methods of Investigation of the Dead Sea Scrolls and the Khirbet Qumran Site: Present Realities and Future Prospects,* ed. Michael O. Wise, et al. (Annals of the New York Academy of Sciences vol. 722; New York, New York: New York Academy of Sciences, 1994) 339-53; William H. Brownlee, *The Midrash Pesher of Habakkuk* (Missoula, Montana: Scholars Press, 1979); John J. Collins, "Teacher and Messiah? The One Who Will Teach Righteousness at the End of Days," in *The Community of the Renewed Covenant: The Notre Dame Symposium on the Dead Sea Scrolls*, ed. Eugene Ulrich and James VanderKam (Notre Dame, Ind.: University of Notre Dame Press, 1994); Frank Moore Cross, *The Ancient Library of Qumran* (3rd ed.; Sheffield: Sheffield Academic Press, 1995) esp. ch. 3; P. R. Davies, *The Damascus Covenant* (Sheffield: JSOT, 1983); idem "Communities at Qumran and the Case of the Missing Teacher," *RQ* 15/57-58 (1991); M. Delcor "Ou en est le probleme du Midrash d'Habacuc?" *Revue d'histoire des religions* 142 (1952) 129-46; Devorah Dimant, "Pesharim, Qumran," *ABD* V 244-51; A. Dupont-Sommer *Les écrits esséniens découverts pres de la Mer Morte* (Paris 1959) 361-68; Norman Golb, *Who Wrote the Dead Sea Scrolls?* (New York and London: Scribner, 1995); Maurya P. Horgan, *Pesharim: Qumran Interpretations of Biblical Books* (Washington D.C.: Catholic Biblical Association of America, 1979); G. Jeremias *Der Lehrerder der Gerechtigkeit* Studien zur Umwelt des Neuen Testaments 2, (Gottingen, 1963) 36-78; Timothy Lim, "The Wicked Priests of the Gronigen Hypothesis," *JBL* 112 (1993) 415-25; Florentino Garcia Martinez, "A 'Groningen' Hypothesis of Qumran Origins and Early History, *RQ* 14 (1989-90) 521-41; H.-J. v.d. Minde, "Thanksgiving Hymns," *ABD* 438-41; J. Murphy O'Connor, ""Teacher of Righteousness"," *ABD* VI 340-41; Elisha Qimron, "*Miqsat Maase HaTorah,*" *ABD* IV 843-44; Lawrence Schiffman, "Temple Scroll," *ABD* VI 348-50; E.P. Sanders *Jesus and Judaism* (Philadelphia, Fortress Press. 1985) 5; A. S. van der Woude, "Wicked Priest or Wicked Priests? Reflections on the Identification of the Wicked Priest in the Habakkuk Commentary," *JJS* 33 (1982); idem, "Once Again: The Wicked Priests in the Habakkuk Pesher from Cave 1 of Qumran," *RQ* 17/65-68 (1996) 375-84; Geza Vermes *The Complete Dead Sea Scrolls in English* (London: Penguin,

as that of the identities of the "Teacher of Righteousness" and the "Wicked Priest" who are mentioned in a number of these texts. Some Christian scholars, looking desperately for historical evidence of Jesus or John the Baptist, have attempted to link the "Teacher of Righteousness" to one of those famous figures. The majority view concerning the history of the sect places the conflict between the founder-organizer of the community, the priestly "Teacher of Righteousness," and his chief opponent, the "Wicked Priest," to the middle of the 2nd century BCE.[2] The "Wicked Priest," described as "good" at the beginning of his career, turned "ungodly" on becoming the High Priestly ruler of Israel. At the end he fell into the hands of his enemies who inflicted vengeance on him.

In studying the relationship between legend and history, one may look for historical kernels in the fanciful. Legends should not be read literally, nor should they be dismissed as worthless, for they may be reflections of reality (even if they have been distorted by ideology or falsity). In the case of the "Teacher of Righteousness" and the "Wicked Priest," scholars have a limited number of references in the Qumran texts with which to work, and these references are obscure at best. The very attempt to sift history from legend may be impossible. And yet the attempt is worthwhile because the stakes are so high. Hidden in such texts are the origins of the sect that created an intriguing community. More important, hidden here and in related apocryphal and rabbinic texts are windows into a mysterious period of history from which Rabbinic Judaism and Christianity emerged.

There is no strong scholarly theory about the identification of the "Teacher of Righteousness." We will suggest a candidate as a model for the ideal or the actual person who was the Teacher. As a model, he would have been quite contemporary and relevant. We will review the popular scholarly theories about the identification of the "Wicked Priest" and, without rejecting them, wonder about the possibility of another High Priest who is not usually considered in this role. Even if our identifications are not accepted, as they may not be, we will have made a small

---

1995); idem *Discovery in the Judean Desert* (New York: Desclee, 1956); idem *The Dead Sea Scrolls: Qumran in Perspective* (London: SCM, 1994) esp. ch. 6; Ben Zion Wacholder, *The Dawn of Qumran: the Sectarian Torah and the "Teacher of Righteousness"* (Cincinnati, Ohio: Hebrew Union College Press, 1983).

[2] See, for instance, Shaye J. D. Cohen *From Maccabees to the Mishnah* (Philadelphia, 1987) 161.

Qumran and Seleucid Parallels

contribution to the background or pre-history of the Dead Sea community concerning two of the important figures in their literature and/or history.

The conflict between the Community and the Maccabaeans seems to have originated in priestly circles. The sect is said to have begun "in the age of wrath," probably the Hellenistic crisis in the early 2nd century BCE, among conservative Jews. The Priests faithful to the Mosaic Law became the leaders of the Community, of the "sons of Zadok," the members of the traditional High Priestly family.[3] The leaders of the Community led a withdrawal from the Temple of Jerusalem not because they were against sacrifices but because they disagreed with the conduct of the priests in control of the Temple. The Community leaders expected to resume Temple service at the end of time, when Jerusalem would be under their control.

The main source for reconstructing the history of the Qumran community is the *Damascus Document*; in cryptic and symbolic language, it seems to indicate that the community began in the first half of the 2nd century BCE. The *Damascus Document* refers to a foreign enemy led by a Hellenistic king or leader ('the chief of the kings of Greece'). The exhortation at the beginning of the *Damascus Document* introduces the theology of the Qumran community by explaining that God left the Temple and sent the Babylonians to punish those who had polluted the Sanctuary. God saved a remnant that would eventually return to Israel when the people would learn how to correctly follow the Law. The true sign of God's blessing would be found in the guide He sent: "And God observed their deeds that they sought Him with a whole heart, and He raised for them a "Teacher of Righteousness" to guide them in the way of his heart." The "Teacher" must show the people the path of righteousness to bring about a time when society will be re-ordered and Israel will be long to her rightful descendants. This "Teacher of Righteousness" has a God-given ability to interpret the Law.

> And God observed their deeds, that they sought Him with a whole heart and He raised for them a Teacher of Righteousness to guide them in the way of His heart. And he made known to the latter generations that which God had done to the latter

---

[3] Over the years this Maccabaean historical reconstruction has gained wide acceptance among Scrolls scholars. A minority view identified the Wicked Priest with the Hasmonaean priest-king Alexander Jannaeus (104-76 BCE), but the thesis, propounded by scholars such as Geza Vermes, that the Qumran-Essene sect was deeply antagonistic to the Maccabaean/Hasmonaean movement, has stayed strong.

generation, the congregation of traitors, to those who departed from the way. This was the time of which it is written, *Like a stubborn heifer thus was Israel stubborn* (Hosea 4:16), when the Scoffer arose who shed over Israel the water of lies. He caused them to wander in a pathless wilderness, laying low the everlasting heights, abolishing the ways of righteousness and removing the boundary with which the forefathers had marked out their inheritance, that he might call down on them the curses of His Covenant and deliver them up to the avenging sword of the Covenant.[4]

Other potential sources for the identification of important figures such as the "Teacher of Righteousness" and the "Wicked Priest" are the various Biblical commentaries that describe contemporary events as the fulfillment of ancient prophecies. The Habakkuk and Psalms *pesharim* have a number of key citations for our purpose here. Works of the *pesher genre* apply the words of the Biblical prophets to current history. These scrolls seem to refer to the time of the Seleucid king Antiochus IV *Epiphanes* (175-164 BCE).[5] The "Teacher of Righteousness" is a priest and the interpreter of the Law. The fact that the "Teacher" is the authority on the Law reflects the pivotal role of Law in the community. In the *Thanksgiving Hymns*, the "Teacher of Righteousness" refers to himself as having the waters of the Covenant confirmed in his heart, for God has "hidden Thy Law [within (him)]."[6] The "Teacher of Righteousness" knows the Law because God has given him the knowledge of it. As in Num. 12:6-8, when Moses receives the Law directly from the mouth of God, the "Teacher" receives the law from the mouth of God.[7] The Community respects the Teacher's legal understanding and uses his interpretations for redemption.[8] Since the "Teacher" is the "Interpreter of the Law," the *pesharim* provide additional insight into the "Teacher." That is, these *pesharim* are the "Teacher's" mode of divine revelation through his interpretation of scripture. By

---

[4] Geza Vermes *The Complete Dead Sea Scrolls in English.* (London, 1995) 127-28. This passage is from the beginning of The Damascus Document (cols. 1, 20; cf. cols. 6, 20.1; CDSSE 125-56; DSSNT 49-74; DSST 33-73).
[5] The Nahum Commentary (4Q169), I 1-5.
[6] *1QH* VIII, 8-10; 12. For other examples, see *1QH* VI 10-12: 'to magnify the Law and the truth and to enlighten] the members of Thy council in the midst of the sons of men' or *1QH* VII 18-21: 'For in Thy righteousness Thou hast appointed me for Thy Covenant, and I have clung to Thy truth and [gone forward in Thy ways].
[7] *1Qp Hab* II 2-3.
[8] CD 28-30.

carefully examining how the "Teacher" interprets scripture, one can learn even more about the figure. The "Teacher" is a priest who has the divine power to interpret Scripture.

The passage mentioned above is quite suggestive in thinking about the historical "Teacher:"

> The well is the Law, and those who dug it were converts of Israel who went out of the land of Judah to sojourn in the land of Damascus...The Staff is the Interpreter of the Law of whom Isaiah said, He makes a tool for His work....
>
> CD, VI

The founders left Judaea and went into Damascus for this "well," the "Law." The powerful metaphor of the "well" as the "Law," indicated that this essential water could not be found in Judaea. The "Teacher" helps found a community that leaves Judaea because the Law cannot "exist" there. Ironically, the water is found in the arid desert. But the people by themselves cannot dig this well in Damascus; they are still unable to find the well. Only the "Staff," the "Interpreter of the Law," finds the water. The "Teacher" interprets the "Law" for the community, thus making it "drinkable."

The "Teacher" repeatedly shows concerns over issues of impurity. Notably, the "Teacher" names three types of impurity that profane the land—fornication, riches, and profanation of the Temple. Included among those things that profane the Temple are menstrual blood, incestuous relationships, and a breach of the Mosaic Covenant. The issues in the sectarian community are purity as understood by Mosaic Law. The relationship between the "Teacher of Righteousness" and the "Wicked Priest" is that of Temple sage or prophet, with a large following, exiled by the High Priest because of his unpopular views. This charismatic figure blames the "Wicked Priest" for polluting the Temple through the priest's inappropriate behavior.

It is interesting for our purpose that there is no evidence in any of these texts to support the idea that the "Wicked Priest" was not legitimate. The "Teacher" struggled with the High Priest over purity rules, rather than for a power position or restoration of a "legitimate" High Priest. In *Pesher Habakkuk*,[9] the "Wicked Priest"

---

[9] *1QpHab* 12:1-10

plots the destruction of the poor, commits abominable deeds, and defiles the Temple. Rather than planning an insurrection or attempt to overthrow the High Priest, the "Teacher of Righteousness" condemns the "Wicked Priest" to an eschatological punishment. In this manner, the "Teacher of Righteousness" fits the model of a prophet acting outside of the court. The "Teacher" laments over the Temple because Temple authorities do not follow the purity laws as dictated by God through Moses.

The "Teacher of Righteousness" was revered, endowed with a special wisdom and revelation; he instructed his devoted disciples in the true meaning of the *Torah*.

> Interpreted, this concerns the Priest, the Teacher of [Righteousness whom] God chose to stand before Him, for He established him to build for Himself the congregation of ...[10]

Miqṣat Ma'ase Ha-Torah (*4QMMT*) has been interpreted as a document written by the "Teacher of Righteousness" and addressed to the "Wicked Priest."[11] In examining this text, one finds that *4QMMT* seems to read like a letter to Alcimus.[12] I will show below that Alcimus' "voluntary defilement" is sexual in nature. After reviewing laws against the mating of different animals and the mixing of different materials in clothing, the letter states:

> But the sons of Aaron are the ho[liest of the holy] [and y]ou know that a part of the priests and of the peo[ple] mingle [and they] unite with each other and defile the [holy] seed [and also] their (own) [seed] with fornications ...

The holiest of the holy, the קדוש קדושים (*qdwšy qdwšym*) would seem to refer to the high priest and those who participate with him. Of special interest here is the fact that the Hebrew verb מתערבים (*mt'rbym*) is used to describe the "mingling" of the priests. The letter goes on to emphasize the holiness of Jerusalem and the

---

[10] Commentary on Psalms *4Q171* III:15-17, referring to Ps.37:23-4.
[11] For very useful articles and full bibliography, see *Reading 4QMMT: New Perspectives on Qumran Law and History* eds. John Kampen and Moshe J. Bernstein (Atlanta, 1996).
[12] In what follows, I am indebted to Dr. Leslie Wilson for her keen eye and insights.

Qumran and Seleucid Parallels

Temple that has been polluted by sexual sins זונות (*zwnwt*).[13] Qimron shows that these terms seem to refer to "mingling' between priests and the laity.[14] The writers of the letter are in a position to criticize because they have separated themselves from such sins:

> [And you know that] we have segregated ourselves from the rest of the peop[le...] [and] from mingling in these affairs, and from associating wi[th them] in these things. ... we [have written that you (sing.) must understand the bo]ok of Moses ...

But all is not lost, the writers say, because there can be forgiveness:

> Remember David, one of the 'pious' [and] he, too, was freed from many afflictions and was forgiven.

David was guilty of sexual sins in his adultery with Bathsheba but God forgave him for his actions.[15] So too Alcimus will be forgiven for his sexual misconduct. Alcimus is worthy of redemption, and of the writers' efforts to change him because he is a pious follower of the Law:

> And also we have written to you (sing.) some of the works of the Torah which we think are good for you and for your people, for we s[a]w that you have intellect and knowledge of the Law. Reflect on all these matters and seek from him that he may support your counsel and keep far from you the evil scheming [s] and the counsel of Belial, so that at the end of time, you may rejoice in finding that some of our words are true. And it shall be reckoned to you as justice when you do what is upright and good before him, for your good and that of Israel.[16]

---

[13] For this term in MMT, see especially John Kampen "4QMMT and New Testament Studies" in *Reading 4QMMT* 135-36.

[14] Elisha Qimron and John Strugnell *Qumran Cave 4: Miqsat Ma'aśe Ha-Torah* Discoveries in the Judaean Desert X (Oxford: Clarendon, 1994) 55, 171-75.

[15] It is a problem in Biblical interpretation that David is not punished more severely for the death of Uriah, Bathseba's husband; that problem is not dealt with in this text which is concerned with sexual sins.

[16] = "Some Observances of the Law" (4Q394-9). I use the text and translation

This letter certainly seems to be written to the religious and political leader of the people. The writers seem to implore Alcimus to listen to Yosi b.Yoʿezer. This explanation demonstrates a relationship between these two important figures that began with mutual respect but may have foundered over issues of impurity that profaned the Temple such as menstrual blood and incestuous relationships. See in this regard the passage in the *Damascus Document* (not coincidentally immediately following the reference cited above to "the builders of the wall") where the Temple is profaned by its leader(s) for some sexually related sin.[17] The "Teacher of Righteousness" blames the pollution of the Temple on the priest's inappropriate behavior.

Let us review what we know about the "Teacher of Righteousness":

- He is a priest;
- He teaches purity rules;
- He interprets the law;
- He instructs his followers in the meaning of the *Torah*;
- He is a major leader of his community; and
- He is persecuted by the "Wicked Priest."

Yosi b.Yoʿezer satisfies all of these criteria. He is a priest who teaches purity rules. He is a teacher, a major interpreter of the law, an instructor in the meaning of the *Torah* and a major leader of his community. As we have seen, he brought new dimensions to the interpretation and promulgation of the Law. We have surveyed the fascinating rabbinic material about Yosi ben Yoʿezer, one of the earliest sages. Following Neusner's form-critical reading of *ʾAvot* 1, it is clear that the original form of that famous chapter stated that Yosi b.Yoʿezer and Yosi ben Yoḥanan were the first of the *zugot*, Pairs of Sages. Perhaps the first *halakhic* dispute, that concerning *sᵉmikhah*, the laying of hands on sacrifices during festivals, was between Yosi ben Yoʿezer and Yosi ben Yoḥanan. The dispute went on for many generations. Yosi came from a respected family of priests, and because of his care in the laws of purity was called "the most pious one in the priesthood" (*Mishnah Hagigah* 2:7). Yosi ben Yoʿezer and Yosi ben Yoḥanan were called "grape clusters" because of their profound erudition and piety. The extensive praise of Yosi

---

[17] *CD* V.

b.Yoʿezer does not constitute a set of quaint compliments. Yosi b.Yoʿezer was a priest and sage. He was the true heir of the chain of tradition. His greatness is established by many rabbinic texts. He is part of the first pair. He is the last "grape cluster." After him, learning would never be the same. He is the man in whom are all things.

The "Teacher of Righteousness" is persecuted by the "Wicked Priest" about whom the *Pesher Habakkuk* speaks:

> Interpreted, this concerns] those who were unfaithful together with the Liar, in that they [did] not [listen to the word received by] the "Teacher of Righteousness" from the mouth of God. And it concerns the unfaithful of the New [Covenant] in that they have not believed in the Covenant of God [and have profaned] His holy Name."
> *1QpHab* II:1-4

If Yosi b.Yoʿezer is the "Teacher of Righteousness," could Alcimus be the "Wicked Priest?"

> Its interpretation concerns the "Wicked Priest" who was called by the name of truth when he first arose. But when he ruled in Israel his heart became proud, and he forsook God and betrayed the precepts for the sake of riches. He robbed and amassed the riches of the men of sin who rebelled against God, and he took the wealth of the peoples, heaping sinful iniquity upon himself. And he performed abominable practices in all sorts of unclean defilement.
> *1QpHab* VIII 8-13

Alcimus was called "in the name of truth," using the words of nothing less than scriptural truth. To invoke the kinds of invective about "lies" that are cast against the "Wicked Priest," the truth that he falsified must have been a great one. One wonders if the priest's defilement matches Alcimus' "voluntary defilement" in 1Maccabees. A similar text can be found in the Psalms *Pesher*:

> Interpreted concerns the Liar who has led astray many by his lying words so that they chose frivolous things and heeded not the interpreter of knowledge...
> *Commentary on Psalms* 4Q171 1:26 - 2:1

Pesher Habakkuk relates that the "Wicked Priest" became arrogant in his power. It accuses him of corruption and oppression of the poor, and violating God's Law. He profaned the holy city of Jerusalem and its Temple with terrible abominations. He caused suffering to the "Teacher" and his followers. The "Wicked Priest's" most heinous crime was his persecution of the "Teacher of Righteousness."

> Interpreted, this concerns the Wicked [Priest] who [watched the "Teacher of Righteousness"] that he might put him to death [because of the ordinance] and the law which he sent to him.
> *Commentary on Psalms* IQ171 IV:8-9

One wonders if some trumped-up charges were not leveled against the *Asidaioi* before they were executed. If the "Teacher" and his followers were persecuted and killed, as were Yosi b.Yoʿezer and the *Asidaioi*, there may have been those who stood and watched:

> O traitors, why do you stare and stay silent when the wicked swallows up one more righteous than he? (1:13b). Interpreted, this concerns the House of Absalom and the members of its council who were silent at the time of the chastisement of the "Teacher of Righteousness", and gave him no help against the Liar who flouted the Law in the midst of their whole [congregation].
> *IQpHab* 5:9-12

The "house of Absalom" may refer to a familial connection, a connection that would be explained by a set of relatives such as Yosi b.Yoʿezer and his nephew Alcimus. Alcimus is the nephew of Yosi b.Yoʿezer. Again, one cannot imagine a reason for Alcimus' enemies to make up the relationship between their sage and hero Yosi b.Yoʿezer and a priest that they despised. From the point-of-view of the later rabbis, the *Asidaioi* or the Maccabees, the shame that Alcimus brought to his people and his family cannot be overestimated. That is, just as Absalom repaid his father King David's mercy and patronage by chasing him out of Jerusalem and usurping his role, so Alcimus' rejection of his uncle would be seen as the worst kind of betrayal.

While there is nothing to indicate that Yosi b.Yoʿezer left Jerusalem at some point, there is also nothing to preclude the possibility. He might have founded a community outside of Jerusalem and then come back (or have been brought back).

Qumran and Seleucid Parallels

We will explain why all of this is so important in this context. Alcimus, Aaronide priest, Yosi b.Yoʿezer's nephew, psalm-writer, should have been a righteous High Priest, another Simeon the Just. Instead, at least according to his detractors such as the Hasmonaeans (represented by the pro-Hasmonaean 1Maccabees), and perhaps the Qumran community, he took a very different and unfortunate path.

What if, as *Genesis Rabba* and *Midrash Tehillim* have it, Yosi b.Yoʿezer was crucified by or with the full collaboration of his nephew, the man on whom he and his colleagues and supporters had placed so much hope? If the death of Yosi b.Yoʿezer is nothing short of a turning point in history, perhaps the manner of Yosi b.Yoʿezer's death made it such a decisive juncture. The trauma of his brutal death may have led to the kind of additional fame that is accorded a martyr.

Alcimus would make an interesting candidate to be the "Wicked Priest" and the "Man of Lies." If he wrote psalms, if he railed poetically at the heathens and their gods and then collaborated with those enemies to the detriment of his people and his religion, then his opponents, the Hasmonaeans and the community at Qumran, as represented by references in the Dead Sea Scrolls, would have ample reason to denounce him.

The death of the "Wicked Priest" may fit well with the death of Alcimus. The "Wicked Priest" rebelled (*marad*) and was punished by means of "judgments of wickedness."

> Interpreted, this concerns the Priest who rebelled and violated the precepts of God…
> to command his chastisements by means of the judgments of wickedness. And they
> inflicted horrors of evil diseases and took vengeance upon his body of flesh.
> *1QpHab.* VIII.16 – IX.2

We remember that 1Maccabees[18] and Josephus[19] say that Alcimus suffered a stroke from God and died after many days of torment. Alcimus, according to the rabbinic notices, died by suicide and not at the hands of the Greeks. According to 1Maccabees and Josephus, he came to a terrible end, stricken with a painful and debilitating paralysis. The suicide contradicts the paralysis. And yet, both stories of

---

[18] 1Macc.9:54ff.
[19] *Ant.* XII.413.

his death are clearly tendentious. In the rabbinic story, he commits suicide in repentance for what he did to Yosi b.Yoʿezer. In the 1Maccabees/ Josephus story, we have a parallel to the death of Heliodorus (1Maccabees 2) who also died in attempting to commit sacrilege to the Temple. Perhaps the third version of his death in the Qumran scrolls, by the hands of his so-called foreign friends, is also tendentious. Alcimus was not killed as such by the Seleucids as this text would insist. In short, there is no reason to accept any of the three versions of the death of Alcimus. If the Qumran text does not concern Alcimus, there is still no reason to accept either a sudden stroke from sacrilege or a suicide in repentance.

We have proposed that Alcimus might be the "Wicked Priest" and that Yosi ben Yoʿezer might fit the role of the "Teacher of Righteousness." The virtue of this theory is that we have two historical figures who were in opposition to each other. One was the High Priest and the other the leader of his community and a priest and lawgiver. Perhaps Alcimus, in trying to assert his power as High Priest, was undermined by the very man who had given him legitimacy, his uncle, Yosi b.Yoʿezer.

If, as Vermes has suggested, the "Teacher of Righteousness" was a Zadokite, and Yosi ben Yoʿezer, like his nephew Alcimus, was a Zadokite, we may have another indication that Yosi b.Yoʿezer was the "Teacher." Vermes compares versions of the *Community Rule* to show that there was a Zadokite takeover of the sect with the arrival of the "Teacher of Righteousness." Vermes states: "The crisis in the Zadokite ranks in the 160's BCE, following the flight of Onias IV to Egypt, provides the likeliest background for these events."[20] In the *Community Rule*, in its later version, we find this clear statement:

> They shall separate from the congregation of the men of injustice and shall unite, with respect to the Law and possessions, under the authority of the sons of Zadok, the Priests who keep the Covenant, and of the multitude of the men of the Community who hold fast to the Covenant Every decision concerning doctrine, property, and justice shall be determined by them.
>
> *IQS* V:2-4

---

[20] Geza Vermes "The Leadership of the Qumran Community" in *Geschichte-Tradition-Reflexion* [Martin Hengel Festschrift] I (Tubingen, 1996) 375-84.

Qumran and Seleucid Parallels

This notice disrupts any historical reconstruction that makes Yosi b.Yoʿezer the "Teacher of Righteousness." We cannot push the evidence too far. Our conclusion is while Alcimus is a good fit for "Wicked Priest," Yosi may have died too soon to fit the "Teacher of Righteousness" chronology. It is possible, however, that the "Teacher of Righteousness" was a colleague, perhaps even Yosi b.Yohanan, or a disciple.

The virtue of our theory is that at least we have some people to talk about. If they were such great and famous leaders, if the disputes were so major, why is there nothing recorded about these people? We have historical figures with known records.

The "Teacher" does not have to be the Community's Founder at Qumran. He could be the spiritual founder of the community that realized, after his death, that it had to get out of Jerusalem.

Scholars have suggested several candidates for the identification of the "Wicked Priest." These are Menelaus,[21] Jonathan;[22] Simon,[23] Alexander Jannaeus[24] and Hyrcanus II.[25]

Since there are allusions that point to at least several of these candidates, some scholars have concluded that the "Teacher of Righteousness" and the "Wicked Priest" are terms that do not just refer to single individuals but to offices/titles.[26] The "Teacher of Righteousness" is both the founder of the community and the teacher who will come in the final age. In several of the citations from the *PesherHabakkuk*, we saw the following: "Its interpretation concerns the "Wicked Priest" who ..." Van der Woude thinks that this means that the interpretation concerns one "Wicked Priest" in distinction from the others.

The "Wicked Priest" referred to in *1QpHab* VIII 8-13 (cited above) was a priest who was acceptable, based on his earlier life, to the community at Qumran. Van der Woude insists that the earlier part of this "Wicked Priest's" life "must have

---

[21] A. Michel *Le maitre de justice* (Avignon, 1954) 232-58.
[22] Geza Vermes *The Dead Sea Scrolls. Qumran in Perspective* 151; G. Jeremias *Der Lehrerder der Gerechtigkeit* 36-78.
[23] Frank Moore Cross *The Ancient Library of Qumran* 127-60.
[24] M. Delcor "Où en est le probleme du Midrash d'Habacuc?" 129-46.
[25] A. Dupont-Sommer *Les écrits esséniens découverts pres de la Mer Morte* 361-68;
[26] W. H. Brownlee "The Historical Allusions of the Dead Sea Habakkuk Midrash" *BASOR* 126 (1952) 10-20.

antedated the rift between the Hasmonaean dynasty and the Qumran community. Indeed in that case we are forced back to the time of the Hasidim from which the Essenes traced their origin."[27] Van der Woude thinks that Judas Maccabaeus may be the "Wicked Priest," asserting that, as Josephus and some rabbinic traditions have it, Judas was a High Priest. The information about the death of the "Wicked Priest" in *1QpHab*[28] fits the death of Alcimus, as we have indicated above. The allusion to the "Last Priests of Jerusalem" in the same passage[29] refers to the Hasmonaean High Priests and separates them from the "philhellenistic High Priests" such as Alcimus. Another passage in *1QpHab* refers to the death of Jonathan:

> *Because of the blood of men and the violence done to the land, to the city, and to all its inhabitants* (2:8b). Interpreted, this concerns the "Wicked Priest" whom God delivered into the hands of his enemies because of the iniquity committed the "Teacher of Righteousness" and the men of his Council, that he might be humbled by means of a destroying scourge, in bitterness of soul, because he had done wickedly to His elect.
>
> 1QpHab 9:9-12

This "Wicked Priest" is delivered into the hands of enemies. Jonathan is the only High Priest that fits the bill; he was betrayed and murdered by the Seleucid general Trypho.[30]

---

[27] Van der Woude "Wicked Priest or Wicked Priests?" 353.
[28] *1QpHab* VIII, 16-IX, 2.
[29] *1QpHab* IX, 3-7.
[30] Jonathan Maccabaeus, the brother of Judas Maccabee and Hasmonaean ruler, served as high priest from 152 to 145 BCE before being captured and killed by a Syrian general, Tryphon. The Hasmonaeans did not reinstate the Zadokites: Jonathan Maccabee claimed the High Priestly office for himself. It remains possible that the Qumran community was founded largely by those disappointed by the turn of events. Josephus first mentions the Essenes in his description of the reign of Jonathan Maccabaeus implying that they were founded then. Jonathan remained in conflict with the Seleucids throughout his reign and would have been given the benefit of the doubt while he was engaged in throwing off the foreigner. At first, was a champion of traditional Judaism against pagan reforms and Seleucid oppression. After he attained leadership, however, he provoked criticism from many circles and was condemned for appointing himself High Priest, an office that had previously been the exclusive birthright of the ancient dynasty of the Zadokites. *Pesher*

Qumran and Seleucid Parallels

The next passage of the *Pesher Habakkuk*[31] refers to Simon, the "master builder" of the Hasmonaeans. *1QpHab* then describes how the "Wicked Priest," probably John Hyrcanus (135-105 BCE), pursues the "Teacher of Righteousness" to his place of exile and then attempts to disrupt his Day of Atonement.

> Woe to him who causes his neighbours to drink; who pours out his venom to make them drunk that he may gaze on their feasts (ii, 15). Interpreted, this concerns the "Wicked Priest" who pursued the "Teacher of Righteousness" to the house of his exile that he might confuse him with his venomous fury. And at the time appointed for rest, for the Day of Atonement, he appeared before them to confuse them, and to cause them to stumble on the Day of Fasting, their Sabbath of repose.
> *1QpHab* XI 4-8

The *Damascus Document* gives a chronological marker:

> And from the day of the gathering in of the unique teacher, until the destruction of all men who turned back with the man of lies, there shall be about forty years.

One can only speculate how this marker should be used. Van der Woude puts the age of the "Teacher of Righteousness" at 40 in 150 BCE and 70 in 120 BCE. If he died at that point, the end was to come in 80 BCE, during the time of Alexander Jannaeus (103-76 BCE). The imperfect tense used in the last columns of the *Pesher Habakkuk* may indicate it is written during that period. Alexander Jannaeus is still in power but his end is predicted:

> Interpreted, this concerns the Priest whose ignominy was greater than his glory. For he did not circumcise the foreskin of his heart, and he walked in the ways of

---

Habakkuk's description of the "Wicked Priest's" fall and death would seem to fit with the end of Jonathan's life, in which he was imprisoned by the Syrian general Trypho who kept him in a dungeon until his execution. For the author of *Pesher Habakkuk*, this end might have seemed to be a just one. A problem to the theory that Jonathan Maccabaeus is the Wicked Priest is that we do not know of any dispute that might have arisen between Jonathan and the "Teacher of Righteousness". Who, in this case, would the "Teacher of Righteousness" be?

[31] IX, 16ff.

drunkenness that he might quench his thirst. But the cup of the wrath of God shall confuse him, multiplying his ... and the pain of ...

1QpHab XI 11-15

Thus we have made a case that Alcimus may have been a "Wicked Priest," perhaps the original one, and that Yosi b.Yoʿezer may have been the original "Teacher of Righteousness."

Are There Any Ptolemaic or Seleucid Parallels?

Obviously, the events involving Alcimus and the Seleucids happened within the larger context of the Seleucid and Ptolemaic rule over lands with continuing native cults. It is imperative that we learn what we can from the relationship of the rulers with the leaders of those cults. [32] Was there a difference between the ways that the Ptolemies in Egypt and the Seleucids over their lands acted in these relationships? Was the sequence of events of the Oniads/Alcimus *intersacerdotium* unique? Did Seleucid and/or Ptolemaic rulers of occupied countries respect the hereditary nature of their High Priesthoods?

One of our questions involves the succession of Alcimus. How unusual was it that a priest other than the hereditary heir became a High Priest? The evidence of the dynasty of the High Priests of Ptah at Memphis during the Ptolemaic period is quite clear in this regard: Hereditary succession was the rule. Esisout, also known as Anemhor, was the first recorded High Priest of this period and seems to have been the founder of a dynasty that lasted for ten generations and thirteen High Priests in hereditary succession of a closed family group.[33] We do not know about his family in earlier generations or who held the office in the period preceding him. We do

---

[32] Dorothy J. Thompson "The High Priests of Memphis under Ptolemaic Rule" in Mary Beard and John North, eds. *Pagan Priests: Religion and Power in the Ancient World* (Ithaca, 1990) 97-116; S.R.K. Glanville in E.R. Bevan *A History of Egypt under the Ptolemaic Dynasty* (London, 1927); D.J. Crawford *Kerkeosiris; an Egyptian village in the Ptolemaic period* (Cambridge, 1971) 134-5; J. Quagebeur "The genealogy of the Memphite high priest family in the Hellenistic period" *Studia Hellenistica* 24, 43-82; E.A.E. Redmond *From the Records of a Priestly Family from Memphis* 1 (Wiesbaden, 1981).

[33] J. Quagebeur "The genealogy of the Memphite high priest family in the Hellenistic period" 43-82.

know that Esisout/Anemhor's wife was Rempnophris. The succession was to his son EsisoutII/PetobastisI and then to his son AnemhorII, who married Heranch, herself a priestess/musician. In the fourth generation, the office moved from AnemhorI's Teos (who predeceased his father, showing that AnemphorII must have retired early) to his brother Harmachis (reminding us of the passing of the High Priesthood of Judaea from Onias III to his brother Jason). It was Harmachis' son EsisoutIII/PsenptaisI who held the office in the fifth generation, passing it on to his son PetobastisII, his son PsentpaisII, his son PetobastisIII, and his son PsenptaisIII. In that generation, the ninth, the office devolved not to PsentpaisIII's very young son Imouthes/PetobastisIV but to the half-brother (and brother-in-law) of PsentpaisIII's wife Taimouthes, PsenamounisI (whose sister Tenepheros, herself a priestess, was married to PsenamounisI). When PsenamounisI died after only two years in office (he may have simply been an elderly place-holder), the office returned to Imouthes/PetobastisIV. His first cousin PsenamounisII, the son of PsenamounisI and Tenepheros, succeeded him. While we saw a case of early retirement in the case of AnemhorII, the rule was that the High Priests died in office and that their sons succeeded them.

What if the legitimate heir were very young when his father died? The evidence we have points to the succession of the heir even if very young. PsenptaisIII was fourteen in 76 BCE when he became High Priest, and his son Imouthes/PetobastisIV was only seven years and ten days old when he became High Priest on July 23, 39 BCE. Thompson concludes, "It would indeed seem likely that hereditary appointment to the office was more important than the capacities of the individual who filled the post."[34]

This makes it even stranger that Onias IV did not become the High Priest after Menelaus' removal and execution. The goal would have been to restore the legitimacy of the High Priesthood. Could it be that the pro-Ptolemaic leanings of Onias III made Onias IV suspect in Seleucid eyes? It is interesting to note that it was not Antiochus IV himself who was the real heir to the throne; it was his nephew, the son of Seleucus. So it may be relevant to note that Antiochus IV, through the violent (and unfortunate) Andronicus, kills the legitimate heir to the throne, the legitimate High Priest Onias III, and that the latter's legitimate heir went unrecognized.

---

[34] Thompson "The High Priests of Memphis" 101.

Did any of these High Priests have double names in their own language as well as Greek? We have already seen that some of the High Priests of Ptah at Memphis during this period, four out of thirteen, did indeed have double names: Esisout/Anemhor, Esisout/Petobastis, Esisout/Psenptais, and Imouthes/Petobastis.[35] This is to be expected in a society where double names, with one Greek name and one native name, seem "to represent a stage in the process of Hellenization for Egyptian members of society."[36] When an Egyptian priest of this period adopted a Greek name, it indicated that he was willing to "compromise."[37] What is striking, however, is that the double names of the High Priests are both Egyptian and never Greek! In the later generations of the family of High Priests at Letopolis (apparently following the lead of the Memphite High Priests), both names were Egyptian. This does not seem to be a "compromise" or an indication of Hellenization but an imitation of royal usage; kings had multiple names. Thus the High Priests might have been claiming special privilege and prestige, but there does not seem to be an indication of Greek influence. Thus a parallel to the two names of our subject, Alcimus and Eliakim, is not found here. Also, the latter set of names seems to be a translation and not a set of double names at all.

If we have indeed found the tomb of Alcimus' wife, and if she had special prestige, we see a partial parallel in the prestige of the wives of the High Priests in Memphis. Many of them had roles as priestesses, and their funeral *stelae* record their lives and families.[38]

Before we leave the subject of comparative contemporary parallels, we can provide some additional general background about the priesthood in Egypt during Ptolemaic times. A priestly order was in existence many centuries before the Greeks arrived in Egypt. This priestly order was not a caste in the most formal sense, because some outsiders could be admitted and sons of priests did not necessarily become priests. Still, the children of priests usually occupied the priestly offices. The priests wore special garments and possessed the sacred lore. The Greeks who arrived in Egypt saw men who had shaven heads and faces and wore white linen

---

[35] D.J. Crawford *Kerkeosiris: an Egyptian village in the Ptolemaic period* (Cambridge, 1971) 134-5.
[36] Thompson "The High Priests of Memphis" 103.
[37] Thompson "The High Priests of Memphis" 103 and see n. 11.
[38] Thompson "The High Priests of Memphis" 102.

robes. The higher priesthood was divided into four groups that the Greeks called *phylai* ("tribes"). The tribes rotated on a monthly basis in performing the priestly duties. The priesthood was further divided into grades according to function. The highest grade was that of the High Priests. The second was that of "Ministers of the God" who were called "the prophets" by the Greeks, though it is not certain why.[39] The third grade was that of "robers" who had the duties of dressing and painting the idols. The fourth grade was the "sacred scribes" who supervised new hieroglyphic inscriptions. A sub-class of these scribes was that of the "feather-wearers." There were other, lower classes of priests that are beyond our interest here.

The Greeks arrived to find this very structured system in place. They would have been anxious to know if there were one central head of the Egyptian priesthood. The answer seems to be in the negative: there is no reference to one central High Priest, even on a temporary or rotating basis. At each of the larger temples, there was a High Priest who was elected by the other priests and who normally held the position for one year. This High Priest had a council of priests consisting of five priests from each of the tribes for a total of twenty. There does seem to have been a general synod that met on an occasional basis to make regulations binding on all Egyptian temples. The synod met at Canopus in the reign of Ptolemy III and later at Memphis.

The temples were, of course, great and powerful economic institutions. The land owned by the temples may not have been a third of the cultivated land as suggested by Diodorus, but it was one of the economic facts facing the Ptolemaic rulers. The Ptolemies, as well as the Seleucids, ruled a country as a modern corporation would, for financial advantage. Egypt, like Judaea, was a breadbasket, an agricultural country that could do much to enhance an emperor's coffers. If the temples owned a great deal of the land and owned a great many substantial industries (linen, prostitution, breweries, bakeries, mills, etc.), the Ptolemies needed to think carefully about their approach to these institutions. Special considerations for taxes were common for the priesthood during this period. Politically speaking, these alien rulers wanted to have the priesthood on their side, lest it help rouse nationalistic fervor and revolt. The Ptolemies demanded annual deputations of priests to Alexandria to pay homage to their rulers. The kings would ceremonially install at

---

[39] Edwyn R. Bevan *The House of Ptolemy : A History of Egypt Under The Ptolemaic Dynasty* (Chicago, 1968) 177. For what follows, see 177-88.

least some of the higher levels of priests into their offices. The text of the Rosetta Stone is an example of how the rulers would then pay homage to the gods and temples. The Ptolemies paid an annual stipend (*syntaxis*) to each individual priest. The family of priests from Memphis detailed above did so well in accommodating themselves to their rulers that they held office from the era of Ptolemy I to that of Augustus Caesar. The hereditary stability may have both caused and been affected by this relationship.

And yet for all of this, we see that the Ptolemies did not always succeed in holding the loyalty of the priests. During the latter reigns of the dynasty, Upper Egypt was the scene of revolts that seemed to have the support of the priesthood of Amon-Ra at Thebes. These priests may have remembered the glory days when their ancestors held sway over the land.

The parallel here forces us to think about Alcimus, a hereditary heir to the Oniads, who is ready to accommodate himself to the alien rulers in exchange for religious autonomy and the right to continue in power.

CHAPTER III

DID ALCIMUS WRITE PSALM 79?

The Dating of Psalms
As we turn back to the question of whether Alcimus wrote Psalm 79 and what this means for the study of his life, we must first provide background on this specific subject.[1]

Is it possible that as late as Maccabaean times, psalms were still being written? When was the Book of Psalms as we have it canonized?

That David wrote all of the Psalms is an important tradition. The Babylonian Talmud states: "David wrote the Book of Psalms including in it the work of the ten elders."[2] 2Maccabees refers to "the books of David."[3] Seventy-three psalms are specifically labeled as "Davidic." To this number, the Greek translation added Davidic superscriptions to many other psalms, even if superscriptions already existed for those psalms: Psalms 39 and 77 were already ascribed to *Jeduthun*, 42, 44-49, 84A and 87A to the *Sons of Korah*, 50 and 70-83 to *Asaph*, 72 and 127 to *Solomon*, 88 and 89 to *Heman and Ethan the Ezrahites*, and 90 to *Moses*.

For Wellhausen and his school, the Psalms, so obviously monotheistic, could not be from a time earlier than that of the prophets, the 9th-8th centuries BCE. The concepts in the psalms are borrowed directly from the prophets.[4] As Wellhausen puts it, "It is not a question of whether there are any post-exilic psalms, but rather, whether the Psalms contain any poems written before the exile."[5]

Duhm answered this question in the negative, claiming that Psalm137, a clearly exilic psalm, was the earliest psalm. He did not think that any psalms other than

---

[1] For the Talmudic references, see BT *Pesahim* 117a; cf. Benno Jacob *ZAW* XVI (1896) 162f.; Harry M. Orlinsky *Ancient Israel* (Ithaca: 1954) 76f.
[2] BT*Bava Bathra* 14b cf. 15a. The number ten is interesting. It seems to think of the Sons of Korah as being three as indicated by Exodus 6:24.
[3] 2Macc. 2:13. See Solomon Zeitlin *The Second Book of Maccabees* Dropsie College edition (New York: 1954).
[4] Julius Wellhausen *Prophets of Israel* xxi-xxii.
[5] Julius Wellhausen in *The Sacred Books of the Old Testament* ed. by Paul Haupt (Leipzig-Baltimore: 1898) 1963.

137; 8; 19A, 46; 48; 76; and 84A were definitely earlier than the Greek period;[6] the only other pre-Maccabaean candidates were 87; 16; 51; 3; 4; 11; and 62. Kennett thinks that the very idea of psalms began in Maccabaean times and that all psalms were written between 168 BCE and 141 BCE.[7] Cornill writes, "All honest exegesis must recognize that there are Maccabaean psalms.[8] The background of most of the psalms, according to these scholars, is the controversies between the parties of the Pharisees, Hasmonaeans, and Sadducees.

Other scholars such as Gunkel and Birkeland, however, demonstrate that the enemies in the psalms of lamentation are mostly foreign.[9] Baethgen makes a very strong canon-historical approach to state that there could not have been a substantial number of Maccabaean psalms.[10]

Buttenweiser's work, as idiosyncratic as it may be, is interesting to consider. He thinks that by 250 BCE, Hebrew was no longer a living language. Four-fifths of the psalms were written, he says, in the Persian era between the Exile and the Hellenistic age.

Mowinckel thinks that most of the psalms come from the First Temple period.[11]

A similar conclusion based on a completely different approach to the subject of dating the psalms comes from Yehezkel Kaufmann, one of the great original thinkers in Biblical scholarship. Kaufmann compares the themes found in the Book of Psalms with those found in the prophetic literature. The prophetic emphasis on morality over ritual and the terms of prophetic eschatology cannot be found in Psalms. Either Psalms comes from a milieu unaffected by the prophets or they were written before the classical prophets began to influence the nature of the religion. Psalms, for Kaufmann, must be pre-exilic: they do not include prayers for the

---

[6] B. Duhm *Die Psalmen* Freiburg i.B. 1899 xix.
[7] R. H. Kennett *Old Testament Essays* (Cambridge: 1928) 119-228.
[8] C. H. Cornill *Einleitung in das Alte Testament* (Introduction to the Canonical Books of the Old Testament) 6 (Aufl. Tubingen, 1913) 408.
[9] H.Birkeland. *The Evildoers in the Book of Psalms* ANVAO II (1955); Gunkel Ps.St. I
[10] Fr. Baethgen *Die Psalmen* 3rd Edition, HKAT, xiii ff. (Aufl. 1904) 3.
[11] S. Mowinckel *The Psalms in Israel's Worship* (Oxford, 1962) II 152.

Did Alcimus Write Psalm 79?

coming of the Messiah or for the ingathering of the exiles.[12] Psalm 137, seen by Duhm as the earliest of the psalms, is now seen as the latest.

In a short monograph specifically devoted to dating each of the Psalms, Treves[13] dates all of these poems to the period 170-103 BCE. In an exercise full of scholarly imagination, Treves attributes the various psalms to Onias, Judas, Jonathan, Simon, and John Hyrcanus. He establishes these criteria for his dating:

1. Since before Josiah's centralization of 621 BCE more than one hill was holy, and since in pre-Exilic days the king's palace was more important than the Temple in Jerusalem, all psalms that refer to a singular "hill" or "mountain" must be post-Exilic.
2. Since the Jewish people did not have an army between the years 585-167 BCE, any psalms that refer to war must be later than that date. If the psalm speaks of a war between the righteous and the ungodly, it must refer to a religious war and be from the years 167-140 BCE.
3. Psalms that exhibit words or phrases from the prophets are later than those prophets.
4. While certain terms can be found in earlier literature, those terms have different meaning in these later contexts. *Ḥokhmah* meant "skill" in earlier texts but referred to the *Torah* in the Maccabaean period. So words that are often taken to indicate an early date for Psalms are really indicators of lateness.
5. Psalms that exhibit phrases that echo Greek literary usages are mostly from the 2nd century BCE.
6. Other Biblical books, such as the Second Isaiah and much of Zechariah, can also be traced to the Maccabaean age and then compared to certain psalms.
7. The Ḥasideans are mentioned 24 times in the Psalms, three times in 1 and 2Maccabees and only a few other times in canonical literature. This sect was founded to defend Judaism from persecution. "Since no one rushes to defend what is not threatened," this sect must have been organized around 170 BCE. The

---

[12] Yehezkel Kaufmann *The Religion of Israel* ed. by Moshe Greenberg (Chicago: 1960) 306-311 and the fuller treatment in the original, unabridged Hebrew version *Toledoth Ha-Emunah Ha-Yisre'elith* II (Tel Aviv: 1947) 646-727.

[13] Marco Treves *The Dates of the Psalms: History and Poetry in Ancient Israel* (Pisa, 1988).

"Manual of Discipline" from Qumran was the constitution of the Ḥasidean community, not the Essenes. The Essenes were pacifists; the Dead Sea Scrolls contain plans for war. "Belial" is a reference to Antiochus *Epiphanes*.
8. "The reign of God" is a phrase that was only used in post-Exilic writings, after there were no Judean kings.
9. Since psalms imitate each other, one can determine priority by seeing where a phrase fits the most naturally in its context. A later psalm will borrow a phrase but will leave hints that it is an imitation through awkwardness or exaggeration.

We have reviewed the Treves "proofs" of Maccabaean psalms as an example of what gives a bad name to the whole effort to find psalms from this late period. Treves' #1, 2, 4 and 8 would need full monographs to substantiate. Still, some of these items are interesting. If one could show #5, Greek echoes, that would obviously be a proof that there at least late glosses. #3, echoes from the prophets, are also good clues to lateness. How one determines what is an echo, and what it the earlier text, is more difficult than Treves would make it seem. It is also harder to trace priority in #9, the relationship between psalms, than Treves would have it. #7 is the subject of whole sections of books (such as Kampen) and is worthy of study. But #6 works from circular logic and assumes a late date for a text such as Second Isaiah to which few scholars would agree.

When Was the Book of Psalms in Its Final Form?

In stating that 1Maccabees does not see the Book of Psalms as scripture, Goldstein[14] opens up a very interesting subject for our considerations here. If the Book of Psalms were not yet canonized, if it were not, at the time of Alcimus and the Maccabees, part of Holy Writ, then that highlights the possibility that psalms were still being written at this time and that Alcimus could be the author of Psalm 79, as 1Macc.7:17 says he was. Canonization of the Bible is, of course, a major topic in the field, and we need to at least briefly survey some of the relevant scholarship.[15]

---

[14] Goldstein *I Maccabees* 5.
[15] M. de Buit "Le David des Psaumes" *Le Monde de la Bible* 7 (1979) 6-7; Thomas Kelly Cheyne *The Origin and Religious Contents of the Psalter* (London, 1891); Avi Hurvitz

Did Alcimus Write Psalm 79?

The prologue to the Greek translation of Ben Sira states that when the author's grandson arrived in Egypt in 132 BCE, all of the books of the Bible, in its three parts, were translated into Greek. Gunkel asks whether the third part of the canon was complete by 190, the time of Ben Sira. He thinks that the Psalter is one of the oldest components of the third part of scripture. He mentions our reference in 1Macc.7:17 to Ps.79:2-3 as "the first citation of a psalm as holy scripture" and says that this text can be dated around 100 BCE.[16] Haran, for instance, assumes that the Psalter was in its final form by the second half of the second century BCE.[17] Fragments of Ben Sira found at Masada in 1964 reflect the style of a highly educated Jew c. 200 BCE. When compared to the style of the Psalter, says Haran, the latter seems to be from a much older period.[18]

The Ben Sira reference does not necessarily mean that the Psalter collection had reached its current form at the time of Ben Sira. On the other hand, the Psalms of Solomon, which may be from Maccabaean times, are very different from the Psalms of the canon. The Psalms of Solomon from the first century presupposes a canonical Psalter.

The Book of Psalms was an evolving entity. A Book of Psalms could have been copied into Greek at an early point, say 200 BCE. But this does not mean that the 150-psalm book, Books I-V, were all in that Psalter.

The evidence from the Dead Sea Scrolls is extremely important in this regard.[19] The fragments from these psalms the order and titles seem to correspond to the order in our extent versions. The fluidity that is found in the Qumran Psalter is found, Sanders says, in the latter two sections of the Book of Psalms (Books IV and

---

The Identification of Post-Exilic Psalms by Means of Linguistic Criteria (Jerusalem, 1966).

[16] Hermann Gunkel *Introduction to Psalms: The Genres of the Religious Lyric of Israel* (completed by Joachim Begrich, translated by James D. Nogalski (Macon, Ga., 1998) 336.

[17] Menachem Haran "*11QPs* and the Canonical Book of Psalms" in Mark Brettler and Michael Fishbane *Minhah Le-Nahum* JSOTSup. 154 (Sheffield, 1993) 193.

[18] Yigael Yadin *The Ben Sira Scroll from Masada* (Jerusalem, 1965).

[19] M. Burrows *More Light on the Dead Sea Scrolls* (New York, 1958) 169 ff.; Frank Moore Cross Jr. *The Ancient Library of Qumran* (New York, 1961) 164-65.

V, Pss.90-150).[20] Sanders states, "The observation that 1Macc.7:17 appears to quote a phrase from Ps.79:2-3 is simply no longer impressive in discussions of the date of the *MT-150* collection, nor the mention in the prologue of Ben Sira of the "other books."[21] He offers the hypothesis that the Qumran sect "arrested the process of stabilization as it was in the period before they left Jerusalem to seek their own identity, and in the then fluid third portion of the Psalter came to accept as "Davidic" what were actually Ḥasidic and proto-Essene (their own identity poems, which were at least biblical in style..."[22]

While the evidence from Qumran would seem to point against the possible authorship of Alcimus for Psalm 79, one should not be too quick to judge against the possibility on this basis. There is nothing in the Qumran evidence or the statement in Ben Sira to preclude this possibility. On the contrary, Sanders' suggestion that the fluid third portion of the Psalter includes poems that were "actually Ḥasidic and proto-Essene" is intriguing. If the third part of the Psalter that includes Psalm 79 was still fluid, if some of the psalms in it were being written by Ḥasidic writers, if Alcimus were a prominent religious personality who became High Priest with Ḥasidic support and perhaps the close lineage of a great Ḥasidic leader, then the possibility of Alcimus' authorship of Psalm 79 increases in validity.

It is important to note the contribution of Flint on this issue.[23] In an up-to-date and meticulously thorough study of all of the Psalms scrolls from Qumran, there is no copy or fragment of a copy of Psalm 79 whatsoever. Indeed, Flint can only find one reference to Psalm 79 in any of the Dead Sea Scrolls, and that is *4QTanhumim*, which is not a psalms scroll at all but a late *pesher*. The Book of Psalms was stabilized in two stages. Flint is uncertain as to the dividing line between the psalms collection that was initially stabilized and that which was established later. For our purpose here, it is uncertain as to whether Psalm 79 would be part of the first or the second collection, although it would be safer to admit that it was part of the first.

---

[20] J. A. Sanders "Cave 11 Surprises and the Question of Canon" *McCormick Quarterly* 21 (1968) 284-98; reprinted in Sid Z. Leiman *The Canon and Masorah of the Hebrew Bible: An Introductory Reader* (New York, 1974) 37-51.
[21] Sanders "Cave 11 Surprises" in Leiman *The Canon and Masorah* 45 n. 16.
[22] Ibid. 47
[23] Peter W. Flint *The Dead Sea Psalms Scrolls and the Book of Psalms* (Leiden, 1997).

Did Alcimus Write Psalm 79?

Flint also concludes that several different collections of psalms can be found among these manuscripts.

Again, there is nothing in all of this to preclude the authorship of Psalm 79 by Alcimus. Schurer states that not only were there Maccabaean psalms but that there is no "plausible reason for thinking otherwise."[24] The Book of Daniel is a strong proof that the canon was not closed and that great religious feeling found great artistic expression. When one thinks about what is described in Psalm 79 about the desecration of the temple and the laying waste of Jerusalem, one must think about the Maccabaean period.

At what point in time was the Biblical text issued with the sanction of authority that gained it acceptance as a standard text, leading to the rejection or even suppression of other recensions? Segal's answer is of great interest here:[25] The time of Judas Maccabaeus. As evidence, he cites passages from both 1 and 2Maccabees:

> And they rent in pieces the books of the law which they found, and set them on fire. And whosoever was found with any a book of the covenant, and if any consented to the law, the king's sentence delivered him to death. Thus did they in their might unto Israel, to those that were found month to month in the cities.
>
> 1Macc.1:56-58

According to 1Macc.3:48, the enemies of the Judaeans also defiled the holy scrolls by depicting the likenesses of their idols on them. Segal concludes that this destruction of sacred scrolls must have led to a terrible scarcity of scriptural books in Judaea at that time. After the Maccabaean victory, however, there would have been a great and immediate desire for new copies of these books. Segal presumes that scribes would have worked with the authority of Judas Maccabaeus. Judas, a priest, was a devout student of the scriptures,[26] and it would make perfect sense to think that he instructed scribes to create a new inventory of biblical books. So says 2Maccabees:

---

[24] Schurer *The History of the Jewish People* Second Division Volume III 15-16.

[25] M. H. Segal "The Promulgation of the Authoritative Text of the Hebrew Bible" *JBL* 72 (1953) 285-297; reprinted in Leiman *The Canon and Masorah* 285-297.

[26] According to 1Macc.4:30, 7:41 and 2Macc.8:19, 23, 15:22.

And in like manner Judas also gathered together for us all those writings that had been scattered by reason of the war that befell and they are with us. If therefore ye have need thereof, send some to fetch them unto you.
2Macc.2:14-15

That is, other communities in need of scrolls could receive them from Jerusalem because of the scribal activity at this time. Those who went to Qumran apparently took many copies with them, and they are now known as the Dead Sea Scrolls.

Segal concludes that, "the work of compiling the authoritative text must have begun immediately after the restoration of the Temple service in 164 *ante*."[27]

One cannot help but suggest that it was at this time of great scriptural activity that Alcimus made his mark, as an author of psalms and a staunch supporter of scriptural activity. There is nothing to suggest that Alcimus would have done anything but a promoter of these efforts. Indeed, the statement of 1Macc.7:17 may be all the more ironic because Alcimus was a man of scripture.

The Psalms Of *Asaph*

If 1Macc.7:17 is correct, Alcimus wrote Psalm 79. If the superscription is correct, he wrote it in the tradition of the *Asaph*-psalms.[28] This tradition emphasized times of crisis. Alcimus applies this tradition of enemies all around and hopes for God's deliverance in his own time.

There are twelve psalms that contain a heading with the ascription "Of *Asaph*." This would seem to indicate that the authors of these particular psalms, or the redactor of the Psalms, saw these psalms as parts of a tradition. That is, either the psalms were written with a sense of this tradition or a unity was superimposed on them. Eleven of the *Asaph* psalms were placed in consecutive order, 73-83, and only one, 50, is found in a different place. According to some, the psalms share certain linguistic and stylistic characteristics.

From this perspective, one would look for unities or resemblances between these psalms. It is striking that the verb *zkr* "remember" occurs thirteen times in the main

---

[27] Segal "The Authoritative Text" 42.
[28] H. P. Nasuti *Tradition History and the Psalms of Asaph* SBLDS 88 (Atlanta, 1988); David C. Mitchell *The Message of the Psalter: An Eschatological Programme in the Book of Psalms* (Sheffield, 1997).

group of *Asaph*ite psalms.[29] In the rest of the Book of Psalms, it only occurs thirty-eight additional times. This preponderance of the uses of this verb in this tradition must mean something. To remember means to remember the past, the saving acts of God and the destructive acts of the enemies of Israel. From this point, Mitchell[30] develops an interesting thematic connection between the *Asaph* psalms:

- Psalm 50 is a command to gather Israel for judgment so that God can pronounce the sentence that the wicked will be destroyed and the righteous will be saved on the day of hostility.
- Psalm 73 states that while the wicked ones now prosper, they will be punished when God acts.
- Psalm 74 describes how the nations have destroyed the Temple. By recounting these evil deeds, the psalmist-*mazkir* hopes that God will be exhorted to punish the enemies accordingly.
- Psalm 75 is a psalm of praise to God that His time of judgment is near.
- Psalm 76 is a remembrance of, at least according to the LXX heading, Sennacherib's siege of Jerusalem.
- Psalm 77 is a cry to God by the psalmist-*mazkir* in a day of hostility. God should remember His past love of Israel and act on Israel's behalf.
- Psalm 78 is a recollection of Israel's sins and God's mercies.
- Psalm 79 speaks of the invasion of the nations. The enemies have shed much blood in Jerusalem where they remain, pouring scorn on the people.
- Psalm 80 is a cry of the *mazkir* for God to deliver the people.
- Psalm 81 is the music of the *mazkir* before a battle. The people are surrounded by enemies.
- Psalm 82 states that God judges the deities of the nations.
- Psalm 83, like Psalm 50, speaks of a day of hostility; a ten-nation confederacy assembles for war against Israel.

In 1Chr.26:1, *Asaph* is a Levite from the *Korahite* clan. The *Asaph* psalms seem to be connected to the *Asaph*ite guild of levitical prophet-musicians. It should be

---

[29] (74:2, 18, 22; 77:4, 7, 12, 12; 78:35; 39, 42; 79:8). I am not including the three uses of this root in the "deutero-Asaphite psalms" of Pss.105-106 (105:5; 106: 4, 45).
[30] Mitchell *The Message of the Psalter* 59.

noted that "of *Asaph*" could not have referred to the original name of the author, for in addition to this superscription, Psalm 88 names *Heman* as the author.[31] There were families of singers in the Second Temple which were named the '*sons of Korah, Asaph, Heman, Ethan* and *Jeduthun*; these guilds were either descended from, or regarded their descent to be from, these famous ancestors.[32]

Chronicles links the Levites of the northern tradition and the *Asaph*ite singers.[33] It is interesting to note that the name and figure of Joseph is found in four *Asaph* psalms.[34] Ps.78:9, 67 and 80:3 mention Ephraim, the most prominent Joseph tribe. Ps.105:17, called 'deutero-*Asaph*ic', contains a brief history of Joseph. But what does this mean? Delitzsch wonders whether *Asaph*, the founder of the tradition, were from a Levite city in Ephraim or Manasseh.[35]

Buss posits a northern origin for the *Asaph* psalms,[36] and has been followed by Nasuti[37] and others. A particularly notable development is Rendsburg's attempt to establish the northern Hebrew dialect that he calls "Israelian Hebrew" and to investigate the origins of certain psalms on this basis.[38] Rendsburg candidly admits that with the exception of Psalm 74, none of the *Asaph* psalms contains a large concentration of what he has determined to be Israelian Hebrew psalms. Even more striking for our purpose here is the fact that Rendsburg never mentions Psalm 79 in his entire monograph.

Critically speaking, however, the psalms need not be ascribed to *Asaph* any more than all of the psalms need to be credited to David. Indeed, Oesterley speculates that the *Asaph* collection was not completed until about 150 BCE.[39]

---

[31] Cf. the superscription to Ps.39.
[32] 1Chr. 6:18ff.; 16:41f.; 25:1ff.; 2Chr. 5:12; 35:15; etc..
[33] Anderson *Psalms* I 45; Buss "The Psalms of Asaph and Korah" *JBL* 82 (1963) 382-92.
[34] Pss.77:16; 78:67; 80:2; 81:6. See E. C. B. MacLaurin "Joseph and Asaph" *VT* 25 (1975) 27-45.
[35] F. Delitzsch *Biblical Commentary on the Psalms* trans. by D. Eaton II (London, 1887) 438.
[36] Buss "The Psalms of Asaph and Korah" 394.
[37] Nasuti *Tradition History and the Psalms of Asaph* 14.
[38] Gary A. Rendsburg *Linguistic Evidence for the Northern Origin of Selected Psalms* (Atlanta, 1990).
[39] See William Oesterley *The Psalms* Vol. I (New York: 1939) 4, 72.

Did Alcimus Write Psalm 79?

Psalm 79

We can now turn to the question of Alcimus' possible authorship of Psalm 79. Let us first review the issue. When, according to 1Maccabees7:12-14, Alcimus has sixty *Asidaioi* executed, the narrator tells us:

> As soon as he had won their trust, however, he arrested sixty of them and had them executed all in a single day, in accordance with the verse which he himself wrote, "The bodies and blood of Your saints they have poured out around Jerusalem, and there is no one to bury them."

As noted above, Goldstein details the various manuscript readings and states that, "modern editors have been correct in taking as most reliable the unidiomatic original text of S, *ton logon hon egrapsen auton*, literally "the verse which he wrote it."" The "verse" is actually a paraphrase of Ps.79:2-3 (we have italicized the key components):

> O God, heathens have entered Your domain, defiled Your holy temple, and turned Jerusalem into ruins. They have left Your servants' corpses as food for the fowl of heaven, *and the flesh of Your faithful* for the wild beasts. *Their blood was shed like water around Jerusalem, with none to bury them.* We have become the butt of our neighbors, the scorn and derision of those around us.

Since the author of 1Maccabees despises Alcimus, he would not have made up the fact that Alcimus had written this psalm. He is using Alcimus' own sacred words against him. At one point, Alcimus had decried the spilling of Jewish blood but now, according to the author of 1Maccabees, he has caused the spilling of Jewish blood himself. At the very point that 1Maccabees aims its harshest possible attack on Alcimus, it also openly speaks of Alcimus as the author of a psalm. If Alcimus wrote the psalm, the reference may be to the sack of Jerusalem by Antiochus IV in 169 BCE or to the expedition of the Mysarch in 167. The land has been invaded and the Temple defiled, a horror that receives poetic expression in 1Maccabees:

> It was an ambush against the temple, And continually a wicked adversary against Israel. They shed innocent blood around the sanctuary and defiled the temple.
> 1Macc.1:36-37

Again, the possibility that Alcimus may be the author of this psalm is the intriguing idea that is at the heart of this study. The thought experiment is to examine whether one can accept 1Maccabees' statement as a fact, to see what commentators throughout the ages have said about the authorship of Psalm 79 and to consider whether Alcimus might have been the author of other psalms as well.

The Interpretation of Psalm 79

For the sake of convenience, we will cite the *NJV* translation in its entirety:[40]

1) A psalm of Asaph.
O God, heathens have entered Your domain defiled Your holy temple, and turned Jerusalem into ruins.
2) They have left Your servants' corpses as food for the fowl of heaven, and the flesh of Your faithful for the wild beasts.
3) Their blood was shed like water around Jerusalem, with none to bury them.
4) We have become the butt of our neighbors, the scorn and derision of those around us.
5) How long, O LORD, will You be angry forever, will Your indignation blaze like fire?
6) Pour out Your fury on the nations that do not know You, upon the kingdoms that do not invoke Your name,
7) for the have devoured Jacob and desolated his home.
8) Do not hold our former iniquities against us; let Your compassion come swiftly toward us, for we have sunk very low.
9) Help us, O God, our deliverer, for the sake of the glory of Your name. Save us and forgive our sin, For the sake of Your name.
10) Let the nations not say, "Where is their God?" Before our eyes let it be known among the nations That You avenge the spilled blood of Your servants.
11) Let the groans of the prisoners reach You; reprieve those condemned to death, as befits Your great strength.

---

[40] W. Bruggemann *The Message of the Psalms: A Theological Commentary* (Minneapolis, 1984) 71-74; E. Janssen *Juda in der Exilszeit: Ein Beitrag zur Frage der Entstehung des Literatur Judentum* FRLANT 69 (Gottingen, 1956) 19-20; Nasuti *Tradition History and the Psalms of Asaph* 193-200.

Did Alcimus Write Psalm 79?

12) Pay back our neighbors sevenfold for the abuse they have flung at You, O LORD.
13) Then we, Your people, the flock You shepherd, shall glorify You forever; for all time we shall tell Your praises.

In briefly studying the history of the interpretation of this psalm, we will notice that some traditional and modern commentators have sensed a connection to the Maccabaean period.

Ancient and Traditional Commentators

Ancient commentators such as Eusebius[41] and Athanasius[42] spoke of Psalm 79 as a prophecy of Antiochus ' persecution. In recognizing the connection between the psalm and this period, these commentators could only call it a prophecy because they could not say that it actually was written during Antiochus' persecution. Within these restrictions, even these commentators clearly saw the relationship to this era.

Traditional Jewish interpretation begins with the idea that *Asaph* wrote the psalm. Since this sad poem describes the destruction of the Temple, it would seem to be more appropriate to call it "a dirge of *Asaph*" rather than a *mizmor*, "a *song* of *Asaph*." A rather platitudinous answer is that since in His anger God only destroyed the Temple and not the people as a whole, the psalm is a song of praise to God for His mercy.[43]

BT*Sanhedrin* 47a, the only reference to Ps.79:2-3 in the entire Babylonian Talmud, explains that *ḥasidekha* in 79:2b refers to those who were already pious. However, *ʿavadekha* "your servants" refers to those who were wicked before death. Since the good and wicked alike were killed, the wicked were redeemed through their suffering and were now considered God's servants. How did the Gentiles enter the Sanctuary and emerge unscathed? After all, Nadav and Avihu died when they entered the Sanctuary without permission[44] and Uzziah was stricken with leprosy because he offered incense to God in the Sanctuary.[45]

---

[41] Eusebius *Demonstratio evangelica* x 1.12. Cited in Goldstein I Maccabees 332.
[42] Athanasius *Expositio in Psalmun* LXXVIII, vol. XXVII, col. 359 Migne. Cited in Goldstein *I Maccabees* 332.
[43] BT*Kiddushin 31b*.
[44] Lev.10:1-2.
[45] II Chr.26.

Benjamin E. Scolnic

In traditional medieval commentary on the Psalms, examined by Uriel Simon,[46] there are different approaches to the issue of the authorship of the various psalms. Simply put, the reference to the defilement of the Temple in Psalm 79 clearly concerns a time quite distant from the period of King David. Thus Ibn Ezra, in reviewing the different approaches, speaks of one view that all of the *Asaph* psalms are David's "prophecies about future events."[47] A second view is that the Psalms do not include prophecies of future events; *Asaph* was a poet who lived in Babylon and not the *Asaph* who was the chief musician in the time of David. Speaking of Psalm 79 in particular, the commentator Moses Ibn Giqatilah finds a Babylonian background. Ibn Ezra himself believes that the entire book is divinely inspired and that "a psalm of *Asaph*" is indeed by the *Asaph* who lived in David's time, as 1Chr.25:2 indicates ("who prophesied by order of the king").

Of interest is the interpretation of the term *mizmor* at the beginning of many psalms, including Psalm 79. How can a song of complaint and supplication like Psalm 79 be referred to as a "song"? In his commentary on Ps.79:1, Ibn Ezra responds: "Some say that *mizmor* [means] something that is cut off and severed from many, perhaps they were dirges." Psalm 79, in this view, was a dirge cut off from a dirge cycle. But Ibn Ezra himself thinks that *mizmor* is a term that means, "a poem [performed] in accordance with the musical art, and adapted fully to its purpose and time, be it joy or sadness."[48] Psalm 79 is his example of a sad song. The commentator offers yet another explanation, that since *Asaph* was a contemporary of David, and 79:1's description of a Jerusalem in ruins cannot refer to the distress of the psalmist himself, Psalm 79 begins with a prophecy, alluded to by the joyful term *mizmor*. The past tense of "the heathens have entered Your domain" is the prophetic past.[49] Psalm 79 is a song of praise to God who will save the people from a calamity that will bring them terrible distress far in the future.

Traditional Jewish commentary is somewhat limited in its flexibility by its literal understanding of psalms of *Asaph*. While it can see the possibility that Psalm 79 is a prophecy of the destruction of the First Temple, it cannot seem to see that it could

---

[46] Uriel Simon *Four Approaches to the Book of Psalms: From Saadiah Gaon to Abraham Ibn Ezra* translated from the Hebrew by Lenn J. Schramm (Albany, 1991).
[47] Simon *Four Approaches to the Book of Psalms* 330.
[48] Simon *Psalms* 225.
[49] Simon *Psalms* 228.

just as easily have been a prophecy of a later time. This may be because the destruction of the First Temple is within the scope of Biblical literature while the time of the Antiochene persecution was not.

Modern Study

In modern form-critical study, Psalm 79 is seen as a collective lament. The communal lament is the most obvious psalm-genre in the psalms of *Asaph*. Aside from Psalm 79, Psalms.74, 80, and 83 are accepted as collective laments by most form critics.[50] A communal lament was molded by tradition; this would account for both the parallels in other psalms (e.g. Psalm 89) and the fact that we are reminded of passages in other books.[51]

A common modern theory is to say that Psalm 79 was written in the time after the fall of the First Temple in 587-86 BCE. Kidner[52] sees this psalm as a cry that comes from eyewitnesses of the fall of Jerusalem in that year.[53] Apparently noticing that there is nothing here about exile, he suggests that the writer was not a deportee like the singers of Psalm 137 but someone who stayed in the area of Jerusalem after its fall. Kidner does not treat the problem of the *Hasidim* in v.2 except to say that the word means "loyal" and not "holy." Kidner correctly emphasizes the horror of a dead body lying unburied as in v.3. He refers to David's honoring of Rizpah for fighting off the indignity done to her sons in 2Sam. 21:10-14 and the prophecy of doom to Jehoiakim with this image in Jer.22:18f. A decent burial seems to be a natural right in the Bible.[54] Kidner describes the tone of the psalm as being one of "indignation."

While one could imagine this tone as appropriate to a people living in their homeland, indignant with the poor treatment of their overlords, it is hard to see the poor survivors of the fall of Jerusalem in 586 BCE as the authors of this psalm.

---

[50] See, for instance, Claus Westermann *The Psalms* (Minneapolis, 1980) 29.
[51] Jer. 10:25; Lam. 5.
[52] Derek Kidner *Psalms 73-150*: A Commentary on Books III, IV and V of the Psalms (London, 1975) 286-88.
[53] See also, for instance, Marvin E. Tate *Psalms 51-100* Word Biblical Commentary 20 (Dallas: 1990) 298-99.
[54] Kidner *Psalms* 286-87.

Most of the scholars who take this position, however, also admit that the language is so stereotypical that one cannot come to any definitive conclusion.[55] For instance, Weiser[56] lists a number of possibilities, from 587 BCE to an unknown catastrophe in the time after Ezra to the religious persecution under the Seleucids. For the latter era, Weiser mentions the events recorded in 1Macc.1:30 ff., 3:45, and 2Macc.8:2ff. Whatever its origin, Weiser takes the psalm as a "prayer of the persecuted cult community in the times of the Maccabees" and references 1Macc.7:17. He stops short, however, of saying that the psalm was written at this time.

While Weiser states that he cannot ascertain whether it was the period of the Maccabees or not "in default of concrete allusions," he nevertheless points to the enemy invasion, Temple defilement, a ruined Jerusalem and the fact that "a horrible massacre has been perpetrated amongst the cult community; the ghastly spectacle of corpses lying around unburied meets the eye everywhere."[57] One does have to wonder what other calamity fits this series of events aside from that of the Antiochene persecution. Indeed, what savage irony there would have been if the writer of this psalm later participated in another horrible massacre of the cult community? For this psalmist, in supplicating God and asking forgiveness for sins, seeks revenge on the enemies who perpetrated this catastrophe. Again, how ironic that the writer of the psalmist might have gone on to be appointed and supported by the people he would kill.

Maccabaean Glosses on an Earlier Psalm

Some modern commentators, who will be represented here by Briggs,[58] say that the psalm was written earlier and then revised to fit the Maccabaean period. Briggs constructs his own theory that Psalm 79 was originally a lament for the destruction of Jerusalem in 586 BCE that now contains many glosses by Maccabaean editors who sought to make it appropriate to the desecration of the temple and the cruelty

---

[55] Kraus *Psalmen* II 550-51; Weiser *Psalms* 554.
[56] Arthur Weiser *The Psalms: A Commentary* translated by Herbert Hartwell OTL (Louisville, 1962) 544.
[57] Weiser *The Psalms* 544.
[58] C. A. and E. G. Briggs *Psalms* Vol. 2 ICC (London, 1907).

by Antiochus. The original psalm, according to Briggs' understanding and translation, would have read as follows:

> The nations have come into Thine inheritance
> They have defiled Thy holy temple,
> They have laid Jerusalem in ruins.
> They have given the dead bodies of Thy servants
> As food to the birds of heaven,
> Thy pious ones to the wild beasts of the earth.
> Remember not the iniquities of our forefathers.
> Quickly let Thine acts of compassion come to meet us.
> Help us, O God of our salvation,
> For the sake of the glory of Thy name.
> We will give thanks unto Thee forever;
> To all generations tell Thy praise.

Verses 1-2 clearly refer to the destruction by Nebuchadnezzar. The use of the verb *ṭm'* (to defile) in v.1 takes us to the realm of the Deuteronomist, the Holiness Code, the Priestly stratum, and Ezekiel, with reference to Jer.7:33 and Ezek.9:7. The former is a prophecy of doom decreed against the people of Judah for their sins in the Valley of Ben-hinnom:

> The carcasses of this people shall be food for the birds of the sky and the beasts of the earth, with none to frighten them off.

It is a prophecy of the destruction of Jerusalem that was fulfilled in the catastrophe of 587 BCE. Ezek.9:7 is part of a vision of the prophet of that same destruction:

> And He said to them, "Defile the House and fill the courts with the slain. Then go forth." So they went forth and began to kill in the city.

It would appear likely that vv.2-3 are, one way or another, a unit, and that at least that much is proven by our passage in 1Maccabees. If Briggs is right and vv.1-2 are indeed part of the original psalm and v.3 is a Maccabaean gloss, why are vv.2-3 a unit at a time before that so-called gloss could have been added?

Benjamin E. Scolnic

The Maccabaean glosses, according to Briggs' scheme, are vv.3, 9cd, 10bc, 12:

(3) Their blood was shed like water around Jerusalem, with none to bury them.
(9cd) Save us and forgive our sin, for the sake of Your name.
(10bc) Before our eyes let it be known among the nations that You avenge the spilled blood of Your servants.
(12) Pay back your neighbors sevenfold for the abuse they have flung at You, O Lord.

According to Briggs, the Maccabaean editors also inserted citations from other scriptures in order to make the psalm more appropriate for religious use. These citations are vv.4-7, 8c, 10a, 11, and 13ab:

(4) We have become the butt of our neighbors, the scorn and derision of those around us.
(5) How long, O Lord, will You be angry forever, will Your indignation blaze like fire?
(6) Pour out Your fury on the nations that do not know You, upon the kingdoms that do not invoke Your name,
(7) for they have devoured Jacob and desolated his home.
(8c) for we have sunk very low.
(10a) Let the nations not say, "Where is their God?"
(11) Let the groans of the prisoners reach You; reprieve those condemned to death, as befits Your great strength.
(13) Then we, Your people, the flock You shepherd,

The whole approach here assumes that it can separate later citations from the original poem. The problem is that even the so-called original poem itself, as we saw in the relationship between Ps.79:1-2 and Jer.7:33 and Ezek.9:7, seems very close to a series of citations. One could go further and dwell on the meaning of quotation or citation. Since most Biblical poetry has so much intertextual relationship, very little does not bear some kind of resemblance, in form and content, with other passages. Look at this partial list of verses in our psalm that relate to other passages:

- v.1c see Jer.26:18; Mic.3:12
- v.4 see Ps.44:15
- v.5 see Pss.6:4; 13:2; 89:47

Did Alcimus Write Psalm 79?

- vv.6-7 see Jer.10:25
- v 8c see Pss.142:7;
- v 9d see Pss.23:3; 25:11; 31:4; 54:3: 106:8; 109:21: 143:11
- v 10ab see Pss.115:2; 42:4; Joel 2:17
- v.11a see Ps.102:21
- v.11c see 1Sam.26:16
- v.12 see Pss.89:51-52; 44:14; Gen.4:15, 24; Lev.26:18, 21, 24.

Again, if one were to accept all of these links, it is not necessarily clear whether Psalm 79 or the other passages have priority. That is, if one were to see the relationship between Ps.79:8c and Ps.142:7, one could easily say that the latter echoes the former. We can assume a relationship between citations without knowing what that relationship is.

Treves is convinced, along with Kent and Cobb, that Psalm 79 was written during the persecution of Antiochus Epiphanes. The fact that the Temple is not destroyed but defiled makes certain that this psalm should not be ascribed to 587 BCE. Also, the psalmist does not lament about a war but a massacre. The fact that the *Hasidim* are mentioned is another key clue pointing to the Maccabaean period. Yet there is no reference to the Maccabees or to their rebellion, so this psalm must have been written in 167 BCE, the first year of the persecution. The description of the martyrs who have not been given burials points to the same year, as we learn from the atrocities discussed in 1Maccabees, 2Maccabees, and *Antiquities*:

> With this loot he [Antiochus Epiphanes] returned to his own country, having polluted himself with massacres.
>
> 1Macc.1:24

> Two years later, the king sent a Mysarch against the towns of Judas, and he came against Jerusalem with a strong army. Treacherously, he addressed the people in peaceful terms, so that they trusted him, and then he hit the city hard with a surprise attack, killing many Israelites....They shed innocent blood around the sanctuary and defiled the temple.
>
> 1Macc.1:29-30, 37

Other Jews hastily assembled nearby in the caves to observe the Sabbath in secret. On being denounced to Philip they were all burned to death because they refrained from defending themselves ...

2Macc.6:11

but the worthiest people ... held their country's customs of greater account than the punishment with which he threatened them if they disobeyed; and being on that account maltreated daily, and enduring bitter torments, they met their death. Indeed, they were whipped, their bodies were mutilated, and while they were still alive and breathing, they were crucified ...

Ant. XII. 255-56

Of these citations, the clearest connection to Psalm 79 is 1Macc.1:37. The same images of innocent blood being spilled in the sanctuary and the defilement of the Temple are found in both texts. The question is what this means. Treves takes the link as a historical one; both texts reflect the same events. First the psalmist and then the author of 1Maccabees, perhaps under the psalm's influence, describes these events in similar terms.

The prisoners mentioned in this psalm[59] may refer to those mentioned in *Ant.* XII:251.

Treves thinks that 79:2 quotes the first lines of the *Iliad*. Treves lists these resemblances to other texts:

- v.1 - Jer.9:11and 26:18 (he does not mention Mic.3:12)
- v.2 – combines Jer.19:7 and 14:6;
- v.4 - comes from Ps.89:41 (he says that 44:15 is an echo of this)
- v.5 - echoes Ezek.36:5, 38:19 and Is.26:11 (Ps.89:47 recalls this psalm)
- vv.6-7 see Jer.10:25;
- v.8 may echo Jer.10:10 or Lev.26:39-40;
- v 10 - Pss.115:2 and Joel 2:17 (which Treves dates to 300 BCE);
- v.12 - Lev.26:18, 21, 24; Prov.6:31;
- v.13 is a liturgical addition.

---

[59] And in Pss.59, 102, 142 and 146.

Did Alcimus Write Psalm 79?

While we cannot accept all of Treves' points (e.g. his dating of Joel), one must admit that scholars such as Briggs and Treves are finding interesting relationships between Psalm 79 and other Biblical passages.

Nasuti takes a very different approach and sees the *Asaph* psalms as containing elements proper to the Ephraimite stream of tradition. [60] His study of our psalm begins with the idea that Psalm 79 is a collective lament like Psalm 74. Like Kraus[61] and Weiser,[62] Nasuti thinks that the language is so stereotypical that it cannot necessarily be related to the catastrophe of 587. Nasuti traces the term *'iyyim* in Ps.79:1 to Micah 1:6 and especially 3:12 where it refers to the predicted destruction of Jerusalem, which would make it a perfect antecedent for this psalm. If this were the only reference, one might see a link to Judahite prophecy. Since Nasuti wants to see the psalms as stemming from the traditions of Northern Israel, he shows how the use of *'iyyim* in Jer.26:18 quotes Mic.3:12. Jeremiah himself was an Ephraimite prophet and was involved with Jerusalemite circles that transmitted pro-Deuteronomic, and therefore Northern, traditions. In 79:2, the word *n^{e}belah* which can mean either "carcass," as in Leviticus and Ezekiel, or "human corpse," as in the Ephraimite corpus (such as Deuteronomy and the Deuteronomic history), is used for humans. The links to Psalm 74 are strong.

Speaking form-critically, there does seem to be a connection between Pss.74 and 79 and the destruction of the temple, thus placing the time of authorship as the exilic period.[63] Willesen, on the other hand, uses near eastern parallels to speak of "temple lamentations."[64] These lamentations were connected with the New Year's festival or ceremonies involved with the purification or re-purification of the temple. Ringgren shows a commonality of reference between the creation myths indicated in Babylonian examples of this type and Psalm 74.[65] Nasuti, while expressing reservations about these connections, sees it as a theoretical possibility that Psalm 79 is written for the restoration or rededication of the temple. He finds it interesting to note that Psalm 79 is an *Asaph* psalm and that there is "explicit

---

[60] Nasuti *Tradition History and the Psalms of Asaph* 193-200.
[61] Kraus *Psalmen* II 550-51.
[62] Weiser *Psalms* 544 and above.
[63] Kraus *Psalmen* II 514-15 and 550-51.
[64] Folker Willesen "The Cultic Setting of Psalm LXXIV" *VT* 2 (1952) 290-306.
[65] Hemer Ringgren *The Impact of the Ancient Near East on Israelite Tradition* VTSup 23 (Leiden, 1972) 41.

*Asaph*ite involvement" in laying the foundation of the new Jerusalemite temple, as Ezra 3:10 indicates:

> When the builders had laid the foundations of the Temple of the LORD, priests in their vestments with trumpets, and Levites sons of Asaph with cymbals were stationed to give praise to the LORD, as King David had ordained.

Yet the songs sung at that time were of thanksgiving and praise and certainly not of lamentation. Still, since the term *Asaph* clearly means something, that it is associated with temple re-dedication is intriguing. Again, however, we stress the situation of the psalmist of Psalm 79 at the time of authorship. The Temple has been defiled and is still in the state of defilement. There is nothing about restoration or re-dedication. Instead, the psalmist is looking forward, with anger and hope, to that restoration, but it is at best in the distant future after the enemies have been defeated.

Nasuti, in trying to link Ephraimite tradition with Psalms 74 and 79, attempts to posit a prophetic connection to these psalms. He does see the objection that 74:9 laments the fact that there is no prophet at this time.

Nasuti actually makes a case for the other side in emphasizing 74:9, which indeed sounds like a late lamentation from a time when there are no prophets. There is nothing in Nasuti's work to dissuade us from the possibility that Alcimus wrote Psalm 79.

McCann agrees that Psalm 79 is one of the communal laments, like the psalms that precede and follow it, which gives one the impression that Book III of Psalms has been shaped by the experience of the Babylonian Exile.[66] The theology of Zion and the Davidic Covenant had to be reconsidered in the light of historical events. McCann does recognize that scholars have seen the origin of this psalm in the desecration of the temple by Antiochus *Epiphanes*. McCann says that portions of 79:2-3 "appear in the second-century 1Maccabees as a comment on the murder of sixty faithful Jews (1Macc.7:17)."[67]

---

[66] J. Clinton McCann "Psalms" in *The New Interpreter's Bible Volume IV* (Nashville, 1996) 993ff.
[67] McCann "Psalms" 994.

Did Alcimus Write Psalm 79?

While it is true that 79:2-3 is quoted in a comment about the massacre, this does not mean that Psalm 79 would, in this theory, be written after that event. Instead, the point is that Alcimus, who had previously written the psalm, is quoted against himself with savage irony to match his savagery.

Following *NRSV*, McCann renders the important phrase in 7:16 as "the word that was written" and infers that the psalm as a much earlier origin.

One then has to understand why this is the only such citation in all of 1Maccabees. In addition, a psalm that "was written' was not necessarily written hundreds of years earlier.

McCann recognizes that the psalm had "its origin in a specific ancient event."[68] Still, it had a rich afterlife in Jewish and Christian tradition. It is used to this day in the liturgy of *Tish ʿah b ʾAv*, the commemoration of the destruction of Jerusalem on the 9th of *Av*. It is alluded to in *Rev.*16:6. Jerome cited it in response to the invasion of Rome by the Visigoths.

McCann's point seems to be that since this psalm written for a specific event has been applied as a lamentation for other events, we should not emphasize its specificity too much. That is, its details should not be scrutinized to the point that we cannot see the psalm as an expression after the destruction of the First Temple. McCann says that the "defilement" of the Temple in v.1, which would not seem to fit with the theory that the psalm is from c.586 BCE, refers to the fact that Jerusalem, God's holy place, is in ruins, and alludes to Jer.26:18 and Mic.3:12.

These allusions, however, would seem to indicate that Psalm 79 comes from a later period than those texts, as others have suggested. The defilement is made worse by the bodies that have been left unburied, an image that brings Ezek.22:1-12 to mind.

McCann, then, does not see Alcimus as the writer of Psalm 79 but does not offer any cogent arguments against this possibility. Dahood says that Psalm 79 is cited in 1Maccabees as Scripture. He concludes that since the citation is known to readers as a quote from a psalm, it must be a well-known psalm that has already been canonized as Scripture.

We could use the same fact, that Psalm 79 is considered Scripture, to make the opposite point. Alcimus wrote a psalm that was included in the Psalter and then he turned around and, at least according to the author of 1Maccabees, became the

---

[68] McCann "Psalms" 996.

enemy of the Jews. The idea that the psalm was well known could also mean that it was a recent and popular lament written during and for this time.

Conclusion

All of these theories pale before the clear statement of 1Maccabees. The background of the writing of the psalm would be Antiochus' sack of Jerusalem in 169 BCE or perhaps the Mysarch's expedition in 167 BCE. The land of Israel has been invaded, the temple has been defiled; Jerusalem lies in ruins and pietist Jews have been massacred.[69] At this point, the pagan cult has not yet been imposed.

Notice that the entire psalm is written from within the context of a persecution that is active at the present time. There is no reference to exile of any kind; indeed, the people seem to be in their homeland with neighbors looking in, mocking with derision at their sorry state. There does seem to be reference to religious persecution; in v.12, for instance, speaks of the abuse thrown at God Himself. The psalmist does not pray for the restoration of the state or the return of the exiles.

An important point is that the Temple here is not burned as it was in 586 BCE. As bad as defilement is, burning is obviously much worse. Some scholars respond that there is also no mention of the burning in Ezekiel 25 or Lamentations. There is, however, a great deal about the fire of God's judgment[70] and this should not be ignored.

Alcimus writes as a devout Jewish priest, decrying the evils that have befallen his people.

Some of the scholars who reject the idea of Maccabaean psalms do not seem to understand that 1Macc.7:17 states that Alcimus was the actual author of the psalm. The idea of "Maccabaean psalms" is that there are psalms from the Maccabaean period. Still, the term "Maccabaean psalms" is ironic; Alcimus was hardly a Maccabee.

A problem for the theory that Alcimus wrote this psalm would seem to be its condemnation of the enemies and the petition for revenge upon them. Alcimus became the agent of those very enemies. This argument doe not preclude Alcimus as author of this psalm, however, because he could have written the psalm before he became a religious/political leader. Indeed, at this earlier stage he may have been

---

[69] Vv 1-2 and 7.
[70] Lam. 1:12; 2:3; 4:11.

associated with his uncle Yosi ben Yoʿezer. He may have become High Priest with the acceptance of Yosi ben Yoʿezer and his colleagues (whether they were the *Asidaioi* or some proto-rabbinic group), and then, because of his role as High Priest and responsibilities to what he thought was best for the Temple and his people, began to collaborate with the very enemies he had once denounced. This psalm may have been a major part of his resume for the job in the eyes of the traditional Jews, and may have been unknown to, or ignored by, the Seleucids.

CHAPTER IV

THE RE-EVALUATION OF ALCIMUS

Who Was Alcimus' Predecessor as High Priest? Was He the High Priest at *Hanukkah*, The Rededication Of The Temple?
While the rededication of the Temple and the resulting holiday of *Hanukkah* is familiar to all as it has been perpetuated by Judaism, there is little to no discussion as to the identity of the High Priest at that festival. There are a number of choices:[1]

1. Menelaus
2. Judas Maccabaeus
3. Alcimus
4. No one held the office at that time.

The answer from the ancient sources would seem to be Menelaus. 1Maccabees states that the dedication occurred in the winter of 164 BCE and Alcimus did not become High Priest until 162 BCE. The question not only of the identity of the High Priest at the rededication of the Temple, but also during the time in between the rededication and the appointment of Alcimus, remains open in this text. 2Maccabees discusses the institution of *Hanukkah* in 10:3-7 but the removal of Menelaus in 13:3-8. Thus Menelaus would still have been the High Priest at the rededication. Alcimus becomes High Priest well after Menelaus is deposed. Josephus has Alcimus selected well after the rededication.[2] When Onias III is killed, Onias IV is not of age and goes to Egypt. It is only after the execution of Menelaus that Alcimus is made High Priest. Judas is appointed High Priest after Alcimus dies.

Most modern scholars conclude that Menelaus was the High Priest *de jure* and Judas the High Priest *de facto* during the re-dedication of the Temple. Schurer and Sievers say that Menelaus is nominally still the High Priest but is unable to function in the presence of Judas, who may not have been the High Priest during the rededication of the Temple but certainly was in control of the restoration of the cult

---
[1] Emil Schurer *The Jewish People in the Time of Jesus* 317 n. 16 and see 318 n. 30.
[2] *Ant.* xii.5.1.

The Re-evaluation of Alcimus

at that time and the removal of all other forms of worship in the Temple. Graetz, however, says that as part of the restoration of order, Antiochus V and Lysias raise Judas to the position of High Priest. Judas is not only the *de facto* High Priest at the time of *Hanukkah* but also the duly appointed High Priest *de jure* as well.

It seems clear to everyone, with the exception of Graetz, that Judas was not the High Priest of *Hanukkah*. And yet, Judas would seem to have the following text from 2Maccabees behind his candidacy to be the High Priest at the rededication:

> Maccabaeus and his men, with the LORD leading them, recovered the sanctuary and the city. They destroyed the illicit altars which the foreigners had built around the marketplace and also the illicit shrines. After purifying the temple, they made another altar. Using fire they got by igniting stones, for the first time in two years they offered sacrifices and incense and installed the lights and set out the showbread. That done, they prostrated themselves and prayed to the LORD that they never again would come to suffer such disasters. Rather, if they should ever sin, let them be chastised by the LORD himself, with clemency, and not delivered over to the hands of blasphemous and barbarous gentiles. On the very same date on which the temple was profaned by foreigners occurred the purification of the temple, on the twenty-fifth of the ninth month (that is, Kislev). Joyfully they held an eight-day celebration, after the pattern of Tabernacles, remembering how a short time before they spent the festival of Tabernacles like wild beasts, in the mountains and in the caves. Therefore, holding wreathed wands, and branches bearing ripe fruit, and palm fronds, they offered songs of praise to Him Who had victoriously brought about the purification of His Place. By vote of the commonwealth they decreed a rule for the entire nation of the Jews to observe these days annually.
>
> 2Macc.10:1-8

If Judas was not the High Priest at this time, why was he not? He had defeated the Seleucids, he was in control and he had the power to *create* the holiday of *Hanukkah*. What could have stopped him from becoming High Priest? One might say that it is plausible that the office did not make any difference to him, that he simply did not care. If so, then one must reckon with his ambitions that, as the record of his subsequent actions proves, included political independence for his people, presumably with him not only as High Priest but also as king. If the suggestion should be made that he could not become High Priest without the appointment of the Seleucid king, this would mean that he still recognized that authority, even at his moment of triumph. This man who was willing to die in order to fight for political independence, who would not accept the restoration of religious autonomy as sufficient, would not have been concerned with the acceptance of the foreign enemy. In fact, accepting the office of High Priest would have made the very strong statement that he, and not the Seleucids, had authority over the nation.

If Judas did not become High Priest, then, it was only because his lineage was insufficient. Historically speaking, there were two ways to become High Priest: In the prescribed traditional Jewish manner, through hereditary Zadokite succession, and by the appointment of the Seleucids, who had placed the non-priest, and certainly non-Zadokite Menelaus in the office. Judas could not replace the illegitimate Menelaus with his own illegitimate candidacy. Again, it is not that he did not aspire to this goal; in fact, he aspired to be High Priest and king. It is interesting that he put "pure" priests into the role of priests at the rededication:

> He appointed unblemished priests, lovers of the *Torah*, who purified the sanctuary and removed the stones of the loathsome structure to an unclean place. They deliberated over what they should do with the profaned altar of the burnt offering...
> 1Macc.4:42ff.

Why were Judas and his brothers not qualified for these roles? While both primary and secondary sources may infer that Judas had become High Priest, he never held this office. This is why he Alcimus, who was indeed a Zadokite, no matter what any sources say, was appointed.

Since we know that Judas Maccabaeus was a priest, and since we know that he was not apparently eligible to become High Priest, what do we know about his lineage? We know that eventually the high-priestly line will become that of the Hasmonaean family, originally from the course of Joiarib. It stayed in the Hasmonaean family until Herod the Great decimated the Hasmonaean family, and executed the last Hasmonaean High Priest, Aristobulus, in 35 BCE. In attempting to determine the possible legitimacy of Judas, we can trace this lineage through several ancient sources. First, 1Maccabees:

> During that time, Mattathias son of John son of Simeon, a priest of the clan of Joarib, left Jerusalem and settled in Modein. Mattathias had five sons: John

The Re-evaluation of Alcimus

nicknamed Gaddi; Simon, called Thassi; Judas, called Maccabaeus; Eleazar, called Auaran; and Jonathan, called Apphus.[3]

1Macc.2:2

The key phrase here is that Mattathias was of "a priest of the clan of Joiarib."[4] We know of this priestly clan from several Biblical passages. In 1Chron.9, a list of returnees from Babylonia, the priests are mentioned in v.10ff.:

> Of the priests: Jedaiah, Jehoiarib, Jachin, and Azariah son of Hilkiah son of Meshullam son of Zadok son of Meraioth son of Ahitub, chief officer of the House of God ...

According to 1Chron.24:7ff., the lots of the priests are as follows:

> The first lot fell on Jehoiarib; the second on Jedaiah; the third on Harim; the fourth on Seorim; the fifth on Malchijah; the sixth on Mijamin; the seventh on Hakkoz; the eighth on Abijah; the ninth on Jeshua; the tenth on Shecaniah; the eleventh on Eliashib; the twelfth on Jakim; the thirteenth on Huppah; the fourteenth on Jeshebeab; the fifteenth on Bilgah; the sixteenth on Immer; the seventeenth on Hezir; the eighteenth on Happizzez; the nineteenth on Pethahiah; the twentieth on Jehezkel; the twenty-first on Jachin; the twenty-second on Gamul; the twenty-third on Delaiah; the twenty-fourth on Maaziah.

In Nehemiah 11, a list of those who lived in Jerusalem during that period of restoration, we read:

> Of the priests: Jedaiah son of Joiarib, Jachin, Seraiah son of Hilkiah ...

Neh.11:10

It is possible that these texts have been tampered with in order to raise the prominence of this clan.[5] If so, this tampering may have been done later, because it was not sufficient to help Judas with his ambitions. While Judas was from an

---

[3] Note the Greek names, as I have discussed above.
[4] 1Macc.14:29 is also careful to trace this line.
[5] See the discussion in Goldstein *I Maccabees* 17.

ancient and well-known priestly family, his lineage was simply not good enough, however, to legitimize him as High Priest.

Let us say that Judas was the High Priest *de facto* at *Hanukkah* but then lost it to Alcimus *de jure*. At some point, Judas would have every reason to become angry that he was no longer in control of the temple that he had restored. He may not have initially been angry with Alcimus, whom he would not have seen as a political force. It is possible that Judas' hands were tied because he himself had appointed Alcimus to a prominent priestly position (though not the High Priesthood itself). If Judas did not trust Alcimus from the start, there seems to have been nothing he could do. By the time of Alcimus' appointment by the Seleucids, Judas seems to have been too politically and militarily weak to do anything at all. He could not have been pleased. He was unhappy not just at Alcimus but that things had not gone as he had had every right to hope. Others, such as the *Asidaioi*, did not have Judas' rivalry and ambition problems and were perfectly willing to deal with Alcimus.

With the coming of Nicanor, we now have a triangle, of the Syrian commander, Alcimus and Judas. We follow 2Maccabees here, which would hardly make up a close relationship between Nicanor and Judas.

> Nicanor spent time at Jerusalem and conducted himself irreproachably. He dismissed the undisciplined mobs that had thronged around him. Continually, he kept Judas in his company. He was sincerely fond of the man. He urged him to marry and beget children He did marry; he experienced tranquility; he partook of life's blessings.
> 2Macc.14:23-25

Alcimus, now the odd man out, cannot handle that Nicanor and Judas have become so friendly. He may very well have been suspicious that Judas's friendship with Nicanor was to acquire the High Priesthood for himself. Indeed, it may have been that. After all, what was this relationship about? What if it were exactly as the text says, a relationship of peers, a mutual admiration society? Judas could have become High Priest and leader of his people under the rule of the Seleucid Empire. It is strange that both primary and secondary sources call Alcimus a collaborator at a time such as this when Judas is capable of such a relationship. The entire story might have gone in this extremely positive direction for Judas. Instead, the relationship deteriorated under the pressure of the king, who had been influenced by the charges by Alcimus against Nicanor.

The Re-evaluation of Alcimus

Alcimus, however, on perceiving their mutual goodwill, took a copy of the treaty they had made and came before Demetrius, saying that Nicanor had hostile designs against the state: indeed, he had appointed as his deputy Judas, the plotter against Demetrius' kingdom.
2Macc.14:26

Alcimus' appeal to the king had its desired effect and pressure was brought to bear on Nicanor not only to end the close relationship but also to imprison Judas and send him to Antioch in chains.[6]

To answer our question: Menelaus was the *de jure* High Priest at *Hanukkah*; the event occurred during his appointment by the Seleucids. It does not seem possible that Menelaus could be High Priest during this festival after everything he had done. It would seem that he would be the last person alive to be able to function in this capacity. And yet we cannot even say that Judas was the *de facto* High Priest at *Hanukkah* because he seemed to be limited by his lineage.

Hanukkah was instituted in December 165 BCE. If one says that our choice is between Menelaus and Alcimus, and Menelaus was *persona non grata* at the Temple, that leaves the possibility of Alcimus. In order to make a case that Alcimus was the High Priest of *Hanukkah*, however, one would have to postulate that our primary sources are wrong and keep Alcimus' appointment until later so that he should not be considered the High Priest of *Hanukkah*. Considering the polemical nature of our sources, this is not impossible. We conclude, nevertheless, that Alcimus may have been functioning as a prominent priest at the Temple but would not become the High Priest until appointed by Antiochus V two years later.

When Did Alcimus Become High Priest?

The question of the timing of Alcimus' appointment as High Priest raises a controversy.[7] Was Alcimus already High Priest during the reign of Antiochus V (163 BCE) or did Demetrius I appoint him for the first time in 162 BCE? The problem is that our two most important ancient sources contradict each other. While 1Maccabees states that Alcimus became High Priest in the autumn of 162 BCE, appointed for the first time by Demetrius I (7:5ff.), 2Maccabees tells us that Alcimus was appointed High Priest under Antiochus V after the removal of

---

[6] 2Macc.14:27.
[7] Wolfgang Mölleken "Geschichtsklitterung im I. Makkabäerbuch" (Wann wurde Alkimus Hohenpriester?)" *ZAW* 65 (1953) 205-28.

Menelaus (163-62 BCE), had voluntarily defiled himself and lost the High Priesthood, and was re-appointed by Demetrius I (162 BCE). Alcimus here is High Priest for four years under the reigns of both Antiochus V and Demetrius. It is interesting that 2Maccabees tells us about the earlier appointment as a kind of afterthought. That is, we are only told about the appointment when the later appointment is discussed (2Macc.14:3). Josephus, who (most scholars insist) follows 1Maccabees and may not have even regarded 2Maccabees as important, says that Alcimus is appointed after the disposal and exile of Menelaus. Soon after the rise of Demetrius I to the throne in 162 BCE, the Hellenistic party, led by Alcimus, speaks to the new king of their oppression by Judas and of Judas' murder of the king's adherents. Alcimus is appointed High Priest.

If, as 2Maccabees states and Josephus implies, Alcimus were High Priest well before this appointment is said to have happened in 1Maccabees, why would 1Maccabees not render this event factually? Why does it say that Demetrius I appointed Alcimus for the first time? Scholarly answers are weak at best. Goldstein explains that the omission in 1Maccabees of any reference to the appointment of Alcimus during the reign of Antiochus V shows that "our author reflects the Hasmonaean position that Antiochus V was an illegitimate ruler with no right to appoint a High Priest."[8] Yet since the same author does mention how Demetrius I appoints Alcimus, why does he not mention the appointment of Alcimus during the reign of Antiochus V? The appointment by Demetrius would be as illegitimate as the appointment by Antiochus V. Bunge says that the author of 1Maccabees postpones Alcimus' appointment because he wants to give the impression that the appointment was a reward for murdering the *Asidaioi*. But he is appointed before the massacre, not afterwards; the massacre occurs because the *Asidaioi* trust in the new appointee. Bar-Kochva thinks that 2Maccabees' statement about the appointment by Antiochus V means that the Seleucid authorities officially appointed Alcimus after Menelaus' execution at the end of the expedition by the king and Lysias. This explanation does not make sense. If Alcimus was appointed at the end of Antiochus V's campaign, then Antiochus V appointed Alcimus.

Scholars such as Grabbe, Sievers, and Shafer who follow 2Maccabees and say that Alcimus was appointed by Antiochus V and Lysias after the removal of Menelaus are on more solid ground. In spring 163 BCE, Lysias invaded again and

---

[8] Goldstein *I Maccabees* 325.

defeated Judas decisively. Lysias seems to have realized that there could be no peace with the Jews as long as Menelaus was the High Priest. Lysias had Menelaus executed, appointing Alcimus in his place. When Demetrius I became king, Alcimus asked him for help against Judas who still opposed Alcimus; the new Seleucid king sent Bacchides back with Alcimus.

When Was Alcimus Appointed? A Reconstruction

In attempting to ascertain the timing of Alcimus' appointment, we need to focus on the details of the events during the years 165-162 BCE. Let us review some key dates.[9]

April 4, 165 BCE - Judas' army defeats the expeditions of Apollonius and Seron.

May-June 165 BCE - Antiochus marches to the eastern part of his empire and leaves Lysias in charge of his minor son Antiochus IV and the western part of the empire. In response to an appeal by Philip, the royal commander at Jerusalem, a strong force led by Nicanor and Gorgias attempt to defeat Judas but is soundly defeated by him.

164 BCE - Lysias himself attacks Judas at Beth-Zur. While Lysias takes heavy losses, he seems to withdraw because of the entreaties of both non-Hasmonaean pious Jews and Menelaus.[10] On March 12, Lysias sends a letter offering Jews amnesty, an end to the imposed cult and permission to observe the *Torah*. Judas, in control of the temple and Jerusalem, disallows Menelaus from exercising his High Priestly prerogatives.[11] Pious priests purify the temple and destroy the Abomination of Desolation,[12] they prepare an altar for sacrifice and temple vessels.[13] They remove the illicit lattice from the temple court (*Megillat Ta'anit*). On September 18, 164 BCE, the sacrifice of meal offerings is resumed at the temple (*Megillat Ta'anit*).

Oct. 16th, 164 BCE (the 25th of Kislev) – The rededication of the Temple is celebrated and an annual holiday of *Hanukkah* is instituted. Since Judas does not

---

[9] I base this review on Goldstein's painstaking and thoughtful chronology,
[10] 1Macc.4:28-35; 2Macc.11:1-21, 29.
[11] 1Macc.36-61; 2Macc.10:1-8.
[12] 1Macc.4:42-46; 2Macc.10:3; Dan.11:24.
[13] 1Macc.4:47-48; 2Macc.10:3.

claim the High Priesthood, and since he appointed priests to conduct the rites and supervise its purification, it is perfectly conceivable that one of these priests was Alcimus.

In **November or early December 164 BCE**, Antiochus IV dies in Persia. While Antiochus IV had chosen Philip to replace Lysias as guardian of his minor son Antiochus V, Lysias retains control and Philip has to flee to Egypt (perhaps in early 163 BCE).

Late 164 to April 163 BCE - Judas wins victories against Idumaea and Azotus as well as Seleucid officials.[14] He fortifies the Temple mount and Beth-Zur.[15] It is not a coincidence that Judas has these successes during a time that the Seleucids are preoccupied with a power struggle among themselves.

On **February 8, 163 BCE**, Antiochus V's letter to the Jews reaches Jerusalem.[16] He announces Antiochus IV's death and promises the continued religious autonomy of the Jews and their temple. It is striking, however, that neither Judas not Antiochus V/Lysias views this religious statement as marking an end to political hostilities.

Judas gathers an army and besieges the *Akra* in the **late spring of 163 BCE**. In response, Antiochus V/Lysias attack Beth-Zur. Judas has to lift the siege of the *Akra* to attempt to help Beth-Zur. Judas loses the battle of Beth-Zechariah and Beth-Zur surrenders. The Jews in the temple are besieged.[17]

At some point between June 28, 163 BCE (when the military campaign began) and early 162 BCE (January or March 5, when full peace is made), Antiochus V removes Menelaus from the High Priesthood[18] and appoints Alcimus as the High Priest.[19] 2Macc.13:3 is very clear in stating that Menelaus came before the king at the very beginning of the campaign. He no doubt wanted to be restored to full rights over the Temple, from which he had been excluded by Judas) and the country in general. If we say that Menelaus was deposed by July, we still do not know when Alcimus was appointed.

---

[14] 1Macc.5:65-68.
[15] 1Macc.4:60-61.
[16] 2Macc.11:23-26.
[17] 1Macc.6:48-54.
[18] 2Macc.13:3-8.
[19] 2Macc.14:3.

The Re-evaluation of Alcimus

We can home in on the timing of Alcimus' appointment by ascertaining when Antiochus V and Lysias would have come to Jerusalem and his motives in making the appointment. The large force assembled by the Seleucids seems to have made quick progress in defeating the Jews both at Beth-Zur and Beth-Zechariah. With the Hasmonaeans in defeat, the way was clear for Antiochus V to come triumphantly to Jerusalem, perhaps still in the summer of 163 BCE. Once there, any attempt to end the rebellion and restore order and calm could only benefit by appointing a legitimate High Priest who would be accepted by all. Alcimus fit this description. By *Yom Kippur* **of 163 BCE**, Alcimus would have been the High Priest over the holy rites. It is logical that the appointment of Alcimus, in the context of restoration of traditional ways, must have been based on a High Priestly pedigree or at least prominent priestly lineage. Otherwise, he would not have been acceptable, especially in this context and at a moment of attempted reconciliation and appeasement. In view of all this, Onias IV realized that he did not have any grounds for hope and left for Egypt. If Alcimus would not have been a Zadokite, Onias IV could have still dreamed of being appointed to the office.

> Before leaving to crush an insurrection back at Antioch, Antiochus demolishes the wall around the Temple mount.

In autumn 162 BCE, Demetrius I returns from Rome and becomes the new emperor. He confirms Alcimus as the High Priest and sends Bacchides with him to Judaea. Bacchides slays *Asidaioi* leaders and other rebels and leaves Alcimus in control.

With Bacchides gone, Judas re-emerges in the countryside. Nicanor is sent to help Alcimus. Nicanor and Judas fight a minor skirmish at Dessau that resolves nothing. Nicanor and Judas create a friendly relationship. Alcimus complains to Demetrius and on **March 8, 161 BCE**, Nicanor and Judas have their climactic battle at Adasa and Nicanor is defeated and killed.

Notice that Alcimus remains as High Priest even after Judas' new victory. If he were an unacceptable "Hellenizer," or an illegitimate High Priest in any way, Judas would have been quick to dispose of him. Alcimus must not only have been legitimate but also a proper steward of the sacred rites.

Demetrius I sends Bacchides back to Judaea. He reaches Jerusalem in **April, 160 BCE** and soon defeats Judas' small force at Elasa (1Macc.9:4-21). Judas dies;

Alcimus is still High Priest at the time and will be until his death no sooner than the next year.

The answer to the question is that Alcimus was appointed in 163 BCE during the reign of Antiochus V.

How then, do we reconcile the sources? Compromise positions, such as that of Bevan who says that Demetrius I appointed Alcimus in the spring of 161 BCE and had only held the High Priesthood "for a moment the year before," are an attempt to reconcile the sources. Such theories may not be as ridiculous as they seem. Alcimus, appointed by Antiochus V, may have lost his position through defilement, then to be re-appointed by Demetrius I. The voluntary defilement of 2Maccabees, which we will discuss below, remains interesting, as if it is a compromise position between admitting Alcimus as a High Priest before the rise of Demetrius I and claiming that he was not High Priest before that point. It seems that all of the sources resist admitting that Alcimus was the legitimate High Priest of a purely traditional temple for any length of time.

Who Was Alcimus?

Why was Alcimus chosen by the Seleucids to be High Priest? Was he a priest? Was he an Oniad? Was he the brother of Menelaus? Was he the nephew or stepson of Yoseʿ ben Yoʿezer?

1Maccabees states that Alcimus is a priest "of the stock of Aaron" but does not tell us his father's name or his priestly clan. We do not know anything else about his lineage except that the *Asidaioi* respected it enough to initially trust him. 2Maccabees is even more vague, calling him "a certain Alcimus." Josephus claims that Alcimus was a priest of the stock of Aaron but not an Oniad. He was not a brother of Menelaus (who, according to Josephus, was an Oniad).

From these sources, Alcimus seems to have been chosen as a pious man of the right stock who was neither a Hasmonaean nor a "Hellenizer." We do not know of any connection to Yose ben Yoʿezer from these sources, but the rabbinic texts do make this connection in very dramatic ways.

Was Alcimus an Oniad-Zadokite and thus a legitimate High Priest? Sievers, Grabbe and Schafer think that Alcimus was an Oniad. Neither 1 nor 2Maccabees say that he was *not* an Oniad. He was appointed to an office held by this family. The *Asidaioi* accepted him. Tcherikover points out that 2Macc.14:7 says that Alcimus saw the High Priesthood as an "ancestral inheritance," which could only mean that

The Re-evaluation of Alcimus

he was indeed a Zadokite-Oniad. No simple priest would see the High Priesthood as his due. Tcherikover, Graetz, Schafer and Bevan think that Alcimus was an Oniad "Hellenizer" from among the "wealthy and well born," and thus acceptable to one side; his Oniad pedigree, coupled with the end of the "persecution"/"reform" and the rededication of the Temple satisfied the nationalists/traditionalists who had supported Judas. Zeitlin, supposedly following Josephus, who says nothing of the kind, thinks that Alcimus was "probably the brother of Onias -Menelaus." Rooke disagrees and says that a strong indication that Menelaus was not an Aaronide is the contrast that is made to Alcimus, who was an Aaronide though not a Zadokite. Alcimus would not have greeted with such approval by the *Asidaioi* if he were just another non-Aaronide Seleucid appointee to the High Priesthood or if his legitimacy was not greatly superior to that of Menelaus. Menelaus was a non-Aaronide from the tribe of Benjamin.[20]

Bickerman, Bar-Kochva and Graetz see Alcimus as a "moderate" who was "loyal to the Seleucid authorities." These scholars think that Alcimus was the nephew of Yose ben Yo'ezer of Zeredah. Zeredah is Surda near Gophna. An ossuary found in a burial cave near Gophna[21] has an inscription that says "Salome, wife (or daughter) of Yakeimos." Vincent has suggested that this was Alcimus' wife.[22] There were many priests at Gophna according to PT *Ta'anith* 24b.[23] Thus we may have evidence of a geographic/family link between the two figures.

To answer the question: Alcimus was a Zadokite who was the nephew of Yosi b.Yo'ezer. We have to understand what it was about Yosi b.Yo'ezer that made his death such a decisive incident. In the rabbinic mind, history would never be the same after his death. We would suggest that the manner of his death was a part of this. The trauma of his brutal death may have led to the kind of additional fame that is accorded a martyr. The story transmitted in *Genesis Rabba/Midrash Tehillim* may

---

[20] It is true that Josephus makes Onias III, Jason and Menelaus as brothers but Josephus would also have Onias III and Menelaus with the same name (Onias, before Menelaus changed it). Why would Josephus do this? One possibility is that the text is garbled, but another is that it was unthinkable to Josephus that there was a high priest who was not an Aaronide and so he makes Menelaus a member of the high priestly family.

[21] *CIJ* II, 1172.

[22] H. Vincent "Un hypogee juif a Djifneh" *RB* 10 (1913) 103-6.

[23] E. L. Sukenik "An Ancient Jewish Cave on the Jerusalem-Shechem Road" *Bulletin of the Israeli Exploration Society* I (1933) 7-9.

be a reflection of the process by which Yosi b.Yoʻezer's fame grew. What if, as *Genesis Rabba/Midrash Tehillim* have it, he was crucified by his nephew, the man on whom he and his colleagues and supporters had placed so much hope? Alcimus, Yosi b.Yoʻezer's nephew, should have been the righteous High Priest, another Simeon the Just. Instead, at least according to his detractors such as the Hasmonaeans, he took a different path. So the rabbis became the chain.

Did Alcimus Voluntarily Defile Himself?

According to 2Macc.14:3, Alcimus "had voluntarily defiled himself during the time of peace." What does this mean? Modern scholars interpret this verse in very different ways. We must remember that scholars often attempt to reconcile the different sources. In 1Maccabees, Alcimus approaches Demetrius to gain or regain the High Priesthood. What is different in 2Maccabees is that there is no massacre of the *Asidaioi* or anything like it.

> Perceiving that there was no way for him to be secure or to have access henceforth to the holy altar, (4) he approached King Demetrius I in about the year 151 and presented him with a gold crown and palm along with some of the customary gifts from the temple.

Alcimus has both a political problem, he is not secure in his position, and a ritual one, he cannot gain access to the holy altar and therefore he cannot act as High Priest. We can readily understand Alcimus' political problem because we know how powerful Judas is. But what has he done to defile himself? Since he is High Priest, who is stopping him if he is defiled?

The Ritual Interpretation

One school of thought is that the verse indicates that even though he was not under coercion by the Greeks, Alcimus was a willing participant in the Hellenization of the Temple. For instance, Bevan states "that the High Priesthood was conferred upon a man of proper Aaronide descent Eliakim, who nevertheless belonged to the "Hellenizing" party and had incurred pollution by pagan practices in the days of the persecution."[24] Perhaps Bevan bases the idea that Alcimus

---

[24] Bevan "Syria and the Jews" 517.

The Re-evaluation of Alcimus

polluted himself in pagan practices on the "voluntary defilement" in 2Macc.14:3. It is not clear, however, what either 2Maccabees or Bevan means by this. Is it that Alcimus was a priest before the re-sanctification of the Temple and participated in the pagan cult? Why does 2Macc.14:3 talk about Alcimus' action "in the time of peace," that is, not during the persecution? If Alcimus were defiled, why would the *Asidaioi*, or any of the Judaeans who were against the pagan cult, have accepted him as High Priest? If we are speaking not of the time of the persecution but after the Temple had been re-sanctified, what did Alcimus do wrong? Would these sources not have been eager to level a specific charge against him?

The Political Interpretation

Sievers, speaking of the various responses to persecution, describes Alcimus as one who responded to the persecution of the Judaeans by Antiochus Epiphanes with "voluntary compliance." He connects the "voluntary defilement" of 2Macc.14:3 to this category and says that it may refer to Alcimus' actions before, during, or after the persecution. According to Gruen, the Jews who were hated collaborators with the Seleucids were sometimes referred to as "impious." Josephus also calls Menelaus "impious."[25] Alcimus is one who "carried the stigma of "impiety" from the vantage point of the Maccabees. But Gruen states that, "he had certainly not forsaken Jewish traditions for the lure of the Greek culture."

Goldstein explains that the last part of v.3, even with its textual complexity, can be used to elucidate its political nature. There are different manuscript readings of v.3. L' (a group of Lucianic manuscripts), 58 (a minuscule), 311 (another minuscule), La^{-BM} (an Old Latin manuscript) and Sy (the Syriac version) read *epimixias* "of peace." On the other hand, the reading *amixias* is found in the uncials A and V and the group of minuscules referred to as *q*; the meaning here is that Alcimus defiled himself in the time of "separation."[26] The matter is even more complex because *amixia* can indicate the unwilling to "mix" with foreigners while *epimixia* is the antonym that means a willingness to "mix" with foreigners. Based on the use of *amixia* in 14:38, however, where in referring to the Jewish elder Razis' martyrdom in the face of persecution it clearly means "war/persecution," *epimixia*

---

[25] *Ant.* 12.385.
[26] For these manuscript readings see Goldstein *II Maccabees* 125-126 and 483. For the different readings also see Doran *Second Book of Maccabees* 285.

here would mean "a time of peace," following the root meaning of a time when people could "mix" together in safety. The question is which reading is original, *epimixias* or *amixias*. Razis, in a time of *amixia*, refused to defile himself. Did Alcimus (at least supposedly) defile himself in a time of persecution or a time of safety? The answer seems to be that as opposed to Razis who would not defile himself even at a moment of severe persecution (*amixia*), Alcimus defiled himself voluntarily at a time of *epimixia* when he was under no pressure to do so. The manuscript readings that use *amixia* may have been influenced by v.38 or their own expectations.[27]

Doran states that the text is not speaking of ritual defilement at all but of a disgrace, a disgrace avoided by Judas when he left Jerusalem "in order to keep clear of defilement" (2Macc.5:27). Judas and his followers need to stay clear of the uncleanness that is apparently brought by Apollonius the Mysarch. There may be a play on words here since *Mysós* in Greek means Mysian and *mýsos* means "unclean"; indeed, the Syriac here translates "Mysarch" as "chief of the unclean." The author of 2Maccabees may be consciously contrasting Alcimus' actions to the behavior of both Judas and Razis (cf. 14:38) in avoiding defilement and/or disgrace.

Thus, one theory is that Alcimus never did defile himself in any way and that Jason of Cyrene is, very simply, making it up in order to pursue his goal of undermining a High Priest that he despised. After all, if Alcimus had truly ritually defiled himself, would 1Maccabees have refrained from saying so? Defilement here means collaboration with the Seleucids, and yet, as much as 1 and 2Maccabees condemn such acts, they do not constitute ritual defilement. This explanation is contrary to the text, which clearly says that Alcimus did not have access to the holy altar because of his defilement. To stay with the meaning of 2Maccabees, then, we have to insist that Alcimus had defiled himself through his actions and that a general state of disgrace is not the sense of the text.

Defilement through Murder

Some such as Habicht[28] think that the killing of the sixty *Asidaioi* constituted this defilement. However, it is illogical to say that 2Macc.14:3 is a reference to the murder of the *Asidaioi* that has not yet happened. If Alcimus had gone through a

---

[27] See Goldstein *II Maccabees* 484 n. 3.
[28] C. Habicht *2 Makkabaerbuch* JSHRZ 1/3 (Gutersloh, 1976) 271.

The Re-evaluation of Alcimus

"voluntary defilement," it could not be before he first became High Priest. The Seleucids would not have selected a problematic candidate. They wanted a respected and pious priest about whom everyone could agree, one about whom even Judas could not say anything negative.

"Defile" is a translation for the Greek verb *molynein*, which is never used in the Greek translation of the Bible for the common Hebrew root for ritual uncleanness, *tm'*. While Goldstein thinks that Alcimus' sin is one of bloodshed, based on a misunderstanding of the use of the verb in the LXX, Alcimus could not have been involved in a murder; anyone involved in a capital crime would have risked his life to enter the temple at all. Alcimus also would have been forbidden to enter the temple if he had worshipped an idol, another capital crime that incurs defilement. Alcimus could not have been rendered unclean by involvement in murder or idol worship; once unclean or defiled in this manner, he could not be restored to a state of purity.

Defilement through Traveling to a Gentile Land

Another choice is that the verse is chronologically confused and should indicate that the voluntary defilement occurred when Alcimus went to see Demetrius; he went outside of the land of Israel to the Gentile country of Syria. While the idea of the impurity of Gentile lands originated in early times (Josh. 22:19; Amos 7:17), it became a *halakhah* by the decree of Yosi b.Yo'ezer and Yosi b.Yoḥanan (BT*Shabbat* 14b; cf. Tosefta. *Parah* 3:5):

> Yosi b.Yo'ezer of Ṣeredah and Yosi b.Yoḥanan of Jerusalem decreed (*gzr*) [the capacity to receive] uncleanness (*ṭwm'h*) upon the land of the peoples and on glassware.

Ginzberg thinks that the Yosi's declare uncleanness on both foreign countries and glassware in order to attempt to stem the tide of emigration from Judaea at the time of the persecutions of Antiochus IV.[29] By saying that would-be emigrants would be going to an impure place, Ginzberg theorizes, the Yosi's were trying to keep them in their homeland. Ginzberg also thinks that glassware was expensive but might be preferred to locally made earthenware and metal dishes because the former

---

[29] Ginzberg "The Significance of the Halachah for Jewish History" 77-126.

could not become impure but the latter could. While the theory that this decree was meant to discourage emigration from Israel during the Antiochene persecutions has generally been discounted as not having any basis in the sources,[30] one must still account for a ruling that could not have been taken very seriously by other sages such as Joshua b.Peraḥiah and Judah b.Ṭabbai who went to Alexandria or by the Mishnah that assumes that Jewish people will live in other countries. Why did the Yosi's enact this decree at this time?

The chronological issue is very important to these considerations. If this voluntary defilement were before or during the persecution, why would anyone accept Alcimus as High Priest in the first place? After all, Alcimus became High Priest well after the persecution in a time when the religious persecution had been lifted. The royal governor elevated Alcimus with the full support of an assembly of doctors of the law that he convened (1Macc.7:12). The new High Priest was considered legitimate by everyone, Seleucid authority and Jewish conservative alike. Alcimus, acknowledged by the people and supported by royal troops,[31] ruled the temple state. The Maccabees became renegades who were hunted by the authorities; the people did not follow them at this point. Notice that Alcimus remained as High Priest, even after Judas' new victory. If Alcimus were an unacceptable "Hellenizer," or an illegitimate High Priest in any way, Judas would have been quick to dispose of him. Alcimus must not only have been legitimate but also a proper steward of the sacred rites. Whatever this defilement was, it seems to be something that he did as High Priest.

The assumption seems to be that the writer of 2Maccabees sees defilement as permanent disqualification. Yet it is totally illogical to think that the *Asidaioi* accepted Alcimus at a point when he was still in a state of defilement. If defilement here means what it does in the *Torah*, and Alcimus had served as High Priest or even entered the temple while "unclean," he would been "cut off" according to the clear rulings of Lev.22:3 and Num. 19: 13, 20. Alcimus could not return to his

---

[30] Neusner retorts that glassware was cheap and that the masses did not keep the purity laws (Neusner, *Rabbinic Traditions about the Pharisees* Vol. III 338-339).
[31] 1Macc.9:24ff.,

The Re-evaluation of Alcimus

position if he had been "cut off."[32] Another problem is that, according to both the *Torah* and later rabbinic law, an individual cannot intentionally incur permanent uncleanness.[33]

Since the *Asidaioi* accept Alcimus, the writer of 2Maccabees seems to be talking about a defilement that did *not* mean permanent disqualification. This "defilement" is illogical in terms of the laws of purity. Either the impurity would be of such a great degree that Alcimus could never be restored to his position or of such a low degree that he would have been restored in a matter of hours or days. The time involved in rituals to restore purity is only until evening for the lesser degrees of impurity (Lev.11:24-27) and a mere seven days for the higher degrees (Lev.12:2).

Sexual Defilement

Nevertheless, we insist that Alcimus defiled himself in some sexually related way that would not mean permanent disqualification. "The separation" in *epimixia* is the separation required of one defiled. The consequences of the laws of impurity are only serious for priests who are involved in matters of the temple and its sacred vessels. As Maimonides puts it:

> It is permissible to touch things that are impure and to incur impurity from them, for Scripture warns none but the sons of Aaron and the Nazirite against incurring impurity from a corpse, thereby implying that for all others it is permissible, and that even for priests and Nazirites it is permissible to incur impurity from other impure things, but not from a corpse.[34]

Still, they were of the utmost importance for priests, particularly the high priest. What if Alcimus had disregarded the required period for restoration to purity and had officiated in his role as high priest before fulfilling the purification period? Who, at this time, would have taken Alcimus to task for his defilement rather than Yosi b.Yo'ezer? Yosi was one of the greatest teachers about purity in the history of

---

[32] Later rabbinic law would condemn Alcimus to "death at the hands of Heaven," which might leave matters, so to speak, up in the air, or lynching, a human and therefore certain punishment (Mishnah *Sanhedrin* 9:6; BT *Keritot* 1:5; BT *Sanhedrin* 82b-83a.)

[33] "Purity and Impurity, Ritual," *Encyclopedia Judaica* XIII (1972) 1405-12.

[34] Maimonides *Yad, Tumat Okhelim* 16:8-9, as trans. in "Purity and Impurity, Ritual," 1410.

Judaism. Since *epimixia* is about sexual defilement, then the whole verse is about sexual impurity and not about anything else. I return to the evidence I brought above in discussing the documents from Qumran. In both *MMT* and *CD*, there seems to be a charge of sexual defilement against the current high priest; interestingly, both texts offer the example of David whom God forgave for such sins. While there may have been an initial willingness to forgive Alcimus if he would make the necessary changes, an unwillingness to do so might well have been the issue that divided Alcimus from those holding him to a strict interpretation of purity laws, including his famous uncle.

It is very possible that Jason artificially created a defilement that never was and that the confusion of the sources demonstrates the desperate attempts to condemn Alcimus, a high priest who carried out his duties in a proper and sacred way. Yet I re-iterate the possibility that 2Maccabees' report of Alcimus' defilement, which forced him to beseech Demetrius I in order to regain access to the holy altar and the full position, may reflect a public argument over purity laws that had historical consequences. It was an argument between Alcimus and Yosi b.Yoʿezer that culminated in the death of the latter and perhaps was involved in the creation of the sect at Qumran.

Was Alcimus a Religious Conservative Or a "Hellenizer"?

What religious and anti-religious actions did Alcimus take? Did his religious position change after he took office?

The evidence is mixed and quite complex. According to 1Maccabees, Alcimus seems to have strong ties to the Hellenizers, which indicates his general religious stance before becoming high priest. And yet Alcimus wrote Psalm 79 and may well have been a functioning priest and a religious figure before his appointment as high priest. For Bickerman and Gruen, while Alcimus "carried the stigma of "impiety" from the vantage point of the Maccabees, he had "certainly not forsaken Jewish traditions." The two letters preserved in 2Macc.11:16-38 (from 164 and 163) should be emphasized. In one, the king writes to the Jews, granting them amnesty and a resumption of their religious laws. What is striking is that the king writes the letter because of a visit by Menelaus, who is to return to the entire people, not just the "Hellenizers, "with the letter in hand. Lysias writes the second conciliatory letter on the basis of a cordial exchange with Jewish emissaries (with Hebrew names). The basic agreement expressed in these letters would retain their force even through

The Re-evaluation of Alcimus

the struggles of these years. The Seleucids no longer sought the "abandonment of Jewish faith, let alone conformity with Hellenic practices." Gruen's analysis is extremely important for my purpose here, because Alcimus is appointed at this point in time. It would not make sense for the Seleucids to appoint a "Hellenizing" high priest at the very moment that they had explicitly moved away from religious Hellenization. The pagan impositions on the cult are necessary background for what occurs during the time of Alcimus. It is clear why the Temple in Jerusalem needed to be re-dedicated to God. Alcimus was a priest who had not participated in the pagan cult; if he had, no one, especially the *Asidaioi*, would have accepted him.

Again, notice well 1Macc.4:42's emphasis on the change in personnel that was made: "He (Judas) appointed unblemished priests, lovers of the Torah, who purified the sanctuary." If the Maccabees were priests themselves, why did they need these other priests? The text is clear that the priests were not only "unblemished," which I take to mean undefiled by participation in the new pagan cult, but "lovers of Torah," which might say something about their sectarian affiliation. Could both of these characteristics point to Alcimus? Could Alcimus have been one of the priests mentioned in 1Macc.4:42, indeed, a prominent one among them, who was then in place to be appointed by Antiochus V and Lysias? Perhaps Judas could not object to the appointment because he had appointed Alcimus to a lower position himself.

According to 2Maccabees, his "voluntary defilement" seems to involve some kind of action that leads to ritual impurity, rendering him unfit for the duties of the high priest. Some take this to indicate that Alcimus was not a religious conservative. Yet according to Josephus (following 1Maccabees), proper sacrifices were conducted at the Temple during his term and we do not see any improper worship during this time. The priests in the Temple under his tenure offered a burnt offering for the Seleucid king which considering the resulting disdain and threats from Nicanor, may indicate that Alcimus' temple was traditional in its mode of practice.

Alcimus wanted to tear down the wall of the inner court of the Temple, usually seen as an action against a religious stance of barring non-priests from the most sacred area, an important traditional rule. The controversy is seen as a demonstration of a conflict between Jewish ideas of separateness and Gentile ideas of assimilation. Alcimus' action is seen as a major action supporting the latter side. He did so to erase the distinction between Judaeans and Gentiles, and to allow pagans free access to the inner court. Rooke says that Alcimus' action in the Temple was based on "a policy of anti-particularism which would make freer access to the

Temple for everyone, and is usually thought to be an attempt to demolish the wall separating the court of the Gentiles from the rest of the Temple." The layout of the temple as well as the strict observance of purity regulations was considered to be of great importance in certain circles.

For Graetz, however, while Alcimus is reproached by some sources and historians for the violation of the Temple, this action, "on careful examination, hardly seems to have been a sin against the religion of the Judaeans."[35] Could Alcimus' action be one involving a sectarian controversy? When he destroyed the wall of the "Temple Court," which the pro-Hasmonaean narrator of 1Macc.9:54 condemned, Alcimus may actually have been acting in accord with the interpretation of Essenes who condemned "the builders of the wall."[36] After Judas died, Alcimus was in a position of great strength, without a major rival. Whatever it was that he attempted to do with Temple architecture, he could do it because he did not have a problem with other factions. While the ancient sources may say that his death was a punishment for this action, it is interesting to note that there is no record of a human controversy about it (unless the Qumran references to "the Builders of the Wall" point to such an argument). It would be interesting if Alcimus' action has been completely misunderstood and was actually done to placate the Qumran sect who had become so disaffected with his policies. At worst, Alcimus may have eventually succumbed to political pressure in committing a controversial act but there is no reason to think that he did anything of the kind before that moment in 159 BCE.[37]

---

[35] Graetz *History of the Jews* 492.

[36] CD 4:19; 8:12, 18.

[37] The fact that his death is described as punishment for this act makes this all the more suspect, historically speaking. 1Macc.9:54ff. and Josephus *AJ* XII.413 say that Alcimus suffered a stroke from God and died after many days of torment. Alcimus, according to the rabbinic notices, died by suicide and not at the hands of the Greeks. According to 1Maccabees and Josephus, he came to a terrible end, stricken with a painful and debilitating paralysis. The suicide contradicts the paralysis. Both stories of his death are clearly tendentious. In the Rabbinic story, he commits suicide in repentance for what he did to Yosi b.Yo'ezer. In the 1Maccabees/Josephus story, we have a parallel to the death of Heliodorus[37] who also died in attempting to commit sacrilege to the Temple. Perhaps the third version of his death in the Qumran scrolls, by the hands of his so-called foreign friends, is also tendentious. The Seleucids did not kill Alcimus, as this text would insist.

The Re-evaluation of Alcimus

159

Despite the fact that all of these sources are clearly anti-Alcimus, notice that we do not have here an outright general denunciation of Alcimus' religious position.[38] Thus, with the exception of his last action concerning the wall of the Temple, which may or may not have been a violation of Jewish practice, we do not see any evidence that Alcimus was a "Hellenizer."

Did Alcimus Write a Psalm?

If Alcimus wrote a psalm, he was a religious figure with poetic and spiritual feelings and expressions that were well known.

According to 1Maccabees, Alcimus himself wrote Psalm 79. 1Maccabees cites it as *kata logon hon egrapsen auton* "according to the word which he himself had written." Grimm sees this as a reference to the fact that the psalm was already Holy Scripture.[39] What does Psalm 79 refer to? Since Alcimus wrote it, the reference to what the enemy has done to Jerusalem may be to the sack of Jerusalem by Antiochus IV in 169 BCE or to the Mysarch's expedition in 167 BCE. There is nothing in either 2Maccabees or Josephus either to support or reject this possibility.

The implications of the Dead Sea Scrolls are intriguing here. While the evidence from Qumran would seem to point against the possible authorship of Alcimus for Psalm 79, one should not be too quick to judge against the possibility on this basis. There is nothing in the Qumran evidence or the statement in Ben Sira to preclude this possibility. On the contrary, Sanders' suggestion that the fluid third portion of

---

In short, there is no reason to accept any of the three versions of the death of Alcimus. If the Qumran text does not concern Alcimus, there is still no reason to accept either a sudden stroke from sacrilege or a suicide in repentance.

[38] For Zeitlin (and Sievers), Alcimus, "while a Hellenist, did not entirely subvert Judaism." Graetz agrees and says that Alcimus, while a leader of the Hellenizers, did not belong to the extreme Hellenists. He was merely an ambitious man who always worshipped the rising power. Finkelstein says that Alcimus was of the old high-priestly nobility that believed that peace could be restored without the oppressive decrees of *Epiphanes* and with the Temple functioning according to Jewish law. Bevan states that, "Alcimus was at first welcomed by the godly, as a man of the house of Aaron, though opposed, of course, by the Hasmonaean brethren and their partisans....Yet Alcimus soon forfeited the goodwill of the godly by his conduct."

[39] C. L. Grimm *Kurzgefasstes exegetisches Handbuch zu den Apokryphen* (Leipzig, 1853) 111.

the Psalter includes poems that were "actually Hasidic and proto-Essene" is intriguing. If the third part of the Psalter that includes Psalm 79 was still fluid, if some of the psalms in it were being written by pious writers, if Alcimus were a prominent religious personality who became High Priest with the support and perhaps the close lineage of a great leader of the pious, then the possibility of Alcimus' authorship of Psalm 79 increases in validity.

Segal states that it was during the time of Judas Maccabaeus that the Biblical text was issued with the sanction of authority that gained it acceptance as a standard text, leading to the rejection or even suppression of other recensions.[40] Citing 1Macc.1:56-58 and 1Macc.3:48, Segal points out that the destruction of sacred scrolls during the persecution must have led to a terrible scarcity of scriptural books in Judaea at that time. After the Maccabaean victory, however, there would have been a great and immediate desire for new copies of these books. Segal presumes that scribes would have worked with the authority of Judas Maccabaeus. Judas, a priest, was a devout student of the scriptures,[41] and it would make perfect sense to think that he instructed scribes to create a new inventory of biblical books (2Macc.2:14-15). Communities in need of scrolls could receive them from Jerusalem because of the scribal activity at this time. Those who went to Qumran apparently took many copies with them, and they are now known as the Dead Sea Scrolls. Segal concludes that, "the work of compiling the authoritative text must have begun immediately after the restoration of the Temple service in 164 *ante*."[42]

One cannot help but suggest that it was at this time of great scriptural activity that Alcimus made his mark, as an author of psalms and a staunch supporter of scriptural activity. There is nothing to suggest that Alcimus would have been anything other than a promoter of these efforts. Indeed, to vary Segal's thesis a bit, it would have been Alcimus, as head of the Temple hierarchy and with close ties to the scribal community, who would have had the resources and the authority to copy and transmit the sacred scrolls. The statement of 1Macc.7:17 may be all the more ironic because Alcimus was a man of scripture.

---

[40] M. H. Segal "The Promulgation of the Authoritative Text of the Hebrew Bible" *JBL* 72 (1953) 285-297; reprinted in Leiman *The Canon and Masorah* 285-297.
[41] According to 1Macc.4:30, 7:41 and 2Macc.8:19, 23, 15:22.
[42] Segal "The Authoritative Text" 42.

The Re-evaluation of Alcimus

Since the author of 1Maccabees despises Alcimus, he would not have made up the fact that Alcimus wrote a psalm. He is using Alcimus' own sacred words against him. At one point, Alcimus had decried the spilling of Jewish blood but now, according to the author of 1Maccabees, he has caused the spilling of Jewish blood himself. At the very point that 1Maccabees aims its harshest possible attack on Alcimus, it also openly speaks of Alcimus as the author of a psalm. Alcimus wrote Psalm 79.

Alcimus and the *Asidaioi*

Why did the *Asidaioi* accept Alcimus as High Priest?[43] Did Alcimus deceive and then massacre the *Asidaioi* leaders, and if so, why? These issues are of central importance to our understanding of Alcimus' attitudes and actions.

According to 1Maccabees, the *Asidaioi* accepted him because he was of Aaronide descent and they did not believe that anyone of this line could commit evil against them. According to 1Macc.7:12, "an assembly of scribes" confirms Alcimus' legitimacy. This assembly's decision may have influenced the *Asidaioi* in their acceptance of Alcimus. In 2Maccabees, neither this acceptance of Alcimus by the *Asidaioi* nor his massacre of their leaders is found in this work. Josephus never even mentions the *Asidaioi*. Josephus says that those who survived the Sabbath massacre joined Mattathias and appointed him their leader.[44] He places the responsibility for the killing of the sixty on Bacchides.[45] Yet in *Ant.*12.400, Josephus states that Alcimus "had put to death many of the good and pious men of the nation." While Josephus may seem to place the blame for the massacre of the *Asidaioi* on Bacchides and not Alcimus, this may be because Josephus assumes that Alcimus is simply a puppet of the Seleucids. Josephus' change is certainly not based on any other source of information than 1Maccabees.

For Kampen, the *Asidaioi* should not be considered a sect but a "group of persons who share a common identity." The term *Asidaioi* should not be limited to a military definition; "leading citizens" might be another translation. That 1Macc.2:42 describes the *Asidaioi* as "devoted to the law" supports the conclusion that they are

---

[43] In this section, I will replace the other terms used for the *Asidaioi*, such as Asidaioi and Hasideans, with the Greek term.
[44] *Ant.*12.275.
[45] *Ant.*12.396.

leading citizens who supported the Maccabees because they opposed those who were acting against tradition and the sanctity of the Temple. The hypothesis that the *Asidaioi* approach Alcimus in 1Macc.7:12-13 because he is a legitimate hereditary successor to the High Priesthood should be tested. This hypothesis assumes that Menelaus was not a priest and that therefore Alcimus, a priest, became a welcome candidate for the office. On the contrary, Kampen says, Menelaus was "from legitimate priestly lineage" and Alcimus was of Aaronide lineage but not from the line of the Oniads. When the *Asidaioi* agreed to negotiate with Alcimus, it is not because they accepted his legitimacy but because they had a specific problem in that Bacchides and Alcimus were approaching with a huge army bent on destruction unless peace negotiations were successful. The "justice" they sought was simply trustworthiness in negotiations. While Antiochus V had broken an oath in 1Macc.6:62, the *Asidaioi* felt that Alcimus could be trusted. It is not so much that he was a legitimate heir to the Oniads as that he was a countryman. This is exactly what Josephus says when he says of Alcimus "who was a countryman."[46]

There is an interesting parallel between this passage in 1Macc.7 and an earlier one in 1Macc.1. Compare the two:

> Two years later, the king sent a Mysarch against the towns of Judah, and he came against Jerusalem with a strong army. Treacherously, he addressed the people in peaceful terms, so that they trusted him, and then he hit the city hard with a surprise attack, killing many Israelites....They shed innocent blood around the sanctuary And defiled the temple.
>
> 1Macc.1:29-30

> He (the King) sent him with the wicked Alcimus, whom he confirmed in the high priesthood, with orders to wreak vengeance on the Israelites. They set out on the march with a large force against the land of Judah. Bacchides sent a message to Judas and his brothers, treacherously couched in peaceful terms...indeed, Alcimus spoke to them in peaceful terms and swore to them that "We intend no harm to you or to your friends." As soon as he had won their trust, however, he arrested sixty of them and had them executed all in a single day, in accordance with the verse which he himself wrote, "The bodies and blood of Your saints they have poured out around Jerusalem, and there is none to bury them."

---

[46] *Ant.*12:395.

The Re-evaluation of Alcimus

The parallel shows that while the Maccabees had understood the lesson of the earlier event, the *Asidaioi* had not, because they trusted in their countryman Alcimus.

One will turn Kampen's argument on its head if one remembers that 1Maccabees is polemical literature designed, in this case, to slander Alcimus. One begins to wonder if the story of the massacre of the *Asidaioi* by Alcimus is not written as an artificial copy of, and not just a parallel to, the story in 1Macc.1. Since 1Maccabees was written from the point of view of the Hasmonaeans in order to legitimize that dynasty, we should turn to the period of its creation. 1Maccabees was written during the period in which there was a rift between the Hasmonaeans and the Pharisees over policies toward the Seleucid Empire. The author of 1Maccabees may very well have seen a parallel between his own time and that of Judas Maccabaeus. The *Asidaioi* were allied with the Maccabees during the early stages of the revolt but then naively thought that Alcimus, a "leading Jewish figure" could be negotiated with. The Hasmonaean historian was discounting the importance of the *Asidaioi* in history. Thus the *Asidaioi* and the Pharisees play parallel roles in their disagreements with the Hasmonaeans.

Kampen, Graetz, Schurer, Schafer and Gruen all accept the story of the massacre of the *Asidaioi* as factual. Graetz and Kampen include Alcimus' uncle Yosi b.Yo'ezer in the group who were executed. Schurer states that Alcimus orders the execution of the *Asidaioi* in order to assert himself in his new position. The result of the massacre was that, with Lysias back in Syria, Alcimus and Judas had the opportunity to measure their respective strengths.[47] Schafer and Zeitlin comment

---

[47] As Sievers points out in detail, while there is a general consensus that Judas controlled Jerusalem during the last years of his life, a closer analysis shows that this is not correct and that Alcimus controlled the area. 1Macc.7:8-19 states that Bacchides entered Jerusalem without conflict; 7:22-24 states that Alcimus had a large following and that Judas was relegated to causing problems in the countryside. Alcimus seeks help because the countryside is dangerous for his followers. Indeed, after Nicanor loses a battle at Capharsalama (1Macc.7:32), he returns to the safe haven of Jerusalem and threatens the priests of the Temple. 2Maccabees' description of the friendship between Nicanor and Judas (2Macc.14:23-25), which Sievers completely accepts as historical, shows that Judas could come to Jerusalem during this time but only because he was Nicanor's guest. When Judas realizes that Nicanor's attitude toward him has changed, he runs to Samaria (2Macc.15:1). There is no evidence in 1Maccabees to say that Judas did control

that we do not know why Alcimus ordered the execution of the sixty *Asidaioi*, but the result, rather than consolidating Alcimus' power as others have understood, was that Alcimus was now in open conflict with the Maccabaean. Gruen points out that the *Asidaioi*'s attempt to find reconciliation with Alcimus shows that they did not find an appointee of the Seleucids as unacceptable as High Priest. Thus even the most pious could seek accommodation with those who were involved with the Hellenic kings. The appointment of Alcimus and its acceptance by the *Asidaioi* show how Hellenic rule and Jewish religious rights could co-exist.

Grabbe does not assume that the story of the massacre of the *Asidaioi* is historical. The *Asidaioi* were interested in religious freedom and had achieved it. They did not share Judas' broader nationalist goal. Because of the bias of our sources on the subject of the massacre of the *Asidaioi*, it is difficult to evaluate precisely what happened and why. If those *Asidaioi* were executed, as alleged, then it would no doubt have driven the group back into the arms of Judas. For exactly this reason, however, it was hardly in Bacchides' self-interest to provoke a section of the population that was willing to accept his orders; furthermore, we do not have any indication that the *Asidaioi* as a group returned to Judas's camp. On the contrary, it appears that the Jews as a whole were willing to recognize Alcimus as High Priest and accept Syrian domination, in return for freedom of worship.[48] In short, the story does not make sense.

This skepticism about Alcimus' massacre of the *Asidaioi* is very important for our considerations. If we combine the logic of Grabbe who says that the story of the massacre does not make sense and analyze the references brought by Kampen we can conclude that the story could have been made up. It is important to note again that 2Maccabees does not have the story at all and that Josephus, who does, does not blame Alcimus. Thus one possibility is that the story is artificial and an attempt by 1Maccabees to turn Alcimus into a villain.

Jerusalem during this time, so we can assume that he was forced into the mode of guerilla warfare near Modi'in. The territory under his control diminished, as did the number of his followers. Even if the numbers are not accurate, one can compare his force of three thousand men in 1Macc.7:40 and 9:5 with the 6,000 of 2Macc.8:1, the 10,000 of 1Macc.4:29, and the 11,000 of 1Macc.5:18-20. The relative numbers tell the story of diminishing strength. 1Macc.6:54 says that many had left Judas for Alcimus.

[48] 1Macc 7:20-22.

If, on the other hand, the story of the massacre is correct, why were the *Asidaioi* so eager to meet with him? Alcimus wrote Psalm 79, a lament that refers to the event of Apollonius' treachery and ruin of Jerusalem. The *Asidaioi* would not have suspected this type of betrayal from the very man who had condemned those events.

The study of the references to the *Asidaioi* in 1 and 2Maccabees leads to the conclusion that they were leading citizens of Judaea, scribes "devoted to the law," who supported Mattathias and his sons in their resistance to the measures taken by Antiochus IV against the Judaeans and their religion. The *Asidaioi* had their own different religious standards but there is no dispute between their actions/interpretations and the *halakhah* of the Sages. The early *Asidaioi* may have been members of the group referred to in 1 and 2Maccabees. This early dating might indicate that Yose ben Yoʿezer was one of these *Asidaioi*. This last point is very instructive for our purpose here. This would mean that the dots that we have attempted to connect might indeed be connectable. The Talmudic references that connect Alcimus to Yosi b.Yoʿezer may have historical validity. Yosi b.Yoʿezer, a priest related to the High Priest Alcimus, may have been the link between Alcimus and the *Asidaioi* and may have been important in Alcimus' rise to power.

Why Was There an Extended *Intersacerdotium* After Alcimus?

1Maccabees states that at Alcimus' death in 159 BCE, there is no mention of a replacement until the appointment of Jonathan in 152 BCE. Bacchides feared Jonathan's military prowess and popularity among the traditionalists and constructed a line of fortifications around Jerusalem and strengthened the *Akra*.[49] When Alcimus died (1Macc.9:55-56), there seems to have been a balance of power between Hellenists and traditionalists; this is indicated by the fact that no High Priest seems to have been chosen to succeed Alcimus. Neither 1 nor 2Maccabees, both pro-Hasmonaean sources, say anything about Judas holding this position. 1Maccabees puts Judas' death at Berea in 160[50] with Alcimus dying the following year.[51] If Judas died before Alcimus, there was no opening for him to fill. Josephus contradicts himself on this issue: In *Ant.* 12.414, 419, 434, Alcimus dies after he has been High Priest for four years and "the people bestowed the High Priesthood on

---

[49] 1Macc.9:50-53.
[50] 1Macc.9:3-4, 18.
[51] 1Macc.9:54-6.

Judas"; in *Ant.* 13.46, Josephus says that after Judas' death, the High Priesthood was empty for four years in a later passage; in 20.237, Josephus says that the position was vacant for seven years. Thus the conclusion would seem to be that Judas did not succeed Alcimus and that there was an extended *intersacerdotium* after him. The question is why.

While Stegemann says that The "Teacher of Righteousness" was the High Priest in the interim,[52] Graetz, Rooke, Schafer, and Sievers all agree that the Syrian court left the office of High Priest open for seven years. Where they differ is the reasons for the *intersacerdotium*. Graetz states that the Temple may have been controlled by a substitute, referred to as a *sagan*. The intention of the Syrians was "removing even the semblance of Judaean independence" by forbidding even a Judaean titular leader. Thus Graetz bases his theory on the idea that after the death of Alcimus, Bacchides withdrew to Antioch. He did this despite the fact that he had recently strengthened the fortifications of Judas and Jerusalem.[53] This shows "the reciprocity of the Seleucid relationship with the High Priesthood." Without the help of a friendly High Priest who would rally their side, the Seleucids could not function in the face of the Maccabaean opposition. The Seleucids could not appoint a successor to Alcimus because they were too weak to do so. Judaeans did not have the power to appoint a High Priest without Seleucid approval and the Seleucids preferred no High Priest to a rebellious one.

This seems strange at best. Was there absolutely no one who could become the High Priest? Alcimus was a prominent religious and political leader who had the full military backing of the empire. Did Alcimus not have a deputy, a *sagan* of some kind, a relative that he was grooming to succeed him? Rooke attempts to explain the gap in the High Priesthood by saying that no one was acceptable to both sides. Yet Jonathan, who would be appointed at the end of the period, was the leader of one of those sides. Jonathan, as a non-Zadokite, may not have been acceptable to traditionalists. Some condemned Jason, Menelaus and Alcimus because Seleucid kings appointed them, yet there is no criticism of Jonathan when he is appointed in this very way. It was only following a defeat to Jonathan in that later campaign that Bacchides began to negotiate a settlement with the Maccabaean leader.

---

[52] H. Stegemann *Die Entstehung der Qumrangemeinde* (Bonn, 1971) 210-25.
[53] 1Macc.9:50-3.

The Re-evaluation of Alcimus

Schafer thinks that the seven-year vacancy in office may simply be a result of the fact that Josephus did not have anything in his sources about the identity of the High Priest in those years. Sievers insists that this situation is not unique and that there were other situations in which there was no High Priest. Since Menelaus was nominally the High Priest in 163 BCE on *Yom Kippur* and then on *Hanukkah*, the rededication of the Temple, but since one cannot imagine that he would have been allowed to function in this capacity when the temple was under Judas' control, there was, in effect, no High Priest at that time. In the same way, there may not have been a High Priest before Jonathan became High Priest on *Sukkot* in 152 BCE.[54] Sievers is incorrect: The Menelaus example is not a parallel to an *intersacerdotium* in the years 159-152 BCE. There was an official High Priest, Menelaus, who, because of a violent takeover of Jerusalem, may not have been allowed to function. Sievers states that Bacchides left for Antioch without leaving anyone in charge and that this move would "keep both parties on good behavior." This seems quite naïve, especially given the violent nature of the conflict that had been raging, without conclusion, for so long.

The evidence for the *intersacerdotium* is strong, but the reasons for it remain puzzling. After Judas died, Alcimus was in a position of great strength, without a major rival. When Alcimus died, therefore, there was no reason for the Seleucids to refrain from appointing a successor who would continue his policies. We do not know why Bacchides did not leave anyone in charge, although he probably did. Indeed, two years after Alcimus' death, Bacchides returned from Antioch, encouraged by supporters in Judaea. These supporters had leaders; one of those leaders, whether an *Aaronide* like Alcimus or a powerful and wealthy leader like Menelaus, could have been High Priest. The Seleucids may have appointed Jonathan as High Priest when they were in a position of weakness, but they were in no such position after Alcimus' death.

The *intersacerdotium* may have implications for the question of Alcimus' identity. During these years, as in the years following the disposal of Menelaus, the assumption by all was that a legitimate High Priest had to be a Zadokite. This is why Judas, and his brother Jonathan, as non-Zadokites, did not even attempt to occupy the position. Jonathan spent the years following Judas' death in 160 gaining political and military power but did not become High Priest until October, 152. If

---
[54] 1Macc.10:21.

Alcimus were a non-Zadokite, as some scholars believe, another non-Zadokite could have replaced him. Demetrius I, even during his years of strength, did not want to appoint a High Priest without the appropriate credentials; such an appointment would only cause him greater problems with a difficult people. With no Zadokite to appoint, he preferred to leave the office open. It would be AlexanderI *Balas* in 152 who would appoint the ambitious Jonathan as High Priest. Time has its own ways of changing what is acceptable; the years that had passed without a High Priest apparently convinced many of the traditionalists that an Aaronide High Priest such as Jonathan was better than a non-Aaronide such as Menelaus or no High Priest at all. The *intersacerdotium*, the period in which there was no High Priest because there was no legitimate Zadokite candidate, points back to the fact that Alcimus was a Zadokite.

Re-Evaluating Alcimus

In attempting to understand the time of the Maccabees from the perspective of Alcimus, we need to understand Alcimus' position and actions. If there is a way to present his side of the story, we will be back inside the situation in a new way. The model of "good Jews vs. bad Jews" becomes much more sophisticated. Now we have at least three positions:

1. Those who wanted to go beyond religious revolt to a political revolution (led by Judas Maccabaeus);

2. Those who wanted neither religious freedom nor political revolution (usually referred to as "Hellenizers"); and

3. Those who wanted religious freedom but did not seek political independence (perhaps the silent majority of the country, including the *Asidaioi*)

One faction in the third group, represented and led by Alcimus, had power, were loyal to the sovereign Seleucids and did not seek a political revolution. They were not Maccabees, *Asidaioi,* or Hellenizers. They did, however, have a vital interest in maintaining the sanctity of Judaism and the temple.

Clearly, a re-evaluation of Alcimus must deal both with a huge negative, the account in 1Maccabees of Alcimus' role in a massacre of the *Asidaioi* leaders who had come in a diplomatic delegation and who had trusted him, and a moving positive, the statement in 1Maccabees that he wrote a psalm. To put it plainly, anyone who can write psalms cannot be "all bad." For a person's work to be

The Re-evaluation of Alcimus

included in the greatest Jewish anthology of spirituality indicates something about his authority and devotion. How shall we reconcile these two matters?

One possibility is to simply deny the negative and point out that since neither 2Maccabees nor Josephus accuse Alcimus of this atrocity, and since it seems unlikely that he could have maintained any support in the nation if had done it, and since the event itself may be an artificial construction based on an earlier parallel, Alcimus should not be blamed for this event, which may not have happened at all. This type of selective thinking is well attested in scholarly writing by historians who display a prejudice for one side or the other.

A more interesting possibility is to assume that the massacre did occur and that, following Josephus, Bacchides is to blame. Perhaps Alcimus was duped and used by Bacchides to set up a negotiation that turned into mass executions of rebel leaders.

In the ancient sources, Alcimus is portrayed as a traitor and collaborator. According to many scholars, his so-called voluntary defilement was his political collaboration made into a religious evil. And yet we think of Judas' friendship with Nicanor as described in 2Maccabees during the very time that Alcimus was High Priest; Judas was not "defiled" by this contact. Political controversy is turned into religious controversy. Even on the basis of 1Maccabees, 2Maccabees and Josephus we can say that Alcimus was anti-Maccabee but never violated Judaism. These sources show him appealing for help from the Seleucids against the Maccabees. Alcimus did see Judas as both a personal threat and as one who would do harm to the Judaeans. We certainly have sources that place Alcimus and Judas in bitter rivalry.

A complex picture of Alcimus begins to emerge. On the one hand, he seems to have been a devout and spiritual priest from a long and cherished tradition. On the other hand, he may have participated in the massacre of his potential enemies and ordered a change in Temple architecture which was controversial and un-traditional.

The question becomes: Did Alcimus or Judas fit better into the flow of history? Judas won a posthumous victory; after the *intersacerdotium*, the Hasmonaeans became the High Priests and eventually the kings of the independent state of Judaea. Actually, however, the Hasmonaeans were the anomaly, lasting for a few generations and only because the Seleucids were in constant conflict and Rome had not yet made its move into the region.

Let us think again about Josephus' political world-view of a priestly aristocracy with religious autonomy, under the rule of a foreign sovereign. Alcimus' political position followed this philosophy. Josephus claims to be a descendant of the Maccabees and views them as heroes, even claiming that Judas was a High Priest. Thus his prejudices do not allow him to recognize that Alcimus' political philosophy paralleled his own.

If we begin with the idea that this High Priest wanted what he thought was best for his people and his religion, why, one might ask, would he be so strongly against Judas Maccabaeus? The answer is that it was really the other way around; Judas opposed Alcimus' legitimate position as High Priest and leader of the people. The real conflict between Alcimus and Judas was a political one over the meaning of independence. As the seed of Aaron, Alcimus, like his famous ancestor, was ready to do what it took to preserve the cult.

We take all of the evidence seriously. In a sense, we are maximalist about Alcimus, for we believe that the sources are all biased but may very well contain basically correct facts about him. We therefore believe that Alcimus was ready to do what it took to preserve the Temple. If the massacre of the *Asidaioi* and the tearing down of the wall are taken at face value and at their worst, still, Alcimus could maintain, the price was not too high for peace, security and religious freedom.

Antiochus IV *Epiphanes'* anti-Judaism edicts were so anomalous that there was no reason to think that the Seleucids would renew his policy of interfering with the local cult. There was every reason to assume that religious freedom under the Seleucids would be secure without political independence. The Seleucids had their own internal dynastic struggles that would divide the empire on a quite consistent basis. The Ptolemies to the south were always a major concern. As long as the southern flank consisted of a loyal and tranquil populace, the Seleucids thought, its religion was immaterial.

Judas knew all this but sized things up differently. He saw the dynastic struggles as well as the growing might of Rome. In reaching out to Rome and receiving what he may have naively taken as strong support,[55] Judas was emboldened to press on with his revolt. Rome seems to have been playing with Judas as a pawn on its chessboard, attempting to create further problems for Demetrius. Before long, Judas, without the support of his countrymen, was dead. When in 153 BCE, Jonathan, Judas' brother and successor, accepted appointment to the High Priesthood by the very same Demetrius, he did so without a promise of political

---

[55] 1Maccabees 8.

The Re-evaluation of Alcimus

independence. Jonathan did procure exemption from taxation from first Demetrius and then from the bastard son of Antiochus *Epiphanes* named Balas. Jonathan won with political acumen and impeccable timing that which his legendary brother could not win with violence. Jonathan did not proclaim independence, but reigned in semi-autonomy over a Seleucid province. In 144 BCE, when the situation required it, Jonathan paid 300 talents to Demetrius' heir Nicator as back taxes for those remitted by his father. Nicator would call him "First Friend of the King."

We could continue this line of thinking but the point is that Judas' methods were not even followed by his own brothers who apparently learned well from his mistakes and demise. Their methods were closer to those of Alcimus than of Judas.

The historian should not judge between two ancient views of the meaning of independence. Indeed, even a strong adherent of Judaism or Christianity could look back at the conflict between Alcimus and Judas and argue it either way. Alcimus, who wrote a moving psalm about the ruination of the Temple, felt compelled to do everything in his power to save the Temple and preserve its sanctity. Despite the harsh verdict of all ancient and most modern historians, he succeeded in his goals.

Alcimus has been either an ignored or denigrated trivial figure in Jewish history. As the *Asidaioi* said, according to 1Maccabees, he was the seed of Aaron who did not want to bring any harm. He should be restored as a leader who attempted to perpetuate his religion and his people.

ALCIMUS: PROSPECTS FOR FUTURE STUDY

Now that we have carefully studied the ancient source material and the important modern scholarly treatments of the actions and life of Alcimus, we face the larger task of placing him in the context of Maccabaean times, the history of the High Priesthood and the early history of the sectarian movements. We will follow different lines of evidence, including one involving the next high priest, Jonathan the Hasmonaean, to support our conclusion that Alcimus was at least the first "Wicked Priest" referred to in the scrolls.

How does Alcimus, as the last of the Zadokite High Priests, compare to his predecessors? What accommodations did the Zadokites/Oniads make with their rulers, both Persian and Ptolemaic/Seleucid? How does Alcimus compare to the Maccabaean High Priests who would follow him? Political independence, Judas Maccabaeus' surprising goal, must have seemed as reckless radicalism to Alcimus, who was more than content with the regained religious autonomy. Whose vision of independence was more common in the context of the Hellenistic world? What accommodations did the priesthoods of the other lands make to the Seleucids and the Ptolemies?

Accommodations, religious or political, were made throughout Israelite and Jewish history in order to preserve the hereditary priesthood and sacred worship. Alcimus looked at the realities of his time and acted to protect his people, his hereditary calling, and his religion. That Judas died trying to re-shape those realities is a romantic story of martyrdom. Alcimus, like the first High Priest Aaron before him, saw his role very differently. Alcimus was a High Priest in the tradition of Aaron who built the Golden Calf while Moses was receiving the revelations of God on Mt. Sinai (Exodus 32). Alcimus also was willing to make accommodations during a time of crisis in order to preserve the institution of the priesthood and live another day. Modern historians should not judge such accommodations harshly; they are the stuff of reality. Perhaps, in the end, Aaron and Alcimus were right; Moses and Judas Maccabaeus are the famous heroes of their people but the priesthood survived and preserved a religion that has contributed so much to the history of humankind.

APPENDIX I

Chronology of Seleucid Emperors and Judaean High Priests

SELEUCID EMPERORS

Antiochus III the Great	233-187 BCE
Seleucus IV *Philopator*	187-176 BCE
Antiochus IV *Epiphanes*	176-163 BCE
Antiochus V *Eupator*	163-162 BCE
Demetrius I *Soter*	162-150 BCE
Alexander I *Balas*	150-145 BCE
Demetrius II *Nicator*	150-145 BCE

HIGH PRIESTS OF JUDAEA

Onias III	c. 187-175 BCE
Jason	175-172 BCE
Menelaus	172-163 BCE
Alcimus	162-159 BCE
Jonathan	152-142 BCE

BIBLIOGRAPHY

Abel, F.-M. *Les Livres des Maccabées.* Paris: Gabalda, 1949.
----- **and J. Starcky**. *Les Livres des Maccabées.* Paris: Éditions du Cerf, 1961.
Avi-Yonah, Michael and Zvi Baras, eds. *Society and Religion in the Second Temple Period*, World History of the Jewish People: First Series: Ancient Times. Jerusalem: Massada Publishing, 1977.
Bar-Kochva, Bezalel. *Judas Maccabaeus: The Jewish Struggle against the Seleucids* Cambridge: Cambridge University Press, 1989.
Barucq, Andre. "Leontopolis" in *Supplement au Dictionnaire de la Bible V* (1957) 359-72.
Beckwith, R. T. "The Pre-history and the Relationship of the Pharisees, Sadducees and Essenes: a Tentative Reconstruction" *RevQ* 11 (1982) 3-46.
Berman, D. "Hasidim in Rabbinic Traditions" in *Society of Biblical Literature 1979 Seminar Papers* vol. 2, ed. P. J. Achtemeyer. Missoula: Scholars Press, 1979, 15-33.
Bevan, Edwyn R. "Syria and the Jews" in *The Cambridge History of the Ancient World* 499-523.
-----. *The House of Ptolemy.* Chicago: Ares, 1968.
-----. *The House of Seleucus* London: E. Arnold, 1902.
Bickerman, Elias. *From Ezra to the Last of the Maccabees: Foundations of Post-Biblical Judaism.* New York: Schocken, 1962.
-----. "Heliodore au Temple de Jerusalem" in *Studies in Jewish and Christian History Pt. 2* ed. O. Michel, M. Hengel and P. Schafer. Leiden: Brill, 1980.
-----. *Institutions des Seleucides.* Paris: Geuthner, 1938.
-----. "Makkabäerbucher" in Pauly-Wissowa et al, eds. *Realencylopaedie der klassischen Altertumswiseenschaft* XIV (1930) 783.
-----. *Studies in Jewish and Christian History.* Part Two. Arbeiten zur Geschichte des Antiken Judentums und des Urchristentums 9. Leiden: Brill, 1980.
-----. *The God of the Maccabees. Studies on the Meaning and Origin of the Maccabean Revolt* Studies in Judaism and Late Antiquity 32. Leiden: Brill, 1979.
-----. "Une proclamation séleucide relative au temple de Jérusalem" *Syria* 25 (1946/48) 67-85.
Bowen, B. A. *A Study of Hesed.* Yale Dissertation, 1938.
Briggs, C. A. and E. G. *Psalms* Vol. 2 ICC. London: T. and T. Clark, 1907.
Bringmann, Klaus. *Hellenistische Reform und Religionsverfolgung in Judaa. Eine Untersuchng zur judisch-hellenistische Geschichte* (175-163 v.Chr.) (Abhandlungen Geschichte der Wissenschaften, Philologisch-Historisch Klasse, Dritte Folge 132 Gottingen: Vandenhoeck & Ruprecht, 1983.

Bibliography

Brooke, George J. "The Pesharim and the Origins of the Dead Sea Scrolls," in *Methods of Investigation of the Dead Sea Scrolls and the Khirbet Qumran Site: Present Realities and Future Prospects,* ed. Michael O. Wise, et al. Annals of the New York Academy of Sciences vol. 722. New York: New York Academy of Sciences, 1994) 339-53.
Brownlee William. H. "The Historical Allusions of the Dead Sea Habakkuk Midrash" *BASOR* 126 (1952) 10-20.
-----. *The Midrash Pesher of Habakkuk.* Missoula, Montana: Scholars Press, 1979.
Broyne, Donatien de. "Le Texte grec des deux premiers livres des Maccabées" *RB* 31 (1922) 31-54.
Bruggemann, W. *The Message of the Psalms: A Theological Commentary.* Minneapolis: Augsburg, 1984.
Buchler, A. *Types of Jewish-Palestinian Piety from 70 B. CE to 70 CE: The Ancient Pious Men.* London: Ktav, 1922.
Bunge, J. G. *Untersuchungen zum Zweiten Makkabäerbuch.* Dissertation, Bonn, 1971.
-----. "Zur Geschichte und Chronologie der Untertangs der Oniaden und des Aufstiegs der Hasmonäer" *JSJ* vi (1975) 9-11.
Burgmann, H. "Das umstrittene Intersacerdotium in Jerusalem 159-152 v.Chr., *JSJ* 11 (1980) 135-76.
Buss, Martin. "The Psalms of Asaph and Korah" *JBL* 82 (1963) 382-92.
Bustanay, Oded. "Seredah, Sererah, Saretan" *Encyclopedia Biblica* VI (1971) 765-68.
Buttenweiswer, Moses. *The Psalms: Chronologically Treated with a New Translation* Prolegomenon by Nahum M. Sarna. New York: Ktav, 1969.
Charles, R. H. *The Apocrypha and Pseudepigrapha of the Old Testament.* Oxford: Clarendon, 1984.
Cohen, Shaye J. D. *From the Maccabees to the Mishnah.* Library of Early Christianity 7. Philadelphia: Westminster, 1987.
-----. "History and Historiography in the *Contra Apionem* of Josephus" in *History and Theory 27: Essays in Jewish Historiography* (1988) 1-11.
-----. *Josephus in Galilee and Rome: His Vita and Development as a Historian.* Leiden: Brill, 1979.
Collins, John J. "Teacher and Messiah? The One Who Will Teach Righteousness at the End of Days," in *The Community of the Renewed Covenant: The Notre Dame Symposium on the Dead Sea Scrolls,* ed. Eugene Ulrich and James VanderKam. Notre Dame, Ind.: University of Notre Dame Press, 1994.
Cross, Frank Moore. *The Ancient Library of Qumran.* 3rd ed.. Sheffield: Sheffield Academic Press, 1995.
-----. *The Dead Sea Scrolls: Qumran in Perspective.* London: SCM, 1994.
Danby, J.C. *1Macc.. A Commentary.* Oxford: Blackwell, 1954.

Davies P. R., "Communities at Qumran and the Case of the Missing Teacher," *RQ* 15/57-58 (1991).
-----. "Hasidim in the Hasmonaean Period" *JJS* 28 (1977) 127-40.
-----. *The Damascus Covenant*. Sheffield: JSOT, 1983.
Delcor, Mathias. "Ou en est le probleme du Midrash d'Habacuc?" *Revue d'histoire des religions* 142 (1952) 129-46.
-----. "Le Temple d'Onias en Egypte" *RB* 75 (1968) 188-203.
Delitzsch F. *Biblical Commentary on the Psalms* trans. by D. Eaton II. London: Hodder and Stoughton, 1887.
Doran, Robert. *Temple Propaganda: The Purpose and Character of 2 Maccabees* CBQMS 12. Washington, D.C.: Catholic Biblical Association, 1981.
-----. "The First Book of Maccabees" in *The New Interpreter's Bible* Vol. IV. Nashville: Abingdon, 1996. 3-178.
-----. "The Second Book of Maccabees" in *The New Interpreter's Bible*. Nashville: Abingdon, 1996. 181-299.
Efron, J. *Studies on the Hasmonaean Period*. SJLA 39. Leiden: Brill, 1987.
Epstein, I. *The Babylonian Talmud*. London: Soncino, 1938.
Ettelson, H. W. "The Integrity of 1Macc." *The Transaction of the Connecticut Academy of Arts and Sciences* 27 (1925) 249-384.
Finkelstein, Louis. *The Pharisees: The Sociological Background of Their Faith*. Phil.: JPS, 1938, 1962.
Flint, Peter W. *The Dead Sea Psalms Scrolls and the Book of Psalms*. Leiden: Brill, 1997.
Gafni, Isaac. "On the Use of 1 Maccabees by Josephus Flavius," (Hebrew) *Zion* 45 (1980) 81-95.
Geiger, Abraham. *Urschrift und Ubersetzungen der Bibel*. 2nd ed. Frankfurt/Main: Madda, 1928.
Ginsberg, Harold Louis. "Daniel, Books of" *Encyclopedia Judaica* 5:1283.
-----. *Studies in Daniel*. New York, 1948.
Ginzberg, Louis. "The Significance of the Halachah for Jewish History," *On Jewish Law and Lore* (Philadelphia, repr. 1962) 77-126.
Goldstein, Jonathan A. *I Maccabees*. The Anchor Bible. Garden City: Doubleday, 1976.
-----. *II Maccabees*. The Anchor Bible. Garden City, Doubleday, 1983.
-----. "Jewish Acceptance and Rejection of Hellenism" in E.P. Sanders and A.I. Baumgarten. *Jewish and Christian Self-Definition* II (1981) 64-87, 318-26.

Bibliography

Grabbe, Lester L. *Judaism from Cyrus to Hadrian Volume One: The Persian and Greek Periods*. London: SCM, 1992.
-----. "The Jewish Theocracy from Cyrus to Titus: A Programmatic Essay" *JSOT* 37 (1987) 125-28.
Graetz, Heinrich. *History of the Jews* 1. New York: George Dobsevage, 1927.
Grimm, C. L. *Kurzgefasstes exegetisches Handbuch zu den Apokryphen*. Leipzig: S. Hirzel, 1853.
Gruen, Erich S. *Heritage and Hellenism: The Reinvention of Jewish Tradition*. Berkeley: University of California Press, 1998.
Gunkel, Hermann. *Introduction to Psalms: The Genres of the Religious Lyric of Israel* completed by Joachim Begrich, translated by James D. Nogalski. Macon, Ga.: 1998.
Habicht, C. *2 Makkabaerbuch* JSHRZ 1/3. Gutersloh: Mohn, 1976.
Haran, Menachem. "11QPs and the Canonical Book of Psalms" in Mark Brettler and Michael Fishbane *Minhah Le-Nahum* JSOT Sup. 154. Sheffield: Sheffield University Press, 1993.
Harrington, Daniel J. *The Maccabean Revolt: Anatomy of a Biblical Revolution*. Wilmington: Michael Glazier, 1988.
Hayward Robert. "The Jewish Temple at Leontopolis: A Reconsideration" *JJS* 33 (1982) 429-43.
Hengel, Martin. *Jews, Greeks and Barbarians* trans. by John Bowden. Stuttgart, 1976.
-----. *Judaism and Hellenism. Studies in their Encounter in Palestine during the Early Hellenic Period* 2 vols. Philadelphia: Fortress, 1974.
Hilbis, A. L. "The Hasmoneans According to the Talmudic and Midrashic Sources" *Sinai* 8, 6-22.
Hirsch, S. A. "The Temple of Onias " *Jews' College Jubilee Volume* (London, 1906) 39-80.
Hoenig, Sidney B. "Onias " *IDB* vol. 3 603.
-----. *The Great Sanhedrin. A study of the origin, development, composition, and function of the Bet Din Ha-Gadol during the Second Jewish Commonwealth*. Philadelphia, 1953.
Horgan, Maury P., *Pesharim: Qumran Interpretations of Biblical Books*. Washington D.C.: Catholic Biblical Association of America, 1979.
Hurvitz, Avi. *The Identification of Post-exilic Psalms by Means of Linguistic Criteria* Jerusalem: Magnes Press, 1966.
Ilan, T. "The Greek Names of the Hasmoneans" *JQR* 78 (1987) 1-20.
Jacobs, Louis. "The Concept of *Hasid* in the Biblical and Rabbinic Literatures" *JJS* 8 (1957) 143-54.

Kampen, John *The Hasideans and the Origin of Pharisaism. A Study in I and II Macc.* Septuagint and Cognate Studies 24. Atlanta: SBL, 1988.
---- and **Moshe J. Bernstein** eds. *Reading 4QMMT: New Perspectives on Qumran Law and History* (Atlanta, 1996).
Kaufmann, Yehezkel. *The Religion of Israel* ed. by Moshe Greenberg. New York: Schocken, 1960 and the original, unabridged Hebrew version *Toledoth Ha-Emunah Ha-Yisre'elith* II (Tel Aviv: 1947) 646-727.
Kieval, P. *The Talmudic View of Hasmonaean and Early Herodian Periods in Jewish History.* Diss.: Brandeis University, 1970.
Lim, Timothy. "The "Wicked Priest"s of the Gronigen Hypothesis" *JBL* 112 (1993) 415-25.
Martinez, Florentino Garcia. "A 'Groningen' Hypothesis of Qumran Origins and Early History" *RQ* 14 (1989-90) 521-41.
Mason, Steve. "Josephus, Daniel, and the Flavian House" in F. Parente and J. Sievers, eds. *Josephus and the History of the Greco-Roman Period.* Leiden, 1994. 161-191
-----. "Josephus and Judaism" in Jacob Neusner, Alan J. Avery-Peck and William Scott Green, eds. *The Encyclopedia of Judaism* Vol. II. New York, 1999. 554-55.
McCann, J. Clinton. "Psalms" in *The New Interpreter's Bible Volume* IV. Nashville, 1996.
McEwan, G. J .P. *Priest and Temple in Hellenistic Babylonia.* Wiesbaden, 1981.
Mitchell, David C. *The Message of the Psalter: An Eschatological Programme in the Book of Psalms.* Sheffield: Sheffield Academic Press, 1997.
Mittwoch, A. "Tribute and Land in Seleucid Judaea" *Biblica* 36 (1955) 352-61.
Mölleken, Wolfgang "Geschichtsklitterung im I. Makkabäerbuch" (Wann wurde Alkimus Hohenpriester?)" *ZAW* 65 (1953) 205-28.
Momigliano, Arnaldo. "The Second Book of Maccabees" in Arnaldo Momigliano *Essays on Ancient and Modern Judaism* ed. by Silvia Berti, trans. by Maura Masella-Gayley. Chicago, University of Chicago, 1994.
Morkholm, Otto. *Antiochus IV of Syria.* Classica et Mediaevalia, Dissertationes 8.
Mowinckel, Sigmund. *The Psalms in Israel's Worship.* Oxford, 1962.
Nasuti, H. P. *Tradition History and the Psalms of Asaph* SBLDS 88. Atlanta: Scholars Press, 1988.
Neusner, Jacob. *Judaism: The Evidence of the Mishnah.* Chicago: University of Chicago, 1981.
-----. *The Mishnah: A New Translation.* New Haven: Yale, 1991.
-----. *The Pharisees: Rabbinic Perspectives.* New York, Ktav, 1973.
-----. *The Rabbinic Traditions About the Pharisees Before 70.* Leiden: E. J. Brill, 1971.

Bibliography

-----. *The Talmud of Babylonia: An Academic Commentary XXII Bavli Tractate Baba Batra B. Chapters VII through XI.* University of South Florida, 1996.
Nodet, E. "La Dedicace, les Maccabees et le Messie" *Revue Biblique* 93 (1986) 321-75.
O'Connor, J. Murphy. "Teacher of Righteousness" *ABD* VI 340-41.
Parente, Fausto and Joseph Sievers, eds. *Josephus and the History of the Greco-Roman Period.* Leiden, 1994.
Parente, Fausto. "Onias III' death and the founding of the temple of Leontopolis" in *Josephus and the History of the Greco-Roman Period* 69-98.
Petrie, W.H. Flinders. *Egypt and Israel.* London: S.P.C.K., 1923.
Qimron, Elisha. "Miqsat Maase HaTorah" *ABD* IV 843-44.
----- **and John Strugnell.** *Qumran Cave 4: Miqsat Ma'aśe Ha-Torah* Discoveries in the Judaean Desert X (Oxford: Clarendon, 1994).
Quagebeur, J. "The genealogy of the Memphite high priest family in the Hellenistic period" *Studia Hellenistica* 24, 43-82.
Rabin, Chaim. *Qumran Studies.* New York: Schocken, 1957.
-----. *The Zadokite Documents* 2nd ed. Oxford: Oxford University Press, 1958.
Rajak, T. *Josephus: The Historian and His Society.* London: Duckworth, 1983.
Redmond, E.A.E. *From the Records of a Priestly Family from Memphis* 1. Wiesbaden, 1981.
Rooke, Deborah W. *Zadok's Heirs: The Role and Development of the High Priesthood in Ancient Israel.* Oxford: Oxford University Press, 2000.
Safrai, S. "Teaching of Pietists in Mishnaic Literature" *JJS* 16 (1965) 15-33.
-----. "The Pharisees and the Hasidim" *Sidic* 10 (1977) 12-16.
Sanders, J. A. "Cave 11 Surprises and the Question of Canon" *McCormick Quarterly* 21 (1968) 284-98; reprinted in Sid Z. Leiman *The Canon and Masorah of the Hebrew Bible: An Introductory Reader.* New York: Ktav 1974. 37-51.
Schäfer, Peter. "The Hellenistic and Maccabaean Periods" in *Israelite and Judaean History* ed. by John H. Hayes and J. Maxwell Miller. London: Westminster John Knox, 1977. 539-604.
Schiffman, Lawrence. "Temple Scroll" *ABD* VI 348-50.
Schunck, Klaus-Dietrich. *Die quellen des I. Und II. Makkbäerbuches.* Halle: Niemeyer, 1954.
-----. "Hoherpriester und Politiker? Die Stellung der Hohenpriester von Jaddua bis Jonatan zur jüdischen Gemeinde und zum hellenistischen Staat" *VT* 44 (1994).
Schurer, Emil. *A History of the Jewish People in the Time of Jesus.* New York: Charles Scribner's, 1961.
-----. *A History of the Jewish People in the Age of Jesus Christ* revised and edited by G. Vermes and F. Millar vol. I. Edinburgh, 1973.

Segal, M. H. "The Promulgation of the Authoritative Text of the Hebrew Bible" *JBL* 72 (1953) 285-297.
Sievers, Joseph. *The Hasmoneans and Their Supporters: From Mattathias to the Death of John Hyrcanus I.* Atlanta: Scholar's Press, 1990.
Simon, Uriel. *Four Approaches to the Book of Psalms: From Saadiah Gaon to Abraham Ibn Ezra* translated from the Hebrew by Lenn J. Schramm. Albany: SUNY Press, 1991.
Steckoll, S. H. "The Qumran Sect in Relation to the Temple of Leontopolis" *Revue de Qumran* 6 (1967) 55-69.
Stegemann, H. *Die Entstehung der Qumrangemeinde.* Bonn, 1971. 210-25.
Stern, Menahem. *Ha Teudot le-Mered ha-Hashmonaim.* Tel Aviv, 1965.
-----. "The Death of Onias III" *Zion* (1960) 25:1-16.
----- and Oswyn Murray. "Hecataeus of Abdera and Theophrastus on Jews and Egyptians" *JEA* (1973) 159-68;
Sukenik, E. L. "An Ancient Jewish Cave on the Jerusalem-Shechem Road" *Bulletin of the Israeli Exploration Society* I (1933) 7-9.
Tate, Marvin E. *Psalms 51-100* Word Biblical Commentary 20. Dallas: Word, 1990.
Taylor, Joan E. "A Second Temple in Egypt: The Evidence for the Zadokite Temple of Onias " *JSJ* XXIX 3 (1998) 298-322.
Tcherikover Victor. *Hellenistic Civilization and the Jews.* New York: Atheneum, 1975.
Thackeray, H. St., J., Marcus, Ralph Wikgren, A., Feldman, L.H., ed. *Josephus* 9 vols. Loeb Classical Library. Cambridge: Harvard University Press, 1926-65.
Treves, Marco. *The Dates of the Psalms: History and Poetry in Ancient Israel.* Pisa, 1988.
Vermès, Géza. *Discovery in the Judean Desert.* New York: Desclee, 1956.
-----. *The Complete Dead Sea Scrolls in English.* London: Penguin, 1995.
-----. *The Dead Sea Scrolls: Qumran in Perspective.* London: SCM, 1994.
-----. "The Leadership of the Qumran Community" in *Geschichte-Tradition-Reflexion* [Martin Hengel Festschrift] I. Tubingen: 1996. 375-84.
Vincent H. "Un hypogee juif a Djifneh" *RB* 10 (1913) 103-6.
Wacholder, Ben Zion, *The Dawn of Qumran: the Sectarian Torah and the "Teacher of Righteousness".* Cincinnati, Ohio: Hebrew Union College Press, 1983.
-----. *Eupolemus: A Study of Judaeo-Greek Literature.* New York, 1974.
Weiser, Arthur. *The Psalms: A Commentary* translated by Herbert Hartwell OTL. Louisville, 1962.
Westermann, Claus. *The Psalms.* Minneapolis: Augsburg, 1980.
Willesen, Folker. "The Cultic Setting of Psalm LXXIV" *VT* 2 (1952) 290-306.
Wirgin, Walter. "Judas Maccabee's Embassy to Rome and the Jewish-Roman Treaty" *PEQ* 101 (1969) 15-20.

Bibliography

Woude, A. S. van der, "Once Again: The "Wicked Priests" in the Habakkuk Pesher from Cave 1 of Qumran" *RQ* 17/65-68 (1996) 375-84.

-----. ""Wicked Priest" or "Wicked Priests"? Reflections on the Identification of the "Wicked Priest" in the Habakkuk Commentary" *JJS* 33 (1982).

Zeitlin, Solomon. "The Semikah Controversy between the Zugoth" *JQR* 7 (1916-1917) 499-517.

-----. *The Rise and Fall of the Judaean State: A Political, Social and Religious History of the Second Commonwealth Volume One 332-37 BCE* Phil.: JPS, 1968.

-----. *The First Book of Maccabees.* Dropsie College Edition. New York: Harper and Row, 1950.

----- and Sidney Tedesche. *The Second Book of Maccabees* Dropsie College edition. New York: Eisenbrauns, 1954.

INDEX

1Maccabees, 3, 7, 9, 12, 13, 15, 16, 17, 18, 21, 24, 25, 26, 27, 28, 29, 30, 33, 38, 40, 44, 46, 47, 48, 57, 63, 68, 69, 71, 101, 103, 116, 123, 124, 129, 131, 132, 134, 135, 136, 138, 140, 143, 144, 148, 150, 152, 156, 158, 159, 161, 163, 164, 165, 168, 169, 170, 171

2Maccabees, 16, 24, 25, 26, 27, 28, 29, 30, 31, 32, 35, 37, 40, 41, 43, 44, 46, 53, 62, 63, 71, 82, 113, 115, 119, 131, 138, 139, 142, 143, 144, 148, 150, 151, 152, 154, 155, 156, 157, 159, 161, 163, 164, 165, 169

Aaron, 2, 9, 15, 24, 42, 46, 48, 98, 148, 155, 159, 170, 171, 172

Alcimus, 1, 2, 3, 4, 8, 9, 10, 11, 13, 14, 15, 16, 17, 18, 19, 20, 21, 22, 23, 24, 25, 26, 27, 28, 29, 30, 31, 32, 33, 34, 36, 37, 38, 41, 43, 44, 45, 46, 47, 48, 49, 50, 52, 56, 57, 58, 62, 63, 66, 67, 69, 70, 71, 73, 74, 75, 76, 77, 78, 79, 87, 89, 92, 98, 99, 100, 101, 102, 103, 104, 105, 106, 108, 110, 112, 113, 116, 118, 119, 120, 123, 124, 134, 135, 136, 138, 140, 142, 143, 144, 145, 146, 147, 148, 149, 150, 151, 152, 153, 154, 155, 156, 157, 158, 159, 160, 161, 162, 163, 164, 165, 166, 167, 168, 169, 170, 171, 172

Antiochus IV, 2, 4, 5, 6, 7, 8, 12, 16, 23, 24, 25, 33, 42, 44, 53, 65, 68, 83, 96, 109, 123, 145, 146, 153, 159, 165, 170, 178

Antiochus V, 2, 7, 8, 9, 13, 27, 36, 37, 38, 41, 44, 139, 143, 144, 146, 147, 148, 157, 162

Asidaioi, 2, 4, 7, 9, 10, 15, 16, 17, 24, 28, 29, 30, 32, 46, 49, 57, 76, 79, 102, 123, 137, 142, 144, 147, 148, 150, 151, 152, 154, 155, 157, 161, 163, 164, 165, 168, 170, 171

Bacchides, 9, 14, 15, 17, 18, 21, 22, 23, 32, 44, 45, 49, 72, 76, 145, 147, 161, 162, 163, 164, 165, 166, 167, 169

Dead Sea Scrolls, 1, 70, 93, 96, 103, 105, 116, 117, 118, 120, 159, 160, 175, 180

Demetrius I, 8, 9, 13, 14, 18, 21, 24, 27, 29, 31, 34, 36, 37, 44, 46, 143, 144, 145, 147, 148, 150, 156

Hanukkah, 1, 2, 8, 10, 24, 26, 36, 37, 49, 66, 138, 139, 142, 143, 145, 167

Hasmonaeans, 1, 14, 23, 24, 36, 37, 46, 57, 62, 64, 82, 92, 103, 106, 107, 114, 147, 150, 163, 169

Heliodorus, 5, 33, 53, 104, 158

Hellenizers, 2, 18, 26, 65, 156, 159, 168

intersacerdotium, 10, 25, 49, 108, 166, 167, 169

Jason, 4, 5, 6, 20, 25, 28, 29, 41, 42, 43, 44, 46, 54, 64, 109, 149, 152, 156, 166

Index

Jerusalem, 1, 4, 5, 6, 8, 9, 12, 15, 16, 17, 19, 21, 24, 25, 26, 29, 33, 35, 36, 37, 38, 41, 44, 45, 47, 50, 51, 52, 53, 54, 58, 60, 61, 62, 63, 64, 65, 79, 80, 81, 83, 84, 86, 87, 90, 93, 95, 98, 102, 105, 106, 115, 117, 118, 119, 120, 121, 123, 124, 126, 127, 128, 129, 130, 131, 133, 135, 136, 140, 141, 142, 145, 146, 147, 149, 152, 153, 157, 159, 160, 162, 163, 165, 166, 167, 174, 175, 177, 180

Josephus, 5, 7, 8, 13, 23, 38, 39, 40, 41, 42, 43, 44, 45, 46, 47, 48, 49, 50, 52, 53, 55, 56, 57, 59, 60, 63, 64, 69, 71, 90, 103, 106, 138, 144, 148, 149, 151, 157, 158, 159, 161, 162, 164, 165, 167, 169, 175, 176, 178, 179, 180

Judas, 1, 2, 7, 9, 10, 13, 14, 15, 16, 17, 18, 19, 20, 21, 22, 23, 25, 26, 27, 28, 29, 30, 31, 33, 34, 35, 36, 37, 38, 41, 45, 46, 47, 49, 57, 62, 63, 71, 78, 80, 82, 83, 106, 115, 119, 120, 131, 138, 139, 140, 141, 142, 143, 144, 145, 146, 147, 149, 150, 152, 153, 154, 157, 158, 160, 162, 163, 164, 165, 166, 167, 168, 169, 170, 171, 172, 174, 180

Judas Maccabaeus, 1, 30, 33, 106, 119, 138, 140, 160, 163, 168, 170, 172, 174

Lysias, 2, 7, 8, 9, 13, 27, 37, 41, 42, 44, 52, 139, 144, 145, 146, 147, 156, 157, 163

Maccabaean, 1, 3, 4, 11, 23, 32, 36, 62, 63, 67, 95, 113, 114, 115, 116, 117, 119, 125, 128, 129, 130, 131, 136, 160, 164, 166, 172, 179

Mattathias, 7, 12, 26, 27, 140, 141, 161, 165, 180

Menelaus, 4, 6, 7, 8, 10, 16, 24, 28, 36, 37, 41, 42, 43, 44, 48, 50, 52, 54, 56, 105, 109, 138, 140, 143, 144, 145, 146, 148, 149, 151, 156, 162, 166, 167

Nicanor, 7, 19, 20, 21, 24, 25, 26, 32, 33, 34, 35, 36, 37, 46, 47, 59, 61, 62, 71, 142, 143, 145, 147, 157, 163, 169

Oniad, 2, 4, 6, 8, 10, 26, 36, 37, 44, 48, 56, 148

OniasIII, 4, 5, 6, 31, 36, 40, 41, 42, 43, 44, 50, 51, 52, 53, 54, 55, 56, 82, 109, 138, 149, 180

OniasIV, 26, 36, 38, 41, 43, 44, 50, 52, 54, 55, 56, 82, 104, 109, 138, 147

Pharisaism, 1, 178

Ps.79, 9, 10, 15, 16, 22, 24, 113, 116, 117, 118, 119, 120, 121, 122, 123, 124, 125, 126, 127, 128, 131, 132, 133, 134, 135, 156, 159, 161, 165

Ptolemies, 6, 42, 50, 53, 54, 108, 111, 112, 170, 172

Qumran, 1, 70, 93, 94, 95, 103, 104, 105, 106, 116, 117, 118, 120, 156, 158, 159, 160, 175, 176, 177, 178, 179, 180, 181

Rabbinic Judaism, 1, 94

Seleucid, 2, 4, 5, 7, 12, 13, 14, 18, 19, 20, 24, 25, 27, 31, 37, 43, 62, 63, 72, 74, 96, 106, 108, 109, 139, 142, 144, 145, 146, 149, 154, 157, 163, 166, 171, 172, 178

Simeon the Just, 80, 81, 92, 103, 150
Simon, 16, 25, 27, 30, 31, 38, 42, 49, 51, 53, 55, 64, 105, 107, 115, 126, 141, 180
soreg, 57, 58, 59, 60, 65, 66, 67, 68, 69, 70
Teacher of Righteousness, 71, 93, 94, 95, 96, 97, 98, 100, 101, 102, 104, 105, 106, 107, 108, 166, 179, 180
Temple, 2, 4, 6, 7, 8, 10, 16, 20, 23, 24, 25, 26, 28, 34, 35, 36, 37, 38, 47, 48, 49, 50, 52, 53, 55, 57, 58, 59, 60, 61, 62, 63, 64, 65, 66, 67, 68, 70, 71, 72, 73, 78, 80, 81, 82, 84, 87, 88, 89, 93, 95, 97, 98, 99, 100, 102, 104, 114, 115, 120, 121, 122, 123, 125, 126, 127, 128, 131, 132, 134, 135, 136, 137, 138, 143, 145, 146, 147, 149, 150, 157, 158, 159, 160, 162, 163, 166, 167, 169, 170, 171, 174, 176, 177, 178, 179, 180
Wicked Priest, 93, 94, 95, 96, 97, 98, 100, 101, 102, 103, 104, 105, 106, 107, 108, 178, 181
Yosi, 71, 73, 74, 75, 76, 77, 78, 79, 80, 81, 82, 83, 84, 85, 86, 87, 89, 90, 91, 92, 100, 101, 102, 103, 104, 105, 108, 137, 149, 153, 155, 158, 163, 165
Zadokite, 2, 4, 10, 23, 50, 56, 68, 69, 70, 104, 140, 147, 148, 149, 166, 172, 179

STUDIES IN JUDAISM
TITLES IN THE SERIES

S. Daniel Breslauer
Creating a Judaism Without Religion. A Postmodern Jewish Possibility. Lanham, November 2001. University Press of America. Academic Studies in Ancient Judaism series.

Jacob Neusner
Dual Discourse, Single Judaism. Lanham, February 2001. University Press of America. Academic Studies in Ancient Judaism series.

The Emergence of Judaism. Jewish Religion in Response to the Critical Issues of the First Six Centuries. Lanham, April 2000. University Press of America. Academic Studies in Ancient Judaism series.

The Halakhah and the Aggadah. Lanham. February 2001. University Press of America. Academic Studies in Ancient Judaism series.

The Hermeneutics of Rabbinic Category Formations. Lanham, February 2001. University Press of America. Academic Studies in Ancient Judaism series.

Rivka Ulmer
Pesiqta Rabbati. A Synoptic Edition of Pesiqta Rabbati Based upon all Extant Manuscripts and the Editio Princeps, Lanham. January 2002. University Press of America. Academic Studies in Ancient Judaism series. Volume III

Edited by Jacob Neusner and James F. Strange
Religious Texts and Material Contexts. Lanham. August 2001. University Press of America. Academic Studies in Ancient Judaism series.

Leslie S. Wilson
The Serpent Symbol in the Ancient Near East. Nahash and Asherah: Death, Life, and Healing. Lanham. December 2001, University Press of America. Academic Studies in Ancient Judaism series.

Jacob Neusner
Talmud Torah. Ways to God's Presence through Learning: An Exercise in Practical Theology. Lanham, January 2002. University Press of America. Academic Studies in Ancient Judaism series.

Jacob Neusner

The Aggadic Role in Halakhic Discourses. Lanham. February 2001. University Press of America. Academic Studies in Ancient Judaism series. Volume I

The Aggadic Role in Halakhic Discourses. Lanham. February 2001. University Press of America. Academic Studies in Ancient Judaism series. Volume II

The Aggadic Role in Halakhic Discourses. Lanham. February 2001. University Press of America. Academic Studies in Ancient Judaism series. Volume III

A Theological Commentary to the Midrash. Lanham. April 2001. University Press of America. Academic Studies in Ancient Judaism series. Volume I. *Pesiqta deRab Kahana.*

A Theological Commentary to the Midrash. Lanham. March 2001. University Press of America. Academic Studies in Ancient Judaism series. - Volume II. *Genesis Raba.*

A Theological Commentary to the Midrash. Lanham. April 2001. University Press of America. Academic Studies in Ancient Judaism series. Volume III. *Song of Songs Rabbah*

A Theological Commentary to the Midrash. Lanham. April 2001. University Press of America. Academic Studies in Ancient Judaism series. Volume IV. *Leviticus Rabbah*

A Theological Commentary to the Midrash. Lanham. June 2001. University Press of America. Academic Studies in Ancient Judaism series. Volume V *Lamentations Rabbati*

A Theological Commentary to the Midrash. June 2001. University Press of America. Academic Studies in Ancient Judaism series. Volume VI. *Ruth Rabbah and Esther Rabbah I*

A Theological Commentary to the Midrash. June 2001. University Press of America. Academic Studies in Ancient Judaism series. Volume VII. *Sifra*

A Theological Commentary to the Midrash. July 2001. University Press of America. Academic Studies in Ancient Judaism series. Volume VIII. *Sifré to Numbers and Sifré to Deuteronomy*

A Theological Commentary to the Midrash. August 2001. University Press of America. Academic Studies in Ancient Judaism series. Volume IX. *Mekhilta Attributed to Rabbi Ishmael*

The Unity of Rabbinic Discourse. January 2001. University Press of America. Academic Studies in Ancient Judaism series. Volume I: *Aggadah in the Halakhah*

The Unity of Rabbinic Discourse. February 2001. University Press of America. Academic Studies in Ancient Judaism series. Volume II: *Halakhah in the Aggadah*

The Unity of Rabbinic Discourse. February 2001. University Press of America. Academic Studies in Ancient Judaism series. Volume III: *Halakhah and Aggadah in Concert*

TITLES

Texts without Boundaries. Protocols of Non-Documentary Writing in the Rabbinic Canon, Lanham, 2002: University Press of America. Academic Studies in Ancient Judaism series. Volume Two. *Sifra*

Texts without Boundaries. Protocols of Non-Documentary Writing in the Rabbinic Canon, Lanham, 2003: University Press of America. Academic Studies in Ancient Judaism series. Volume Three. *Sifré to Numbers.*

Texts without Boundaries. Protocols of Non-Documentary Writing in the Rabbinic Canon, Lanham, 2003: University Press of America. Academic Studies in Ancient Judaism series. Volume Four. *Sifré to Deuteronomy.*

Texts without Boundaries. Protocols of Non-Documentary Writing in the Rabbinic Canon, Lanham, 2004: University Press of America. Academic Studies in Ancient Judaism series. Volume Five. *Genesis Rabbah.*

Texts without Boundaries. Protocols of Non-Documentary Writing in the Rabbinic Canon, Lanham, 2004: University Press of America. Academic Studies in Ancient Judaism series. Volume Six. *Leviticus Rabbah.*

Texts without Boundaries. Protocols of Non-Documentary Writing in the Rabbinic Canon, Lanham, 2004: University Press of America. Academic Studies in Ancient Judaism series. Volume Seven. *Pesiqta deRab Kahana.*

Texts without Boundaries. Protocols of Non-Documentary Writing in the Rabbinic Canon, Lanham, 2004: University Press of America. Academic Studies in Ancient Judaism series. Volume Eight. *Esther Rabbah and Ruth Rabbah.*

Texts without Boundaries. Protocols of Non-Documentary Writing in the Rabbinic Canon, Lanham, 2004: University Press of America. Academic Studies in Ancient Judaism series. Volume Nine. *Song of Songs Rabbah.*

Texts without Boundaries. Protocols of Non-Documentary Writing in the Rabbinic Canon, Lanham, 2004: University Press of America. Academic Studies in Ancient Judaism series. Volume Ten. *Lamentations Rabbah.*

Texts without Boundaries. Protocols of Non-Documentary Writing in the Rabbinic Canon, Lanham, 2004: University Press of America. Academic Studies in Ancient Judaism series. Volume Eleven. *Mekhilta Attributed to Rabbi Ishmael.*

Texts without Boundaries. Protocols of Non-Documentary Writing in the Rabbinic Canon, Lanham, 2004: University Press of America. Academic Studies in Ancient Judaism series. Volume Twelve. *Abot deRabbi Natan.*